The Politics of Compassion

The Politics of Compassion

THE SICHUAN EARTHQUAKE
AND CIVIC ENGAGEMENT
IN CHINA

Bin Xu

STANFORD UNIVERSITY PRESS
STANFORD, CALIFORNIA

Stanford University Press
Stanford, California

Printed in the United States of America on acid-free, archival-quality paper

Library of Congress Cataloging-in-Publication Data

Names: Xu, Bin (Sociology professor), author.
Title: The politics of compassion : the Sichuan earthquake and civic engagement in China / Bin Xu.
Description: Stanford, California : Stanford University Press, 2017. | Includes bibliographical references and index.
Identifiers: LCCN 2017000570 (print) | LCCN 2017003688 (ebook) | ISBN 9781503602106 (cloth : alk. paper) | ISBN 9781503603363 (pbk. : alk. paper) | ISBN 9781503603400
Subjects: LCSH: Civil society—China. | Political participation—China. | Voluntarism—China. | Wenchuan Earthquake, China, 2008. | China—Politics and government—2002–
Classification: LCC JQ1516 .X794 2017 (print) | LCC JQ1516 (ebook) | DDC 303.48/5—dc23
LC record available at https://lccn.loc.gov/2017000570

*For the children who died in their schools
in the 2008 Sichuan earthquake, in memoriam*

For their parents, who have to live without them

Contents

Illustrations

Acknowledgments

This is not an easy book in many senses. I thank the children who died in their schools in the Sichuan earthquake and their parents who have to live without them for making me realize that scholarship is more than knowledge and expertise. In the past eight years, those young victims kept reminding me that, once I knew of their suffering, I should not turn my back on them. I hope this book can serve as a commemoration of their abruptly ended lives, even if it may not soothe their parents' unspeakable pain.

This project started at Northwestern University and then took a zigzag course, generating a few other writings with different themes and materials. It is finally embodied in the present book. It would not have been possible without my mentors' and friends' intellectual and emotional support. I am greatly indebted to them. Gary Alan Fine not only has read and commented on different versions of the manuscript but also has had a profound impact on my study, writing, and career. He inspires me through his writing, our conversations and correspondence, and his insightful observations of human interactions. Special thanks also go to Deborah Davis at Yale, who thoroughly read and commented on an earlier version and provided valuable feedback as well as unfailing support. Wendy Griswold has been of tremendous help through her timely feedback on different versions of the manuscript and my other writings as well. I presented parts of this work in the Culture and Society Workshop Wendy directed at Northwestern. I thank my fellow "workshoppers"— whose names are too many for the limited space here—for their comments. Chas Camic also provided incredibly useful feedback. Dingxin Zhao changed many of my thoughts through his comments on my writing. Peter Carroll as a China historian always reminds me of the historical dimension of Chinese society and urges me to pay more attention to nuances—two very valuable suggestions that changed this initially overly theoretical project. Dingding Chen, Kazuya Fukuoka, and Xiaoyu Pu read earlier versions of some of the chapters and provided comments and suggestions. Many thanks to David Palmer, one of the reviewers of this manuscript, who graciously revealed his identity, for his careful reading and extremely useful comments.

I am also grateful for the institutional support I have received. Much of the final manuscript was written when I was a visiting scholar at Fudan University in Shanghai in 2013 and a postdoctoral fellow at Yale University in the academic year 2014–2015. I am grateful to Fudan's International Center for Studies of Chinese Civilization and Yale's Council on East Asian Studies for their generous financial and institutional support. Duke University Library provided me with a small grant to use its Asian collection in 2011. I thank Luo Zhou for her support and guidance during my library research at Duke. I have presented different parts of the manuscript at talks in various places, including Fudan University, the University of Macau, Yale University, and the University of Hong Kong. I thank Zhang Qi, Dingding Chen, Gonçalo Santos, and Cheris Chan for hosting the talks and giving helpful feedback.

I also want to thank all my informants and interviewees in Sichuan and elsewhere. Fu Han was my key entry point into the world of volunteers and associations in Sichuan. Without his network and "serviced residence" in Chengdu, this book might have been entirely different. I also thank Xiao Fengyi and other members of the Feiteng Group, with whom I spent much time in An County and Beichuan, for their friendship, stories, and pictures.

Finally, a book about sentiments should not be emotionless. My heartfelt thanks go to my family. They have made this book more personally meaningful. My parents, Xu Jinzhang and Zhang Siwei, like many Chinese parents, have had high expectations of my educational achievements. I am the first person in my family to have attended college and even earned a Ph.D. degree, and probably have exceeded their expectations. Behind my overly long education were their years of sacrifice, love, and support. My wife, Li Yao, and my daughter, Meimei, endured hardship and enjoyed happiness with me in China and the United States. It has been more than a decade since I decided to restart my career in an entirely different country as a relatively older graduate student with a family to support. Their love has been the greatest reason for me not to give up amid adversity. I finished this book manuscript during our move from Miami to Atlanta. The old odyssey was coming to an end; we were starting a new journey. Life is always uncertain and liminal. However, to quote Adam Smith out of context, "if the chief part of human happiness arises from the consciousness of being beloved, as I believe it does, those sudden changes of fortune seldom contribute much to happiness" (Smith [1759] 2009, 52).

The Politics of Compassion

Introduction

On May 12, 2008, an earthquake measuring 7.9 on the Richter scale struck Sichuan, a densely populated province in western China.[1] The earthquake resulted from the long-term movement of the Longmenshan Fault, a "convergence of crustal material slowly moving from the high Tibetan Plateau to the west, against strong crust underlying the Sichuan Basin" (United States Geological Survey 2016b). This movement is occurring at a glacial pace, but its path has led to catastrophic quakes and landslides for millions of years. The Sichuan earthquake was one of the deadliest episodes in this process. According to the State Council Information Office, the earthquake killed 87,150 people, 17,923 of whom are still missing and are presumed dead (State Council Information Office 2008b). It impacted more than 45.5 million people in Sichuan and adjacent provinces. About 15 million people were evacuated, and about 5 million were left homeless. An estimated 5.36 million buildings collapsed, and more than 21 million buildings were damaged to varying degrees (Renminwang [People.cn] 2008). The total economic loss was estimated at 845.1 billion yuan (138 billion US dollars) (State Council Information Office 2008a).

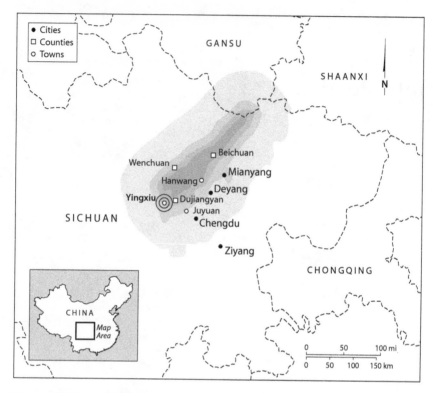

The 2008 Sichuan Earthquake. United States Geological Survey.

The USGS (United States Geological Survey) ranks the Sichuan earthquake as the seventh deadliest quake in the world and third in China in the period of 1900–2014 (United States Geological Survey 2016a). It is the third deadliest disaster of any kind in the history of the People's Republic of China, following the Great Leap Forward famine in the late 1950s and early 1960s, which killed millions, and the Tangshan earthquake in 1976, which killed about 240,000. The Great Famine lasted several years, whereas the Sichuan earthquake accomplished its deadly job in mere minutes. The Tangshan earthquake hit an industrial city and its suburbs; the Sichuan earthquake, in contrast, devastated a mostly rural region, triggering explosive geological reactions not just at the epicenter, but also in other places along the Longmenshan Fault—Dujiangyan, Beichuan, Mianzhu, Qingchuan, and as far as in the neighboring province of Shaanxi. Very few disasters had wreaked havoc over such a large area and affected so many people in just an instant.

Even these striking comparisons cannot adequately reflect the shock and tragedy on the ground. At Juyuan Middle School in Dujiangyan, a building collapsed immediately after the quake, burying several hundred students and teachers. Parents, local government officials, and the Armed Police rushed to the site, trying to rescue them with their bare hands and simple tools, but only twenty students were dug out alive in the first couple of hours. Others were trapped under the rubble, crying for help. Cranes and machinery finally arrived at dusk, as heavy rain poured down on the desperate parents.

Zihou,[2] a middle-aged businessman in Chengdu, was one of the first volunteers to arrive at Juyuan Middle School. He climbed onto the rubble to help rescuers but was extremely depressed by what he saw and heard:

> I was on the rubble and heard a voice from below. It was a cry but indistinct because it was raining [hard]. [I knew] there were people under the rubble but didn't know what to do. Then [the bodies] were pulled out and put onto a one-meter-high pile, covered by striped tarps. When dawn broke, the local residents and soldiers arranged the corpses into a line on the ground.[3]

When a student was pulled from the rubble and carried out on a stretcher, desperate parents dashed toward the body to see if it was their child, usually finding that the student was already dead. The child's parents wailed uncontrollably and fell to the ground, while others staggered back and continued to wait helplessly. The school set up a tarp-covered shelter for the parents to light incense and firecrackers, in accordance with the local mourning custom. So many students were found dead that, according to a journalist from the *Financial Times*, the firecrackers were heard "at regular intervals of about 5, 10 minutes" (Cable News Network 2008). Then, the parents rode away on motorcycles, carrying their children's bodies on their backs, and embarked on a hard trip back home.

Melissa Block, a National Public Radio (NPR) reporter on site the first night, choked up several times when she described the scene:

> Tonight, there were dozens upon dozens of families going through this same grim ritual, their heads bowed in unspeakable pain as they set vigil over small lifeless forms. Many of these young victims would have

been their parent's only children. And in row after row, their parents sat huddled through the rainy night keeping watch, one last time, over their babies. (National Public Radio 2008)

Juyuan was only one of the many schools that toppled in the earthquake. As a report in *Caijing*, a popular magazine, in June 2008 noted, an official from the Ministry of Housing and Construction estimated that 6,898 school buildings had collapsed as of May 16, 2008. This number did not include those in Beichuan and Wenchuan, two devastated counties. Regarding scale, the town of Juyuan was not even the most devastated place, since most of its buildings remained intact or were only slightly damaged. By comparison, many other towns and villages in Sichuan were destroyed or simply swallowed by landslides.

The county seat of Beichuan, for example, located in a narrow valley, was utterly devastated by boulders and landslides from the surrounding mountains. Decades earlier, when the county government decided on the current location as the county seat, the residents worried about the potential "dumpling effect": that landslides from the mountains could easily enclose the town, just as dumpling dough wraps stuffing. This worry turned into reality decades later at the moment of the earthquake. The ground rocked like a boat on a storm-tossed sea, back and forth, up and down. The sky suddenly became dark amid a powerful dust storm, and people closed their eyes and coughed violently. When the storm subsided after two minutes, students and teachers at Qushan Elementary School found that a small hill of earth had appeared on the playground, while buildings in the school were hit by boulders and had toppled into pieces. Not a single building in the town stood intact. People were buried and crushed by falling walls and rubble.

A journalist from *Life Week* (*Sanlian shenghuo zhoukan*), a popular magazine in China, arrived in Beichuan a day after the quake and described it as a "town of death":

There was nothing in the town except for the odor of corpses. No lights, no water. I couldn't speak with the rescuers, and this made me want to cry. The only thing I could do was dig through the rubble with other people. I wanted to save people but could do nothing. I could only watch rescuers doing their job and comfort the relatives of the victims. [In that situation] you feel you're so pathetic, having no ability to rescue a single person. I didn't hear the kindergarteners' cries, but other people said they did. They asked me to listen carefully. All this made me so frustrated and ashamed. (Li 2009, 42)

FIGURE 1. Earthquake survivors walk among the rubble in Beichuan. May 16, 2008. Reuters/Bobby Yip.

Not far from the county seat, at Beichuan High School, students taking a physical education class were on the playground when the quake hit. Suddenly they heard a huge roar and saw a wide crack appear in the ground. All of them were pushed down to the ground as if by a giant hand. They were the lucky ones. The students in the main building were buried under the rubble. Only a few had been able to get out of the building; as they dashed down, the stairs behind them broke into pieces, one after another. The casualties of Beichuan School astonished everyone. More than a thousand students and teachers died--roughly 30 to 50 percent of the total school population.[4] One of the classes had to be merged with others because so few students survived (Feng 2010, 20–24).

The earthquake was not just a local disaster. Nearly half of the country felt its tremors. In Chengdu, the metropolis nearest the affected areas, many residents felt buildings shaking violently, and some reportedly saw frightening waves lift and throw down the roads. Some heard a noise like the rumble of an invisible subway train underneath the city. Those in high-rise buildings immediately ran down into the streets. In an interviewee's words, "people looked at each other with a confused expression; my mind went blank; everyone was trying to find out what happened, but

FIGURE 2. A father cries next to the body of his son in Hanwang, Mianzhu.
May 14, 2008. Reuters/Jason Lee.

no one knew what to do next."[5] City roads and highways were jammed
because drivers had abandoned their cars and run away in fear.[6] After
the first several hours of chaos, they found that Chengdu had survived
mostly intact, but the daily routine in the city had been disrupted. Even
in cities as far afield as Shanghai, Beijing, and Guangzhou, more than a
thousand miles away from Sichuan, residents also felt the tremors.

In China's cultural geography and in popular perception, Sichuan is
famous for breathtaking mountain scenery and rugged roads. Li Bai,
one of the greatest poets in China's history, expressed his admiration for
the scenery and his frustration with the roads in his well-known poem
"Hard Is the Road to Shu": "Oh, but it is high and dangerous! Traveling on Shu's roads is even more difficult than scaling into the sky!"[7] In
some points in history, the mountainous roads protected Sichuan from
invasion and contributed to its prosperity, even when the rest of China
suffered from famines and wars.

This natural blessing, however, turned into a handicap in the wake
of the earthquake. More than 100,000 People's Liberation Army (PLA)
soldiers, countless firefighters, Armed Police troops, and emergency

responders were dispatched to the quake zone. Yet, catastrophic land-slides and falling rocks had destroyed the roads and blocked their access to the most devastated places. Sometimes they had to abandon their vehicles and reach their destination on foot. All my informants who participated in the early emergency response described these journeys as the hardest ones they had ever experienced. Liang, a young volunteer from Shanghai, followed a group of PLA soldiers climbing over several mountains to get to Yingxiu. At some points, exhausted, he tried to sit down and rest, but the soldiers urged him to keep moving—sometimes even dragged him—because, "if I stopped, I probably would have died there because I was too exhausted and had no supplies at all."[8]

To distant observers following the news, the Sichuan earthquake consisted of a series of melodramatic episodes—trapped children and adults were rescued from the rubble, usually followed by cheers celebrating the miracle. But things were not so sensational on the ground. Rescuing a single person took hours, even days. Responders, working in shifts, slept for only a couple of hours every day, usually on the bare ground. The onsite crowd had to be absolutely quiet because the responders needed to listen for any voices rising up from below. Doctors and nurses had to be always prepared to attend to the trapped survivors at a moment's notice. Sometimes they had to perform amputations on the survivors, right on the rubble, to save their lives.

On top of all this was the daunting task of sheltering the fifteen million survivors and evacuees. The local governments used sports stadiums and university campuses as evacuation shelters in major cities like Chengdu and Mianyang, but most survivors had to stay in tents and self-made tarp shelters. Food and water had to be provided, and sanitization had to be taken care of in places with heavy casualties. Hospitals in Sichuan were filled to capacity with the injured and could not take any more; some patients had to be transferred to outside provinces.

The Sichuan earthquake happened in an extraordinary year, 2008, three months before the Beijing Olympics and two months after a series of uprisings in Tibetan areas. China was in the spotlight. International public opinion condemned the government for cracking down on the Tibetan protesters and blocking the foreign media's entry into Tibet. Human rights organizations called for a boycott of the Olympics, and pro-Tibet protesters clashed with Chinese students in overseas cities through which the Olympic torch relay passed. Domestically, the public criticized the government for its inadequate response to a historic snow-storm in January and February. Separatist ethnic groups in Xinjiang were seeking opportunities to stage protests and riots during the Beijing Olympics. The earthquake occurred at a difficult time, posing enormous challenges to the Chinese government and society.

CIVIC ENGAGEMENT AFTER THE EARTHQUAKE

The tragedy, chaos, and difficulties, however, led to many extraordinary happenings, which made the earthquake not only a devastating disaster but also a political drama. One of the most important episodes of the drama was that countless Chinese citizens engaged in public activities to help the survivors, rebuild the communities, commemorate the victims, and demand justice. Social scientists term participation in these kinds of activities "civic engagement" or "civic participation" or "civic action," in which "participants are coordinating action to improve some aspect of common life in society, as they imagine society" (Lichterman and Elia-soph 2014, 809).

No keen observer could miss an extraordinary phenomenon in the wake of the earthquake: a massive number of volunteers either went to Sichuan to help with the relief effort or provided services and collected donations in other places. Nobody knew for sure how many people were involved in this wave of volunteering. Estimates ranged from 200,000, the number of volunteers registered with the Red Cross and the Youth League (which was believed to be significantly lower than the actual number), to 10 million. They rushed to the quake zone, by car, train, or plane from adjacent cities such as Chengdu and Mianyang, and from as far away as Shanghai, Beijing, and Guangzhou. They did whatever work they could do and were assigned to do: cooking meals, taking care of children, unloading supplies from trucks, and cleaning toilets in densely populated public shelters.

This wave of volunteering came as a surprise. To many people, Chinese society had been experiencing a moral crisis or a "vacuum of belief" since the economic reform launched in 1978, becoming a place of "wolves against wolves"--a jungle where people blatantly pursued their own material interests at the cost of public welfare. The older generations frowned on the younger ones—the "one-child generation" or the "little emperor generation"--who immersed themselves in manga, dyed their hair, and seemed uninterested in anything but themselves. The younger generation, in turn, mocked the older ones for their bad manners, meticulous calculations, and equally strong self-interest cloaked in a hypocritical language of Maoist altruism. A *Time* journalist observed:

> For years, China's citizens couldn't watch the evening news without being reminded of their darker side, of the grasping, reckless self-interest that has characterized China's headlong rush to become wealthy and powerful—stories of slave labor and child-kidnapping rings, rampant government corruption, counterfeit products, tainted food, dangerous toys and, lately, the brutal crackdown on dissent in Tibet. But from a monstrous humanitarian crisis has come a new self-awareness, a recognition of the Chinese people's sympathy and generosity of spirit. (Elegant 2008)

Chinese citizens did more than volunteering. A few days after the earthquake, some influential public intellectuals, the liberal media, and netizens advocated a national mourning observance for the earthquake victims. The state eventually accepted the proposal and, for the first time in Chinese history, held a period of national mourning for ordinary people instead of leaders, heroes, soldiers, and officials. On May 19, at 2:28 p.m.--the exact time the earthquake struck seven days earlier--with the national flag throughout the country flying at half-staff, air-raid sirens blared and a three-minute silence was observed. People crowded squares in major cities to commemorate their fellow citizens, and public intellectuals and media celebrated their successful public advocacy.

Some citizens went even further. They were not content with simply alleviating their fellow citizens' suffering; they wanted to address the causes of the suffering. A vexing issue emerged immediately after the earthquake: a massive number of schools collapsed and killed at least 5,335 students, according to official statistics, whereas some nearby buildings survived. People began to ask: Why did so many schools collapse? Who should be blamed for the children's deaths and the parents' suffering? Parents of the student victims and many observers believed that contractors, local officials, and even the whole education system should be held responsible for the tragedy. They speculated that because of the low budgets allocated to school construction and possible corruption involved in the bidding process, contractors had used substandard materials—unreinforced concrete, or sand mixed with concrete, or no concrete at all—to increase their profits. Some parents began to protest about a week after the earthquake. The government conducted some investigations but finally declared (without releasing a formal report) that buildings failed because of the intensity of the earthquake rather than poor construction.

Outraged by the state's denial, artist Ai Weiwei and activist Tan Zuoren mobilized volunteers to collect the student victims' names as a way to enhance the public awareness of the issue and resist the oblivion the state imposed on the public. Volunteers phoned various government bureaus to request the release of the students' information, and, after being denied, they went to the quake zone and visited almost all the schools— town by town, door to door—to verify students' names and other information. Liberal intellectuals and political dissidents made underground documentaries, built alternative memorials, and created artistic works to commemorate the students and to challenge the state's moral authority.

The Sichuan earthquake, therefore, was a social-political drama that played out and made visible the ubiquitous but otherwise little discernible self-organized civic engagement in Chinese society. Public discourses paid much attention to this massive wave of civic engagement but disagreed on how to understand and explain this extraordinary collective act of compassion.

Some explained it as an automatic outburst of sympathy, which was overshadowed by day-to-day life but activated by the catastrophe. In other words, "disaster brings out the best in people." This conventional wisdom corroborated philosophers' assertions about human beings' moral nature. The ancient Chinese philosopher Mencius believed that everyone has an instinctive compassion for other people's suffering (*ceyin zhixin*). Similarly, in his 1759 classic, *The Theory of Moral Sentiments*, Adam Smith described how a European man would respond to an imaginary earthquake that "swallowed up the great empire of China," a country then remote and mysterious to Europe. Smith emphasized, "human nature startles with horror at the thought" of not caring about the tragedy, and often "we dare not, as self-love might suggest to us, prefer the interest of one to that of many" (Smith [1759] 2009, 159). In many disasters, care for other people's suffering motivates civic engagement, including rescue, relief, recovery, public debates, rituals, activism, and commemorations (Fortun 2001; Dynes and Tierney 1994; Eyre 2007). In massive disasters in different historical periods in China, especially in the late Qing and the Republican era, various civic associations—religious, commercial, international, local—actively participated in disaster relief and fundraising for victims of droughts and floods (Cai 2005; Li and Xia 2007).

This view, however, needs qualification. Compassion for other people's suffering is universal, but it needs social conditions to turn into public expressions and actions. Mencius reminded us that compassion in traditional Chinese society aimed to maintain the familial social structure: that we always have greater concern for those socially close to us—family members, relatives, the chief of the village, and so on—than strangers. The "solidarity among strangers" in the wake of the Sichuan earthquake went well beyond the familial framework in the traditional Chinese moral imagination. The charity events in traditional society also relied on various associations—chambers of commerce and religious associations—which had already carved out a social sphere outside the familial structure in the late Qing and Republican era. In modern Western societies, compassion and volunteering for distressed and devastated strangers—the "distant suffering" or the spirit of "good Samaritans"—do not exist in a social vacuum either (Wilson 2000). Ubiquitous post-disaster volunteering never happens automatically but requires certain social and political conditions to become a reality. In Japan, for example, a country with a longer history of civil society than China, large-scale post-disaster volunteering did not emerge until the 1995 Kobe earthquake (Shaw and Goda 2004; Tierney and Goltz 1998). As studies of contentious politics show, disaster-related activism as a form of civic engagement requires particular social and political conditions to emerge, continue, and succeed (Fortun 2001). The civic engagement after the Sichuan earthquake was not an exception; it was not only a "natural outpouring" of sympathy but also a complex political and social process.

Another view in the popular discourses regarded the volunteering as a large-scale activity organized and mobilized by the Chinese state, which intended to use national solidarity to shore up its legitimacy. An obvious problem with this view is that it takes a narrow view of "civic engagement," limited to volunteering in disaster relief and recovery but excluding activism and other contentious forms of civic participation not organized by the state (Eliasoph 2013).

Even within the limits of its narrow definition of volunteering, this state-mobilization view does not grasp something new and important: most volunteers after the Sichuan earthquake were not organized by the state or by state organizations like the Red Cross.[9] Rather, they were mobilized by various civic associations, such as nongovernmental organizations (NGOs), grassroots associations, and small groups. This phenomenon might be taken for granted elsewhere but was significant against its historical background. During the Mao years, after massive disasters, many *danwei* (work units) organized response teams to rush to disaster zones to provide assistance, required their workers to work for extra hours to produce supplies, and deducted donations from their employees' wages (Qian 2008b). Similar state-organized civic engagement existed after the Sichuan earthquake. For example, some local *danwei* in the affected zone set up response teams; state-owned hospitals outside the quake zone sent doctors and nurses to Sichuan; the Red Cross remained a major organizer of volunteering. Nevertheless, many more volunteers went by themselves, with only brief encounters with state organizations, such as registering with the Red Cross, cooperating with the Youth League, and so on. This wave of self-organized, grassroots civic engagement in disaster relief and recovery was indeed unprecedented in the history of the People's Republic of China. From a longer historical perspective, it also differed from the elite- and foreigner-dominated charity activities in the late Qing and the Republican era. It was those self-organized, grassroots actions instead of the state-organized relief, which predictably occurs after every major disaster, that surprised and delighted many observers.

Another view emphasized the role of nationalism in motivating people to participate in the volunteering. A report in *The Guardian* cites a volunteer's enthusiastic words:

> Like many of her generation, Zhang says she is now more patriotic and concerned about China. "I have grown up because so many things have happened," she says. "I used to look at events and think about how they affected me. Now I consider whether they benefit my country." That nationalist ethos pervades the relief effort one month after the quake. (Watts 2008)

This patriotic fervor among volunteers was not new in China or other contexts. Many idealistic American volunteers who joined the Peace Corps were inspired by John F. Kennedy's words "ask not what your country can do for you—ask what you can do for your country." This view made even more sense in the year of 2008. While the Chinese state suffered from an international public relations crisis due to the Tibetan uprising and boycotts of the Beijing Olympics, many Chinese regarded the criticisms of the state as malicious attacks on the Chinese nation. Therefore, the impressive wave of volunteering could have been an outburst of bruised national pride, a symbolic gesture to show the world the sympathetic side of the Chinese.

Nevertheless, as this book will show, nationalism was only one of the cultural terms that people used to understand and interpret their actions. Many citizens understood their actions by resorting to other cultural ideas, such as individualism, religion, and political ideas about civil society and democracy. This diversity became salient only when one listened closely to what they said and observed closely what they did, whereas a brief media interview could lead to little in-depth knowledge because a person could put on a patriotic face in front of foreign journalists.

A more sophisticated view regarded the post-earthquake engagement as an indication that civil society had started becoming an independent and important force in China. In an enthusiastic editorial a week after the earthquake, *Asia Weekly* applauded the volunteers for their "quality and awareness of citizenship," which it considered as "the sprout for a Chinese civil society in the future" (Li et al. 2008). In this discourse, the volunteers had a clearly defined idea of "civil society" or "citizenship," which motivated and guided them to engage in public-spirited activities and build a "civil society." The year of 2008 was claimed to be the "birth year" of civil society in China. People who made this claim certainly knew its historical inaccuracy, because Chinese civil society was born long before 2008, but their statement was intended to celebrate a potentially significant turning point: Chinese civil society would gain more autonomous social space, and the post-earthquake participation, as a "culture of democracy," could empower citizens to pursue a democratic civil society. This discourse prevailed in the media in the mainland and Hong Kong as well as in academia, triggering an upsurge of hope for the future of civil society.

This view rightly identified the "unprecedentedness" of the civic engagement—grassroots participation through civic associations instead of the state system—and situated it in the historical development of Chinese civil society in the post-Mao years. Much evidence presented in this book supports this claim. Nevertheless, its optimism underestimated the complexity of political factors involved in the emergence, development, and consequences of civic participation.

For example, the development of Chinese civil society did not automatically lead to the emergence of the large-scale post-earthquake engagement because this development was often hindered, exploited, and manipulated by the authoritarian state. The state learned a lesson from the East European experience in the 1980s and the color revolutions in the 2000s—in which "civil society" was a rallying cry of autonomous associations and social movement organizations in their march toward democracy (Ekiert and Kubik 1999)—and thus imposed many restrictions on nongovernmental organizations. The number of people also mattered. A big crowd engaged in collective action, regardless of its aims, constitutes in and of itself a political issue. Even if a collective action is tolerated or even initiated by the state, a large number of participants may lead to unintended consequences, turning an officially sanctioned gathering into an antigovernment protest (Pfaff and Yang 2001). The sheer number of volunteers in Sichuan—millions!—and many not organized by the state made the civic engagement in the rescue and recovery the largest collective action since the Tiananmen incident in 1989. The seemingly nonpolitical volunteering turned very political at that moment. Moreover, with the wisdom of hindsight, it is clear that the enthusiastic optimism about the future of civil society was wishful thinking. As I will show in the chapters that follow, the post-earthquake engagement failed to bring significant change to Chinese civil society. In sum, all these restrictive conditions added complexity to the simplistic view of Chinese civil society and begged a more sophisticated explanation.

At a deeper level, the participating citizens did not always understand and interpret the *meanings* and goals of their participation in the same way as this civil society view would have anticipated. By definition, civic engagement aims to improve some aspects of society, and its style and effects largely depend on the participants' understanding of some key issues: What "society" do they want to improve? What is the common good? How should society be improved? (Lichterman and Eliasoph 2014). The classical ideals of "civil society" as a "good society" include several key ideas: independence from the state, tolerance of diversity, equality of opportunities, freedom from tyranny, and so on (Brunkhorst

2005; Taylor 1995; Calhoun 2002; Putnam, Leonardi, and Nanetti 1993, 87–90). Liberal media commentators and dissident intellectuals adhered to these ideas, but public-spirited citizens on the ground did not always understand their actions in this way. Thus, it would be a mistake to substitute reality for liberal interpretations of reality.

Moreover, if we listen to how they talked about the meaning of their actions more closely, we may hear about their painful experiences and the dilemma of how to come to terms with human suffering. Many of these uneasy discussions were about the school collapse issue. On the one hand, the participating citizens tried to reduce people's suffering and help restore them to a normal life by building community centers, teaching summer courses for children, and collecting donations for educational assistance. On the other hand, it was not uncommon for a volunteer to teach in a tent school by the ruins of the old school, which had collapsed almost immediately after the quake and killed hundreds of students. The problem was too obvious to ignore, but would the volunteers have serious public discussions about it? And did they decide to take action to remedy it? To take such a step made people nervous, owing to the likely outcome of political suppression, which might jeopardize their personal lives and careers. But not to take this step was equally difficult––consciously or unconsciously, one might feel guilty for not doing something for the poor child victims under the rubble.

This dilemma is ubiquitous in various contexts; it comes from the tension between two kinds of civic engagement: "harmless and warm" volunteering that is comparable to sticking a Band-Aid on a wound, versus "angry" activism––Jane Addams-style actions that address the causes of social illness (Eliasoph 2013). The earthquake made manifest this dilemma by placing compassion side by side with unsolved problems: volunteers were reading stories to children not in local libraries but by the collapsed schools that had killed other children. This dilemma fell beyond the scope of the optimistic and normative view of civil society.

In sum, all these popular discourses correctly pointed out one or two dimensions of the civic engagement in the aftermath of the Sichuan earthquake, but they left us with more confusion than a clear, comprehensive story of this extraordinary event. The impressive civic engagement after the Sichuan earthquake consisted of a series of public actions embedded in its social and political context. This was something to be explained rather than taken for granted. Research has shown that civic engagement is shaped by group dynamics (Lichterman 2006), macro-level cultural ideas (Wuthnow 1998, 1991), the Internet (Xenos and Moy 2007), social capital (Putnam 2000), participants' demographic characteristics (Beyerlein and Sikkink 2008; Wilson 2000), and political contexts (Schofer and Fourcade-Gourinchas 2001; Skocpol and Fiorina 1999). The last factor is particularly important. Authoritarianism is not an exception to but a variation of political context. As civic engagement is widely seen as a part of a "culture of democracy," the ways citizens participate in civic engagement in an undemocratic context, in which they have to overcome more institutional and cultural constraints, is worth exploring.

In this book, I aim to provide a snapshot of civic engagement in contemporary China by examining the unprecedented, memorable civic engagement in the aftermath of the Sichuan earthquake. I focus on the grassroots civic engagement organized by civic associations. This is not meant to dismiss the importance of state-organized volunteering, which certainly existed and remained strong in the aftermath of the earthquake; its features and outcomes, however, were widely known and fairly predictable. Nor does this focus mean that the grassroots civic engagement could be free from the state's system. Instead, as my analysis shows, it was deeply embedded in and intertwined with the political system and its affiliated organizations. The aim of the book, in fact, is to reveal the complexity of the grassroots engagement and its political context.

I ask several questions: Why was there such large-scale grassroots civic engagement after the Sichuan earthquake but not in previous disasters? How did different types of citizens engage? How did they interact with different levels and sectors of the Chinese state? Against the backdrop of human suffering after the earthquake, how did the civically engaged citizens understand and interpret the meaning of their actions, deal with the moral-political dilemmas they encountered, and take—or not take—actions to address the suffering they witnessed? All these questions boil down to three components of civic engagement: *contexts*, *actions*, and *meanings*. By attempting to answer these questions, my ultimate goal is to understand what I term the "politics of compassion": how political conditions shape expressions of moral sentiments through civic engagement.

CIVIL SOCIETY IN CHINA

The story of Sichuan presented in this book aims to enrich our understanding of Chinese civil society in general.[10] Scholarly interest in Chinese civil society can be dated back to the 1989 Tiananmen protest, which has been explained as a result of the development of civil society and a public sphere in the 1980s (Calhoun 1994). This initial interest was boosted by the then prevalent analogy between China and East European countries, where "civil society" was both a slogan and an ideal for pro-democracy movements, a yearning for a society free from Communism (Keane 1988). This intellectual and political trend converged with the emergence of neo-Tocquevillianism in the 1990s. Neo-Tocquevillian scholars in the United States emphasize voluntary associations' acting independently from and in opposition to bureaucratic state power (Putnam, Leonardi, and Nanetti 1993), although Tocqueville's original intention was to argue against the continuation of a strong state in post-revolutionary France rather than to provide an accurate sociological description of civic life in the Jacksonian America (Skocpol 1997). This trend also triggered a debate among sociologists and historians, presented in a special issue of the journal *Modern China* in 1993 (volume 19, no. 2), about whether the term "civil society" can be applied to China and whether there is or was a civil society in China. The debate generated no consensus. Some emphasized the term's historical specificity, and therefore its inapplicability to China, but others went so far as to argue that there was a civil society / public sphere even in late imperial China, more or less like those envisioned in the classic definition in Western political theory.

Since that debate, there has been a fast growth and expansion of various sectors of Chinese civil society: the public sphere, including the media, urban space, and online space (Yang 2009, 2003; Zhao 2008, 1998); civic associations (Brook and Frolic 1997; Lu 2009; Ma 2006; Spires 2011); and citizens' rights (Diamant, Lubman, and O'Brien 2005; Goldman 2005, 2007). Scholars have come to increasingly question the neo-Tocquevillian theory highlighting civil society's independence from the state and its potential for fostering democratization (Spires 2011; Teets 2013). The "corporatist" approach even explicitly stresses the state's strategies for fending off democracy by controlling NGOs and developing an alternative form with "Chinese characteristics": GONGOs (government-organized nongovernmental organizations) (Unger 2008; Unger and Chan 1995; Hildebrandt 2013).

Many scholars now follow what I term the "complex coexistence" approach and stress complexity, variation, and contingency in state–civil society relations. They have found that civic associations strive to mobilize all possible institutional resources to survive and constantly negotiate with the state (Spires 2011; Saich 2000). The Chinese state is willing to delegate some of its social service functions to civic associations but is also cautious about such associations since they may have a hidden political agenda. This tension between need and control leads to political opportunities unevenly distributed on different issues and in different realms. Civic associations react to those opportunities to expand their space of survival (Hildebrandt 2013). Consequently, as Jessica Teets's recent work shows, it is possible to find cases where the expansion of a relatively autonomous space for civic associations coexists with an upgraded, more flexible state control (Teets 2013). This complexity is reflected in the terms these studies use: "dependent autonomy" (Lu 2009), "contingent symbiosis" (Spires 2011), and "consultative authoritarianism" (Teets 2013). Studies of the public sphere follow the same trend, emphasizing the complex interrelations among the media, market, and state, instead of depicting a dichotomous picture of state versus public sphere (Qian and Bandurski 2011; Yang 2009; Zhao 2008).

The Sichuan earthquake provides much evidence for the complex coexistence approach. My analysis extends and develops this approach by taking it a step further. I shift the focus from organizational and structural relations to actions, in other words, from civic associations to *civic engagement.*

Studies of civic engagement constitute an established field in other intellectual contexts (Putnam 2000; Putnam, Leonardi, and Nanetti 1993; Skocpol 2003; Baiocchi 2013; Bennett et al. 2013; Schudson 2009; Skocpol and Fiorina 1999; Theiss-Morse and Hibbing 2005), but the topic has not attracted much attention from China scholars. The literature does not ignore this topic completely, but it mainly describes civic engagement within the "third sector," particularly within formal NGOs, mostly as organizations' strategic actions carried out by NGO staff members as part of their job (Lu 2009). By contrast, scholars know less about civic engagement from people outside of formal NGOs, particularly activities organized by associations even more "grassroots" than the grassroots NGOs scholars have been studying. For example, small civic groups that never bother to register, self-serving hobby groups, and occasional volunteers who join in a group's or NGO's activities only for a limited time or sporadically. Only a few scholars now are beginning to study volunteering in China, and their work has provided insights on which the present study draws (Fleischer 2011; Ying Xu 2013). However, this body of literature is just starting to accumulate and a clearly defined research agenda has yet to emerge.

In this book, I rely on a cultural sociology to examine civic engagement, particularly focusing on civic culture (Lo 2010). The early studies of civic culture were mainly based on surveys of people's political opinions and attitudes (Almond and Verba 1989). More recent work has redefined civic culture as "the symbols, meanings, and ways of doing things that create and sustain civic life" (Lichterman 2005, 384). In general, the cultural sociology of civic life examines several key elements and their interrelationships: people's *action* of engaging in public affairs, their interpretations of the *meanings* of their actions, and the *context* in which their actions are embedded.

This approach differs from the dominant institutionalism and organizational analysis in that it shifts the focus from organizational relations to actions, including a greater variety of civic engagement, such as citizens' volunteering in social services, public advocacy to enhance awareness of social problems, and activism to remedy those problems. It is people instead of organizations that are at the center of the analysis.

At the core of this approach is uncovering how participants understand and interpret the *meaning* of their actions. Since Max Weber's "interpretive sociology," meaning has been central to sociology. Human beings rely on a "web of significance" to understand the world and take action correspondingly (Geertz 1973). We need meanings to orient ourselves in an uncertain world, to justify our actions, and to understand social reality (Alexander 2003; Wuthnow 1987). Meaning is even more essential to civic engagement. We are all too familiar with Tocqueville's statement about the virtues of joining associational life: "feelings and ideas are renewed, the heart enlarged, and understanding developed only by the reciprocal action of men one upon another" (Tocqueville 1969, 515). In Tocqueville's view, the value of civic engagement lies not in the material benefits it brings about but "feelings and ideas" about goals higher than one's personal interests. A democratic republic in the United States could be maintained, he believed, because people had distinctive "habits of the heart"—the whole moral and intellectual condition of the American people.

Later conceptions of civic engagement, which are rarely so romantic and optimistic, still stress the importance of meaning. For example, Wuthnow defines civic engagement as "acts of compassion"—not physical behaviors, but the actions within a "cultural framework": "the languages we use to make sense of such behaviors, the cultural understandings that transform them from physical motions into human action" (Wuthnow 1991, 45). The aforementioned Eliasoph's and Lichterman's definition, which this book adopts, also emphasizes the centrality of cultural interpretations of ideal society and actions.

Moreover, the emphasis on meaning does not imply that civil society as an empirical entity must be tied with certain normative ideas. The term "civil society" has never been a univocal concept; instead, it has encompassed a wide range of political views and varied across different historical periods (Cohen and Arato 1992; Ehrenberg 1999). In reality, while people participate in civic engagement with the intention of improving society, their actions largely depend on what kind of society they consider a "good society" and which society they want to improve. Moreover, the ideas of public-spirited people who participate in civic engagement may not fit with "classical" civil society values, which draw much on Tocqueville's cherished conviction about the independence of civil society from the state and its positive role in democracy. In non-Western contexts, people use hybrid codes—multiple cultural codes from diverse legacies—to develop civil inclusion (Lo 2010; Lo and Fan 2010; Baiocchi 2006). Within the field of Chinese civil society, Richard Madsen raises a similar idea that the contours and content of civil society vary across contexts and largely depend on local "moral ecologies." A certain moral idea or an institution, which can be seen as essential to Western civil society, may not be so fundamental or salient in a non-Western context (Madsen 1998, 1993).

In this book, I treat meaning empirically instead of normatively. I see meaning-making as a practice in which one mobilizes available items in one's cultural repertoire or schema to interpret, understand, and justify social life (Sewell 1992; Swidler 2001). The available cultural frames in a society shape actors' cultural repertoire or schemas, but each actor

practices his or her agency by mobilizing different and sometimes conflicting items in their cultural repertoire to interpret actions to meet
demands and deal with dilemmas in particular situations. Without getting into an abstract debate about action and culture, I empirically focus
on what people who are civically engaged do, how they do it, how they
interpret the meanings of their actions, how they deal with ethical dilemmas, and how the political context shapes their civic engagement and
their meanings. The meanings in their engagement are not monolithic;
instead, they are filled with paradoxes, contradictions, and dilemmas.

Context, the third component of civic engagement, includes *structure* and *situation*. We have learned much about the structural conditions of civil society from the complex coexistence approach and the
institutionalist approach (Schofer and Fourcade-Gourinchas 2001;
Riley and Fernández 2014). I follow their insights and pay particular
attention to "the nature of connections between powerful supralocal
institutions and local or particular endeavors" (Skocpol, Ganz, and
Munson 2000, 542). Another factor of context is "situation." Situation
can be defined as an occasion on which an interaction happens among
a certain set of actors. Situations play an intermediary role in turning
structural forces into actual actions (Gonos 1977; Diehl and McFarland 2010; Goffman 1974). Scholars in the micro-sociological tradition
have shown that in real interactions civically engaged people do not
necessarily adhere to the dominant civil society values and norms.
They develop their speech norms, action styles, and patterns of behavior which may differ from the general moral codes but are suitable for
the interaction order in particular situations (Eliasoph and Lichterman 2003; Lichterman 2005; Eliasoph 1998). Overall, this emphasis
on context—both structure and situation—constitutes a remedy to the
neo-Tocquevillian normative idea about civil society by showing how
the joint force of structure and situation shapes civic engagement and
participants' expressions of moral meaning.

WHY DISASTER?

Why the Sichuan earthquake, then? Or, more generally, why is disaster a significant situation through which we can understand civic
engagement?[11]

First, a massive disaster usually serves as an ideal situation for examining a greater variety of civic engagements within one single event, and thus provides a lens through which we can see the complexity in civic engagement. Compared to a riot, a protest, a civil war, or any other "contentious crisis," a disaster involves specific external threats and related practical tasks in solving immediate and technical problems (Dynes and Quarantelli 1971). Thus, a disaster usually starts as a *consensus crisis*, "in which there is a general overall agreement about goals and about what should be done" (Quarantelli 1970, 114).[12] Civic associations and volunteers get involved in disaster relief and provide social services for affected communities and tend to cooperate with government agencies (Dynes and Tierney 1994; Tierney, Lindell, and Perry 2001). On the other hand, a disaster makes otherwise hidden problems visible and forces people to confront flaws in the political system and weaknesses in the structure of society (Klinenberg 2002; Oliver-Smith and Hoffman 1999). This usually leads to more contentious civic engagement, such as advocacy, public debates, and activism, which aim to remedy the deeper causes of the problems: for example, the environmental activism after the Bhopal explosion (Fortun 2001), the anti-nuclear movement after Japan's Fukushima incident (Samuels 2013), and the public debates over racial and economic inequality and mitigation problems after Hurricane Katrina (Eyerman 2015; Adams 2013; Angel et al. 2012; Freudenburg et al. 2009; Brunsma, Overfelt, and Picou 2007). As this book shows, the Sichuan earthquake is not an exception—it also contained both consensual and contentious aspects.

Second, a massive disaster accentuates moral issues pertaining to death and suffering and compels the participants of civic engagement to reflect on the meaning of their actions. It leads to a "collective trauma," "a blow to the basic tissues of social life that damages the bonds attaching people together and impairs the prevailing sense of communality" (Erikson 1976, 154). A natural emotional reaction to this trauma is sympathy and then willingness to help. Sympathy enables the devastated community to reconfirm its solidarity by "repairing" itself through rituals and other meaningful actions (Durkheim [1912] 1995, 213; Turner 1967, 62). Therefore, often a "therapeutic community" (Barton 1969) or "brotherhood of pain" (Oliver-Smith 1999) emerges in the aftermath of a massive disaster.

Civic engagement in disaster relief and recovery is one of the common ways to carry out this repairing function. It is not only practical—it provides food, shelter, and assistance—but also meaningful. It is an act of compassion in an emotionally stressful situation, in which the death and suffering of others compel the participants to think about fundamental issues concerning the meaning of their actions: What is the purpose of my volunteering? What is an appropriate response to people's grief? How exactly can I help reduce their pain? Do emotional encounters with their misery threaten or reinforce my previous convictions? At a deeper level, reflections on the meanings of their actions may lead to serious ethical dilemmas, which the participants may not experience or not in an intensive way in everyday life. For example, when a volunteer sees mismanagement, corruption, and injustice involved in disaster response, he or she might contemplate his or her proper reactions: Should I take the issues to the public, to the government, or just talk about them with friends, or pretend I do not see anything? What if the issues are too obvious or too emotion-loaded to ignore, an "elephant in the room" (Zerubavel 2006), such as the school collapse issue in Sichuan, where shoddy construction could not escape even untrained eyes? When everybody knows the risk of speaking out about injustice, how should I get over the guilt of not doing anything for the grieving and discontented, whom I have been trying to help? Or, are we—mostly organizations but sometimes individuals—justified in exploiting suffering in pursuit of our own commercial, political, and individual interests?

In sum, a massive disaster like the Sichuan earthquake makes visible different types of civic engagement and compels participants of civic engagement to face the complexity of reality and think and talk about the meanings of their actions. The issues revealed by massive disasters exist in "normal times," but disasters dramatize them and give us an opportunity to scrutinize them in a much more intensive way than in everyday settings. As an extreme case, a disaster allows us to examine otherwise small-scale but no less essential phenomena (Klinenberg 2002, 23). Studying extreme cases is "a self-conscious attempt to maximize variance on the dimension of interest" to see the "ideal" situation, in its negative and positive sense, in which latent things can be more manifest (Gerring 2001, 102).

PREVIEW OF ARGUMENTS AND CHAPTERS

The chapters that follow tell an analytical story of grassroots civic engagement in the aftermath of the Sichuan earthquake. The story highlights how citizens acted on the ground, how they interacted with the state, how they interpreted the meanings of their engagement, and how the political context shaped their actions and meanings. In this story, I unpack "civil society" into different actors, including not only staff members of formal NGOs and semi-formal associations but also members of small civic groups, individual volunteers, public intellectuals, the liberal media, political dissidents, and emergent networks of some of these actors. I also unpack the "state" to different levels, actors, and their interactions in different situations, all of which constituted the political context of the engagement: the central government, local governments in Sichuan, state organizations (GONGOs), the disaster management system, and the core state media such as *People's Daily*. In sum, the interactions between the participants and the state were multifaceted and multilayered.

The story consists of four intense episodes of the post-earthquake drama, which are presented respectively in four substantive chapters. First, in the emergency period, approximately within one month after the earthquake, all kinds of volunteers and associations participated in disaster rescue and relief and interacted with central and local governments (Chapter 1). Second, several days after the earthquake, some public intellectuals and liberal media pressed the central government to accept their proposal for an unprecedented mourning for disaster victims, which contained rich meaning about the state's symbolic gesture of concern for citizens' suffering and death; as the proposal was accepted by the state, ordinary Chinese citizens around the country actively participated in the ritual (Chapter 2). Third, during the recovery period, because state-business alliances at the local level dominated the recovery projects and parents' protests provoked governments' restrictions, individual volunteers and associations faced more complex and less favorable political conditions (Chapter 3). Fourth, while the government constructed memorials and narratives to forge official memories for political and commercial purposes, an oppositional "tiny public" of dissidents and intellectuals addressed the school collapse issue and constructed alternative memories by activism and artistic objects (Chapter

4). In the Conclusion, I reiterate the major points and contemplate how the Sichuan case can enrich our understanding of civic engagement in China and beyond.

Overall, this book shows that Chinese citizens expressed their compassion for their fellow citizens' suffering through self-organized civic engagement in the aftermath of the Sichuan earthquake. This civic engagement, however, was enabled and constrained by the political context. It was enabled by the opportunities that emerged from the interaction between the long-term development of Chinese civil society and situational conditions generated by the disaster. Nevertheless, such opportunities varied across types of engagement and situations. At the individual level, participants understood and interpreted their engagement in multivocal and diverse ways, most of which did not follow the classical notion of civil society prevailing in the West or the official narrative of altruism propagated by the Chinese state. Moreover, while all the volunteers expressed their sympathy for the affected people's suffering through their actions, many of them avoided talking about the causes of the suffering—for example, why schools collapsed. This silence and apathy can be explained by various political factors, such as censorship, suppression, and nationalism, which constituted a context conducive to a general inability to think about and talk about politically sensitive issues. Only a tiny public of dissidents and liberal intellectuals, through activism and acts of commemoration, addressed the causes of the collapse of schools. In sum, the civic engagement and the meanings the participants attached to it were deeply shaped by the political context in China.

RESEARCHING CIVIC ENGAGEMENT

I first learned about the Sichuan earthquake when I was in the third year of my graduate study at Northwestern University, thousands of miles away from Sichuan. Suspending my daily routine, I, like many other overseas and domestic Chinese, followed the disaster day and night, often in tears. Sometimes, I had to turn off the TV and the computer because it depressed me to see the many dead bodies, usually children. When I shared this feeling with an informant in Shanghai, he described a similar emotional state: "So many children! Dead! I couldn't watch that anymore! I just walked back and forth in my living room and repeatedly murmured: 'What can I do for them?'"

Spectators have several options to "do something," according to Boltanski (1999): talking about the disaster in the public sphere is helpful, and most spectators did; donating money to help the less fortunate, which I and many other Chinese did too. My wife and I printed out hundreds of flyers with information of trustworthy donation-receiving agencies, and stood in front of the Arch on campus, distributing them to students and faculty. Yet, I was still thinking of a more direct way to help.

At that time, the first group of volunteers from adjacent metropolises such as Chengdu and Mianyang had already arrived in the quake zone, and many began to upload pictures to various online forums, depicting the devastation and their activities. Soon volunteers from distant places, as far as Shanghai and Beijing, flew or drove to the affected areas.

I joined the crowd. I arrived in Dujiangyan with a group of Shanghai volunteers two months after the earthquake. My field notes, which were published as part of an essay, recorded my experience:

> We visited several villages. We showed movies at night to entertain the villagers when the only dynamo was working. Perhaps the most practical task was to look after the children who were out of school for the summer. These jobs were not as easy as they sounded. To gather children, we had to hire a three-wheel motor vehicle, driving from village to village. Often our only option was to walk. The trip could be dangerous, especially as the movies ended near midnight. Eight of us packed into a tiny vehicle and drove on dark mountainous roads. When rain threatened, we had to end our activities early in fear that the rain would trigger landslides.
>
> Trust relationships were easily built. When we picked up children for activities, the parents were delighted. They did not know our names and did not check our ID cards—two strategies people usually rely on when interacting with strangers. One day when we missed a lunch during the activities, we went to the construction site's "outdoor cafeteria," asking for a meal, without paying anything except for a few packs of cigarettes as a polite gesture. Once when we were helping children in a tent residence area, a family bought us several bottles of water. Water might be a small expense for us but not for them, who had just lost their homes and property. Toward the end of our stay, we decided to throw a farewell and thank-you party. We walked around to invite everyone. I was assigned to invite the construction workers, with whom I had a pleasant conversation

facilitated by a ritual of cigarette exchange. At night, as promised, they arrived in their bulldozers. (Xu 2009)

I left the villages with a quite naïve notion of this small and cozy world constituted in the wake of the earthquake. I was moved by the suffering; more precisely, I was moved by *myself*. I felt good about myself because I was able to help those "poor people." Strangely, I was *happier* than I was before I went to Dujiangyan, even after I witnessed much more devastation.

A brief visit, however, shattered my self-congratulating and condescending euphoria. On our way back to Chengdu, we stopped by Juyuan School, whose collapse and the parents' protest were widely reported. Our local driver warned us to walk separately and not to linger at the school, in order to avoid attracting the attention of the police. The whole street where the school was located was sealed off. The police did not allow people—especially those with cameras—to get in, except for local residents. I could only glimpse the outline of remaining part of the collapsed classroom building. Other buildings on the street remained intact or had only cracks on their façades. This image of the collapsed school could not be wiped away from my mind and contrasted with the utopian world I had just left.

This contrast kept disturbing me, especially when the national controversy over the school collapse issue later unfolded into activism. For most people, this controversy might have been just another online debate. Yet, for those who had actually been to the quake zone to help the affected people, this controversy had a deeper personal meaning. A question gradually emerged when I contemplated my experience: If my volunteering was motivated by my intention to reduce people's suffering, then was I justified *not* to say or do anything about the apparent injustice and forced silence that inflicted further suffering on those with the deepest grief—the parents? They had sent their children to school in the morning, only to find they were buried under rubble in the afternoon; they heard their children's cries for help, weeping, and, then, silence. Their children's bodies were deformed and their chests crushed. The question had been nagging at me since my Sichuan trip; and it became even more disturbing on a daily basis when I hugged and kissed my then eight-year-old daughter, who was fortunate enough to study in a safe school and sleep in a safe house. I had no answer to the question.

I realized I had inadvertently become part of a significant historical event in which Chinese citizens had organized themselves to participate in the largest public mobilization since the 1989 Tiananmen
incident. What happened to me—the can-do spirit, the condescending,
feeling-good compassion, and the guilt of being unable to change the
situation—also happened to other people who took part in earthquake-
related public activities. The "do-nice-things" volunteering was not as
simple as it looked. Moreover, as it became clear in the second half
of 2008 and 2009, some bold Chinese started activism to enhance the
awareness of the unhealed wound left on the child victims' parents.
My initial simplistic image of a volunteer was getting more and more
ambiguous. I was convinced that civic engagement was a complex
social and political process. I wanted to find out why and how. That
was the starting point of my seven-year researching and writing on the
Sichuan earthquake.

I started my fieldwork in Shanghai in March 2009. I recruited interviewees through a snowball sampling within my personal networks
developed during my volunteering trip in 2008 and previous projects.
At this stage, I tried to balance the availability of interviewees and my
theoretical hypotheses. The basic principle was to maximize the variation in their participation and demographic features. I conducted 27
recorded interviews in Shanghai and a focus group interview in Taicang,
a city adjacent to Shanghai. I also participated in and observed some
earthquake-related activities, mainly meetings and charity evenings. Yet,
trained as an ethnographer, I still felt it was necessary for me to go to the
site, to "where the action is" (Goffman 1969).

At the end of April, I decided to go to Sichuan for a short exploratory
trip to build contacts. One of the tricks about doing fieldwork in China
(and elsewhere) is to find a person with many connections; such a person
can dramatically facilitate one's research. In other words, one has to find
a Doc—William Whyte's companion and major informant in his *Street
Corner Society* (Whyte [1943] 1993). I was lucky enough to find my Doc.
A few of my interviewees told me, "You should talk to F." F is the owner
of a "serviced residence," a family-run hotel in Chengdu, where many
NGOs, journalists, and volunteers stayed after the earthquake. F was
my access point to the world of people involved in the post-earthquake
engagement. In retrospect, it is clear that without him, my fieldwork in
Sichuan would have been much more difficult.

I flew to Sichuan right before the first anniversary of the earthquake and stayed in F's hotel. After the short trip (about ten days) in May, I went to Sichuan twice more and spent two months in Chengdu and the quake zone. Doing fieldwork in China heavily depends on informal relations (*guanxi*) and mutual trust built on those relations (Yang 1994). F often stayed up late to receive guests who arrived at night. I became his frequent companion during his long midnight shift. We usually purchased cheap but delicious dim sum from street vendors. With beer, food, and cigarettes, we chatted, sometimes joined by other guests who could not sleep and who often had something related to the earthquake to talk about.

F's hotel lounge was a place of interaction for different kinds of people, including volunteers, NGOs, mountaineers, dissident intellectuals, and domestic and foreign journalists. Most of my conversations with them in the lounge were not formal, recorded interviews, but they nonetheless provided valuable information that otherwise would have been hard to obtain. Moreover, almost every Chengdu resident had some experience of the earthquake. Sometimes I even started casual conversations about the quake with complete strangers, such as cab drivers, street vendors, and restaurant waitresses. Thus, my Sichuan fieldwork was more like being truly in the field than conducting recorded interviews. The number of recorded interviews in Sichuan was not dramatically higher than in Shanghai: 29 in two months. Nevertheless, informal conversations, social gatherings, and participant observations provided me with ample information that could not be obtained in Shanghai.

In addition to interviews and observations conducted in Chengdu, I traveled extensively in the quake zone. I've been to most of the severely affected counties: Dujiangyan, Wenchuan, Shifang, Beichuan, Mao County, Mianzhu, An County, and Qingchuan. My companions were individual and small groups of volunteers, corporation-organized groups, NGO workers, and journalists. The trips usually involved driving and walking on rugged roads, undertaking the groups' daily duties, visiting affected people, a lot of conversations, formal interviews, and sometimes manual labor (I once helped load about a hundred boxes of books onto a truck that then delivered them to a school in An County). We usually slept in makeshift houses, musty storage rooms, or wherever we were able to find a bed or a bed-like thing. The most "luxurious" place, however, was a hotel in Mao County where we stayed during a charity trip sponsored by a bank. Such trips provided me with the unique chance to obtain information about group cultures of volunteers and other groups with different purposes. In April and May 2010, about half a year after my fieldwork, I felt I needed more interview data about the mourning rituals and volunteers. I conducted 13 online/phone interviews with some volunteers and NGO staff members.

Altogether I conducted 67 formal, recorded interviews, including individual and focus group interviews. Forty of them were with males and 22 with females. Five were focus group interviews. Many of the interviewees were in their twenties (28) and thirties (18). But there were still a good number of older interviewees: 8 in their forties and 8 in their fifties. Their social-economic status varied widely: a wealthy private entrepreneur who owns a hotel and a nightclub, a few white-collar workers who have salaries above 200,000 yuan, ordinary office workers who struggled to pay the rent, NGO employees, college students, a lawyer, a magazine editor, a travel agent, a photographer, a few writers, a university professor, some unemployed, and a few famous dissidents. Their political views, as the book will show, also included the full political spectrum of contemporary China: ultra-left Maoists, ordinary patriotic people, self-identified "liberal" (ziyoupai) intellectuals, and dissidents.

My identity in the fieldwork fell somewhere between an insider and an outsider. As an insider, I myself was a volunteer without research purposes in 2008 and identified myself as a volunteer/researcher during the fieldwork period in 2009. I shared with my "research subjects" many common experiences—joy and sorrow, stress and pain—and thus acquired an empathetic understanding of the stories they told me. More generally, I grew up in China and went to the United States to restart my graduate studies at a relatively old age. My long-time immersion in Chinese society was a blessing for my ethnography. Often wearing sandals, tees, and shorts during my fieldwork, I talked, walked, and acted like an ordinary Chinese man in his thirties, without making an effort to manage my impression. I simply walked into the crowd and disappeared.

In retrospect, my insider identity as a volunteer and my Chinese appearance and habitus also protected me from the political surveillance that usually upset my non-Chinese or overseas Chinese colleagues, whose appearance, accent, and demeanor make them especially visible in the field. Certainly, such habitus had to be sustained and complemented by an in-depth knowledge of what to do and when to stop in a potentially precarious situation, given that the topic of the Sichuan earthquake was politically charged. Working and traveling as a volunteer in the quake zone was not particularly politically sensitive, but conversations, dinners, and interviews with dissidents, almost all of whom had been detained, or jailed, or blacklisted, could be a little more dangerous. I usually followed their suggestions about venues and times of meeting to avoid the attention of the police because they knew much more about the local situation and carefully took into consideration my identity as an "American" scholar. At the same time, I refrained from posting anything about our meetings to online spaces. By doing this, I believed I also conformed to the regulations and ethics of protecting research subjects. Overall, in this book I do not present an "action-movie-hero" story, as some ethnographers do, in which the fieldworker sneaked out information from behind the "iron curtain," because nothing like that ever happened to me. Of course, this does not mean that I ignore the latent and manifest ways political power sets limits on people's perceptions and actions, which in fact are at the heart of this book.

The downside of being an insider might be a lack of emotional and cognitive distance from one's research subjects, which results in too sympathetic a view of their experience. I do not believe any ethnographer can completely free himself or herself from such a dilemma, but in practice and writing, I try to be reflexive by presenting diverse experiences, ironies, and problems. While some of my descriptions substantiate a picture of warm-hearted volunteers, many parts of the book may make the reader ponder their limitations and even doubt their words and actions.

I was also an outsider: a researcher, a Ph.D. candidate from an American university. Usually, I identified myself as a researcher, who wanted to do his work by "experiencing" (tiyan) volunteering in addition to interviewing. This identity did not surprise anyone because at the time I did my fieldwork, a big crowd of researchers from Chinese and Hong Kong universities also flocked to Sichuan to spend their newly acquired funds on projects on community reconstruction, social work, psychiatric therapy, economic development, nongovernmental associations, and so on. I was considered as, and I indeed was, one of them. During some interviews, particularly cold interviews with people with whom I had no previous contact, my "American" identity may have influenced their words and the self-images they wanted to project through their stories.

On one occasion (Chapter 3, the interview with Jiajun), the interviewee expressed his concern with my identity as "someone from the United States" and was reluctant to comment on the school collapse issue. Such a reaction, however, was not evident in other interviews. From a broader perspective, as Chinese youths studying abroad had already become prevalent by 2008, encountering someone who studied in the United States and came back to volunteer in the quake zone was not unusual. Moreover, during my participant observation, my research purpose was mostly forgotten after a few hours.

I aimed to locate the fieldwork in the macro-level historical context by examining the influence of macro-level processes, structures, and situations on the micro-level actions and meanings. To achieve this, I collected textual and visual materials from various sources, including press reports, online texts, government documents, media images, memoirs, online videos, museums, memorials, and the quantitative and qualitative data collected by Chinese social scientists. The textual data were collected during my fieldwork in 2009 and a few research trips to major libraries in China and the United States.

Eight years after I first went to Sichuan, I finished the manuscript of this book. Many things related to the earthquake have happened during those eight years and compelled me to revise the manuscript again and again. After zigzagging through different themes, theories, and analytical frameworks, which, however, resulted in a few articles (Xu 2012, 2016), I finally went back to my original purpose: to understand the participants' experience, the contextual conditions of their actions, the way in which they interpreted their actions, and the dilemmas they faced. To some extent, the book remains unfinished since the things I saw after the earthquake are still developing in other arenas of Chinese society.

CHAPTER 1

Consensus Crisis

In the wake of the Sichuan earthquake, Luqiong, an employee of an NGO in Shanghai, immediately called her parents in Sichuan, who fortunately were safe and sound. Saddened by the tragedy that had befallen other Sichuanese, she incessantly checked the news and rising death toll. The next day, she decided to do something more than just whimpering in front of a computer screen. She called her colleagues in other NGOs in Shanghai, and after a quick meeting, they decided to form a coalition to collect donations and deliver supplies. They named their network New Operation Hump, after the Chinese and American air forces' supply transportation route over the Himalayas during World War II. Their achievements surprised even themselves. Within two weeks, they had collected so many supplies that they had to borrow a warehouse to store them and later managed to find an airline, which generously gave them space in a cargo plane to deliver their materials, free of charge. Rumor had it that "they got an airplane to deliver their stuff!" Modestly, Luqiong attributed their achievements to the donators' "goodness" (*shanyi*) instead of her own efforts.

Many coalitions like New Operation Hump emerged after the earth-quake, gathering together civic associations and volunteers who worked enthusiastically in the disaster relief. Collectively, these associations and coalitions constituted a vast network that served as a hub for volunteering. They demonstrated an ability to mobilize resources and to respond quickly, creatively, and enthusiastically. In the first months after the earthquake, everywhere in the quake zone one could easily bump into groups of people who introduced themselves as *zhiyuanzhe* ("volunteers") from a *gongyi zuzhi* ("public-welfare organization"), both terms that used to be neologisms but now sounded familiar to the local people. With sanitization masks, backpacks, sneakers, and T-shirts emblazoned with uplifting messages like "I ♥ China" or "*Xiongqi* (Be strong!) Sichuan," the volunteers assisted responders and the affected people alike. The volunteers were also everywhere in cities outside of Sichuan. At train stations, with mountains of backpacks and baggage, they waited for trains bound for Sichuan. They stood on street corners and sidewalks, with boxes and little red hats, calling for donations. Years later, this large-scale volunteering remained an emblematic image of the Sichuan earthquake.

The government demonstrated an unusually receptive attitude toward this large-scale public participation. Luqiong said: "I have been interacting with the government since I started my career, but this was the first time that officials didn't repeatedly ask me, 'Who are you? Why are you doing this?' For the first time, they didn't trap me in a maze of telephone calls to make me lose my patience and hope."[1] Before they found the generous airline that provided them with cargo space, the New Operation Hump mustered up the courage to ask the Civil Affairs Bureau in Shanghai for help. To their surprise, instead of interrogating them about their qualifications and registration status, the officials tried to provide them with the best available solutions. Although Civil Affairs did not solve the issue, Luqiong and her colleagues were impressed by their cooperative attitude. Their interactions with various local governments in Sichuan were also unusually smooth. Other NGOs and small groups reported that officials' attitudes were "warm," "reasonable," or at least "not hostile." Press reports and scholarly studies corroborated my interviewees' stories. In the very first weeks, the earthquake prompted local governments, provincial and national government bureaus, and GONGOs to cooperate with NGOs and informal

FIGURE 3. A volunteer plays with children in An County. June 2, 2008.
Reuters/Jason Lee.

groups, often for the first time. A few well-known NGOs with strained
relations with the state, such as Friends of Nature (*Ziranzhiyou*),
undertook some reconstruction programs with local governments in
the quake zone (Zhu, Wang, and Hu 2009, 226). Even B-log, a blog that
attracted "liberal intellectuals" interested in criticizing the government, worked with local governments to distribute the materials they
collected. Given the often strained relations between the Chinese state
and civic associations, such cooperation was unusual. This experience
made Luqiong "feel more confident in this world I live in, my career,
and China's future," because, using a Buddhist image, it "opened my
eyes to many things as beautiful and pure as a lotus."

Sorrow and compassion drive people to volunteer to offer help. Volunteering had happened in previous major disasters in the history of
the People's Republic of China, for example in the 1976 Tangshan earthquake. The official political culture also prized bursts of altruistic behavior in disasters, in the form of donations, assistance from around the
country to the affected place, and mutual help among the victims. This
altruism was encapsulated in a slogan widely used in official discourses

about disaster: "As people in one place are experiencing adversity, people from other places come to help" (*yifang younan, bafang zhiyuan*).

Nevertheless, although we cannot deny the enthusiasm and compassion of volunteers in the Mao years, their post-disaster volunteering was mobilized, organized, and controlled by the state, through a top-down fabric of work units (*danwei*) and party-state organizations like the Youth League. This state-mobilization model still existed to some extent in the wake of the Sichuan earthquake: for example, a significant number of volunteers were organized by state organizations like the Red Cross, and members of the Communist Party were required to pay "special party membership fees," a form of mandatory donation.

What was new after the Sichuan earthquake, however, was that numerous civic associations—from formal NGOs like the one Luqiong worked for to small, hobby groups—rather than state organizations mobilized volunteers and collected incalculable amounts of donations. Most scholars recognize this important phenomenon of grassroots civic engagement and attribute it to the long-term development of Chinese civic associations. Shieh and Deng, for example, suggest that "the widespread participation of volunteers and associations in earthquake relief shows that civil society in China has made significant progress in recent years" (Shieh and Deng 2011, 181). Empirical evidence substantiates this argument. The Sichuan earthquake did not create volunteering overnight. However, it served as a catalyst for realizing the power and ideas accumulated in the rapid development of Chinese civic associations in recent decades. It was a moment when various civic associations and actors stepped onto the national and even international stage to demonstrate their capacity.

Nevertheless, this undoubtedly correct explanation does not tell us much about the catalyst itself, the earthquake. It indicates only a necessary but not sufficient condition. It constructs a direct causal relation between the structural conditions of civil society and civic engagement. A reasonable deduction from this causation is that civic engagement would have occurred in other large-scale events at the same historical moment since the structural features of state-society relations were the same as those in the wake of the Sichuan earthquake. The year 2008 provided two natural comparative cases: the snowstorm in January and February and the Beijing Olympics in August, both of which needed services from civil society. There was no large-scale volunteering after the snowstorm. Many volunteers worked for the Beijing Olympics, but they were strictly organized and trained by the Youth League and other state organizations.

Why was it the Sichuan earthquake, instead of other events at the same historical moment, with the same structural conditions, that made civil society participation possible? Why did large-scale grassroots volunteering not occur after previous disasters? Why did the Chinese state cooperate with civic associations, given its usual caution and restrictions on civil society? In other words, we need to know more about the *contextual conditions* that enabled this unusual level of volunteering.

We also want to know how the participants actually worked in this larger political context. How did they interact with local governments, the Youth League, the Red Cross, and various state bureaus? What resources did they mobilize? How did they gain trust when reaching out beyond their own group? How did they deal with the issues that emerged from their interactions with the state? Moreover, we must listen to how they articulated the meanings of their civic engagement. Volunteering is a meaning-loaded action. Distant volunteering like that in Sichuan could be tedious, costly, and even dangerous. People have legitimate reasons not to volunteer—job, family, budget, time, etc. Thus, they need meaningful ideas and emotions to sustain their commitment. How did they interpret their actions? What did they feel? How did their meaning-making reflect broader cultural changes in Chinese society?

This chapter is devoted to an examination of the structural and situational conditions that enabled the grassroots volunteering, the volunteer groups' and associations' actual actions, and the meanings they attached to those actions. To fully understand the complexity and variation of the interactions, I unpack both the state and civil society. I examine not only different levels of the state (central to local) and different state sectors (disaster management agencies, propaganda departments, state organizations, and the Communist Party) but also different types of civic associations and groups, from formal NGOs to small groups. I also go beyond the macro- and meso-levels of analysis, on which most civil society studies focus, and explore how individual participants understood their actions at a significant historical moment.

CONTEXT

The most important feature of the context in which the Sichuan earth-quake volunteering took place was a "consensus crisis," a type of crisis in which different parties are motivated by a common goal to undertake practical tasks instead of confronting each other. Compared to "conten-tious crises" like riots and ethnic conflicts, disasters create community-wide problems and a consensus on what needs to be done—usually saving lives and relieving suffering. This consensus reduces the possi-bility of conflicts and leads to an upsurge in mutual helping during the emergency (Dynes and Quarantelli 1971). The concept of a consensus crisis is tied to one of the most verified findings in the sociology of disas-ter. Although it has been challenged by some empirical cases of violence and conflicts occurring after disasters, its core insights are still useful: situational opportunities and incentives mediate the structure's influ-ence on action.

The consensus crisis in the wake of the Sichuan earthquake had four features: challenges to the state's administrative capacity; the need for civil society's services; the moral politics involved in disaster response; and a consensus about goals and priorities. Those features weakened some structural factors and strengthened others and finally led to a favorable context for civic engagement.

Challenges to the State's Administrative Capacity

As discussed at the beginning of the Introduction, the Sichuan earth-quake posed many administrative challenges to the Chinese state's disaster management system because of its unparalleled scale. Other challenges were less sensational but equally important. For example, the earthquake seriously compromised and damaged local state appa-ratuses in the quake-stricken area. Many local officials died, lost their families, or were injured. CNN reported on a township official named Zhao Haiqing in Chenjiaba, Beichuan, who, despite having lost his son and parents, still worked around the clock to organize the town's response work. Zhao was just one of the many local officials who lost their immediate relatives but continued to work under tremendous emotional and administrative stress. In Beichuan, where he worked, for example, about 23 percent of local officials died, 200 were injured, and many more lost family members (Deng 2009, 30). When Jing Dazhong, the Beichuan county magistrate, assembled the surviving county officials above *ke* (subcounty) rank and called the roll, most officials were not there because they had either died—including one of the seven vice-magistrates—or were severely injured. Even the surviving officials in understaffed townships were overwhelmed by the daunting tasks ahead. A volunteer who went down to the quake zone said the township officials he encountered apparently worked around the clock. Consequently, they lost their voices, and their faces turned "blackish-red like pig livers."[2]

The local governments' compromised capacity also exacerbated a problem in China's disaster management system: lack of a well-established, community-based response system. The Chinese government did not put emergency management on its major policy agenda until the 2003 SARS crisis revealed the potential political risk of a public health incident (Kleinman and Watson 2006).[3] As the SARS epidemic subsided, the State Council redesigned a comprehensive emergency response plan in 2005, and the National People's Congress passed the *Emergency Response Law* in 2007. In 2006, the State Council set up the China National Commission for Disaster Reduction to coordinate response efforts at the central and local levels. In theory, China's disaster management system runs on the "local management principle" (*shudi guanli yuanze*): the local government is responsible for initiating the response plan and managing the emergency as it unfolds, and has the authority to command government bureaus and even local armed forces. In reality, however, if a disaster is defined as a "particularly massive emergency" (Category I in the Comprehensive Response Plan), the central government will organize a special task force, directed by state leaders at the vice-premier level, to go to the site to lead the response. Consequently, local governments' power is significantly restricted. Some scholars and policy-makers in China view this "whole-country system" (*juguo tizhi*) as an advantage because it enables the central government to bypass institutional barriers and gather resources from throughout the country to manage emergencies in a speedy manner (Gao 2010; Shan 2011).

The centralization, however, overburdens the national agency, which has to take care of many trivial tasks in addition to coordinating more than thirty national bureaus and ministries, as well as all the provincial agencies. By contrast, as experts and even Civil Affairs officials point out

(Chen 2012; Li, Yang, and Yuan 2005, 13–40), local governments do not have adequate incentives to invest in disaster management, especially as economic growth has become the most important criterion for evaluating local officials' performance. Therefore, the local disaster response system, particularly below the city/regional level and in rural areas, lacks basic personnel and equipment. The trained professionals and supply warehouses are mostly based in larger cities, and, as the Sichuan earthquake shows, it takes time for supplies and personnel to reach the disaster zone. This delay was even more critical when the famously rugged "Sichuan roads" were damaged. As an Asian Development Bank (ADB) report on the technical aspect of the Sichuan earthquake response points out, "there were, therefore, significant difficulties in gathering a sufficiently large rescue force to meet the rescue needs presented by the earthquake, even by tapping the entire rescue resources of the country. This led to some major shortfalls in the delivery of rescue services, particularly in rural and mountain areas" (Asian Development Bank 2008, 130). Even professional responder teams at the provincial and central levels were understaffed and underequipped. The China International Search & Rescue Team (CISRT) was one of the few highly trained and professionally equipped response teams in the country, but it had only 214 members (in 2008), all based in Beijing. The level of equipment and training of the provincial response teams varied greatly. For example, in the wake of the Sichuan earthquake, the Sichuan provincial team had to borrow an emergency communications vehicle from the relatively better-equipped Yunnan team (Teng 2008). Overall, as an expert from the CISRT admitted, China's professional response teams very much lagged behind those in developed countries. For instance, in Germany, there are 2.14 professional responders for every 10,000 people. This number is 1.73 in France and 0.15 in the United States, while in China, it is 0.011, less than one-tenth of that in the United States, less than 1 percent of the number in France, and less than 0.5 percent the number in Germany (Shan 2011, 136).

In a real-world disaster response, the Chinese army, the Armed Police, and firefighters undertake major tasks. In the wake of the Sichuan earthquake, the Chinese state demonstrated its impressive mobilizing capability by gathering and dispatching more than 100,000 soldiers and firefighters to the quake zone. Nevertheless, without firsthand data it is hard to evaluate their efficiency. Reports and TV footage show that the soldiers sometimes had to rely on simple tools like shovels and pickaxes to dig through the rubble. The Chinese air force's helicopters also had difficulty landing in places with complex geographic features and weather conditions. The most efficient response, according to technical reports like that by the ADB, was the medical assistance. There were no large-scale epidemics after the Sichuan earthquake. This can be explained by what other responders lacked: the doctors and nurses were highly trained, fully equipped professionals.

In addition to rescues, there was an endless list of small but urgent tasks that had to be undertaken immediately: moving and processing corpses and rubble; sanitizing places with heavy casualties; identifying victims; nursing and caring for senior, young, disabled, and injured people; delivering supplies to remote villages lacking big roads to the outside; transporting the injured to medical facilities; and providing psychological counseling and therapy for traumatized survivors. Many of these tasks fell outside the scope of the official response plan, or were included in it but inadequately executed because of an insufficient number of personnel and lack of attention to the details.

Need for Civil Society's Services

The disaster's administrative challenges compelled the state to mobilize every possible resource to carry out the response tasks. Consequently, public services provided by civil society were needed. What was involved was not a top-down process, however, but a back-and-forth interaction between the state and society at different levels. The overwhelmed local governments in Sichuan immediately sent an unambiguous call for help from society. Several hours after the earthquake, local radio anchors in Chengdu called for blood donations. This led to the widely reported long lines at blood banks in Chengdu. The radio also called on citizens with vehicles to transport injured local people from the overcrowded hospitals in Dujiangyan to Chengdu. Numerous taxi drivers used their internal radio networks to call on each other to rush to Dujiangyan and picked up patients for free.

In the quake zone, village- and township-level governments sent out messengers to seek help from higher levels of government, or indeed, from whomever they met. A local school teacher, Mr. Chen, in Chenjiaba, Beichuan, told me that he was sent out by the township authorities to ask for help from the Jiangyou government or anyone he encountered on his way, the sooner the better. On his way, Mr. Chen met a group of motorcyclists and asked them to use their motorcycles to transport the affected people in Chenjiaba because their small vehicles could get through the broken up roads. When the motorcyclists appeared reluctant, Mr. Chen knelt down in tears to beg them. Many local officials in other places, when interviewed by the media, anxiously, and sometimes tearfully, called for help from all walks of society. Some village and township governments at first habitually attempted to conceal the devastation, as a few of my interviewees' witnesses suggested, but this was quickly discouraged by the central government, which decidedly emphasized openness in information to facilitate an effective response.

This urgency created a temporary opportunity for civic associations to participate in a large-scale public activity. The opportunity, however, did not automatically translate into actual participation. First, the state did not have a clearly designed mechanism to incorporate social organizations into its disaster management system. The *National Comprehensive Response Plan for Public Emergencies* (2006), China's governmental emergency management plan, does have an article about the role of social organizations (Article 1.5[5]): "To strengthen local-based emergency response teams and establish a coordination system, we need to fully mobilize and realize the function of towns and townships, communities, corporations and non-corporate *danwei*, social organizations and volunteers." Nevertheless, as with many other Chinese public policies, the plan does not provide any details about how civic associations could be used to strengthen the local disaster system. As a result, the participation of civic association is not institutionally guaranteed but is subject to the vagaries of particular situations.

Second, in practice, the state usually sought assistance from GONGOs, particularly the Red Cross, which deployed its stored supplies to the affected areas and recruited volunteers through its national network (Deng 2009, 31). Its capacity for organizing volunteers and mobilizing resources from society was quickly overwhelmed by the huge demand, particularly in Chengdu, the receiving end of its response chain. With only seventeen staff members, the Sichuan Provincial Red Cross received and processed 2 billion yuan in donations and numerous materials (Tu 2008). The number of volunteers waiting in front of the Sichuan Red Cross office for an assignment, according to my informants, ranged from several hundred to almost a thousand every day for the first two weeks. Some volunteers registered with the Red Cross or the Youth League but never got a callback. Donated food had gone bad in the poorly managed Red Cross warehouse, because there were not enough vehicles to make deliveries. The overpowered GON-GOs frustrated many citizens, who then joined NGOs and informal groups. One of my interviewees, a volunteer who decided to go by himself, "stole" medicine from the Red Cross's unguarded warehouse and delivered it to the quake zone.

This huge pressure also revealed the Red Cross's management problems. The Red Cross was the biggest official collector of donations, but it only provided incomplete and outdated information about those donations. This lack of transparency inevitably and immediately provoked public criticism. To make things worse, a Red Cross official mentioned in a TV interview that about a thousand tents with a value of 13 million yuan would be delivered to the quake zone. Some people thus calculated that the price for each tent was about 13,000 yuan, significantly higher than the market average. Later, a Red Cross spokesperson clarified that the number was wrong, but people's distrust of the organization had already taken root.

Consequently, situational urgency overrode institutional ambiguities and constraints with regard to the participation of civic associations. Although very few Chinese civic associations have specialized disaster rescue and relief functions,[4] many of them had prior experience of providing social services. Thus, they were able to carry out tasks that required only a few hours of training or no training at all, for instance purchasing, delivering, and distributing food and water; transporting evacuees; updating information online; collecting donations; directing traffic; cooking meals; babysitting, and so on.

The Moral Politics of Disaster Response

The challenges to the state's administrative capacity were also challenges to its moral authority. The heavy casualties and widespread devastation caused by the Sichuan earthquake generated an outpouring of compassion, which made the life-and-death crisis more urgent and put the state's response under more intense scrutiny. This urgency was strengthened by events that transpired before the earthquake.

In March 2008, three months before the earthquake struck, Tibetan monks and laymen launched protests in Tibet and Tibetan areas of other provinces. The state media depicted the uprisings as riots, with Tibetans killing Han Chinese, whereas Tibetan exiles condemned the state's brutal crackdown and its long-term discriminatory ethnic policies that had provoked the unrest. The Chinese state clearly lost the competition for the international moral high ground as it denied the foreign media access to Tibet. Later, in April Tibetan supporters and human rights activists protested and disturbed the carefully arranged Olympic torch relay in several overseas cities and clashed with overseas Chinese. Some international organizations even called for a boycott of the Beijing Olympics (Brownell 2012).

In the wake of these events, on the eve of the Sichuan earthquake, the Chinese state's image was at stake. The central government clearly recognized the political importance of its image in a year of image-making. Two days after the earthquake, an editorial by the pseudonymous Zhong Zuwen published in *People's Daily* analogized the disaster response as a test or even a "great battle,"[5] which must be the top priority of party organizations at all levels, particularly those in the quake zone (Zhong 2008). The apparatuses of the central party-state, including the military, various party organizations, and all bureaus and levels of the government, made similar pronouncements, stressing that the disaster response was first and foremost a *political* task. Moreover, to ensure that local governments strictly carried out the central government's orders, state leaders went to the quake zone to supervise rescue and relief efforts. In addition to Premier Wen Jiabao's widely reported swift appearance in the quake zone only hours after the earthquake, most members of the Politburo Standing Committee went to Sichuan in the first two weeks. According to a tacit logic of Chinese politics, the presence of almost all of the state's leaders conveyed an unambiguous message that the central government "attached great importance to" (*zhongshi*) the disaster response. Local governments and various governmental administrations were expected to strive to do better.

Official discourses emphasized "saving people's lives" as the state's top priority. Wen Jiabao reiterated several times during his visit to Sichuan that even if there was a 1 percent chance of survival, the state would make a 100 percent effort to save every life. About five days after the quake, when people under the rubble had almost no chance of surviving, the central leaders still emphasized that rescuing people was the "most important of important tasks" (*zhongzhong zhizhong*) and ordered a more careful and thorough search (Xinhua News Agency 2008). This effort was technically inefficient, and whether the responders followed the central government's order to search or acted according to their own assessment of the situation remains unknown. Nevertheless, the order made perfect political sense because it was intended to demonstrate the government's care for people's lives and because it served the goal of enhancing the government's moral legitimacy. Consequently, mobilizing every possible resource from society to achieve a better disaster response was not just a management issue but also a moral-political issue.

The state also faced the issue of how to react to the emerging wave of volunteering. The message from local governments clearly indicated their urgent need for whatever assistance was available, and civic associations' work had been proven helpful in the first couple of days. There was no clear sign of political "instability" in the quake zone. The central state had no reason to dampen citizens' enthusiasm. Moreover, the moral values demonstrated in the volunteering—compassion, mutual help, and solidarity—were in line with the official altruism the state propagated, although the official altruism in the Communist political culture prioritized the interests of the party, the people, and the collective (*jiti*).

On May 14, Wen Jiabao shook hands with an American volunteer from an international organization and thanked him for his contributions. Chinese volunteers also appeared several times in reports of leaders' visits to the quake zone. For example, a report by *People's Daily* and the Xinhua News Agency described President Hu Jintao's brief meeting with a volunteer, who had lost her grandfather in the earthquake but "turned sorrow into power" and devoted herself to relief. Hu Jintao held her hands and praised her perseverance and contribution (Sun 2008). These small actions from state leaders conveyed a clearly welcoming message.

Nevertheless, a keen observer can discern political subtlety and ambiguity in these positive messages. Official reports tended to emphasize the contributions of *individual volunteers* or the volunteers mobilized by state organizations, such as the Red Cross and the Youth League, but not civic associations (*China Youth Daily* 2008a). Thus, these reports implicitly signaled that volunteering was certainly much needed but should be in the form of atomistic individuals under the state's control. Various levels of government and state organizations also called for volunteering but emphasized that individual volunteers without "special skills"—such as medical care and disaster response—should not "blindly" go to Sichuan. Volunteers must be organized by the local Youth League or Red Cross (*China Youth Daily* 2008b). In reality, however, the state's ambivalence did not come across. Volunteers rarely—if not never—discern such political subtlety. The ambiguity justified ordinary citizens' participation outside of state-controlled channels. "Volunteer" became a badge of honor and an automatic pass for any helper, although some "volunteers" were in fact NGO employees.

Consensus on Priorities and Goals

In the very first days after the earthquake, a few issues, including the government's response and the collapse of schools, emerged in the public sphere. Nevertheless, public opinion reached an instant consensus, across the political spectrum, on putting aside all debates and criticisms and focusing on saving people's lives. Qian Gang, a renowned liberal intellectual, former editor-in-chief of *Southern Weekend*, an important liberal newspaper, and author of the widely acclaimed *Tangshan Earthquake*, called for immediate action instead of debates:

> Some media friends have started to look for answers to questions about responsibility and problems. What I want to say to you is: yes, what you want to do is correct but now is not the right time. . . . Nothing is more important than human lives. At this moment, when tens of thousands of people's lives are in jeopardy, let us focus on the battle for life. Let us make constructive suggestions to the administrators, cheer on the responders who are going to the epicenter on foot, and pray for compatriots who are struggling in the dark. . . . Any words pale into insignificance now. Take action! The most essential thing is action! (Qian 2008a)

Some dissidents and liberal intellectuals also trimmed their criticisms and joined the crowd of volunteers. B-log, a large blog-hosting website that attracted many famous liberal intellectuals, political bloggers, and dissidents, collected 2,260,642.39 yuan ($327,155 in 2008), organized a response team to fly to Sichuan, and used the money to purchase supplies and deliver them to the quake zone.[6]

A few issues emerged as a result of ambiguities in the structural relations between the state and civic associations, but these were quickly resolved given the consensus on priorities and goals. A major issue was illegal donation collecting. In China, only governments above the county level and a few state-sanctioned public foundations have the legal right to receive donations and organize fund-raising activities (Chinese Ministry of Civil Affairs 2008). In the wake of the Sichuan earthquake, however, numerous civic associations, which did not have the right to collect donations from the public, ignored this regulation and actively engaged in all kinds of fund-raising activities. In addition to formal NGOs, those associations included local chambers of commerce, online forums, volunteers' associations, homeowners' associations, and even small groups that emerged in the wake of the earthquake. They gained the trust of donors partly because most of them, even the online forums that consisted of anonymous users, could provide detailed and timely information about the use and delivery of donations.

On this matter, the state had a moral-legal dilemma. On the one hand, it did not want to dampen the spontaneous enthusiasm, which could complement its official altruism. On the other hand, without regulations, illegal donation collection could spin out of control and potentially serve as a hotbed for fraud. This worry was not unfounded. Right after the earthquake, the police found rampant text message scams and hacked web pages using the Red Cross's name to urge people to send donations to private bank accounts. There was only a fine line between illegal but well-intentioned donation collecting and actual fraud. Both operated online or through other virtual communications, used private bank accounts, and were run by strangers. However, the differences between them were certainly salient to the people involved. Some NGOs and associations already had a well-established reputation. Small groups operated within extended personal networks and thus did not face incidences of fraud. Some online donation-collecting activities were organized by long-time participants in many online and offline activities, whose real identities were already known. However, these local nuances did not make immediate sense to law enforcement.

Therefore, the state had to maintain a balance between legal flexibility and fraud prevention. To prevent fraud, governments at various levels emphasized the government's and state organizations' exclusive right to fundraise. On May 20, about a week after the earthquake, for example, the Sichuan Provincial Earthquake Response Headquarters issued an announcement urging people not to "make donations to informal work units" (*Sichuan Daily* 2008b).

In practice, however, law enforcement adjusted the restrictions to suit the situation. Some interviewees reported being investigated by the police. But such investigations were mainly concerned with potential fraud rather than illegal donation collecting, and were often quickly completed. For example, Caring Babies, a group formed by two young business partners, launched a blog to collect donations. They cautiously refused all monetary donations and only accepted products related to babies and toddlers, mainly diapers and baby formula. They also kept careful documentation. The local police in Shanghai visited their company and investigated alleged "fraudulence" and "human trafficking" because they had also organized volunteers to go to Sichuan. Xiaoli, one of the two members, described the policemen as "friendly" and said that they did not seem to take the charges too seriously. When Xiaoli claimed that they had not done anything wrong, the policemen responded, "Yes, we knew that because we've been following your blog for a while. If you really did something wrong, you wouldn't be just sitting here talking to me."[7] Other groups' bank accounts were frozen temporarily but soon were reinstated after they provided evidence of their donation collecting. Many groups I interviewed held various kinds of public charity activities involving money collecting, such as charity sales, street campaigns, and online donations, but were not even investigated.

This flexibility was also manifested in a few minor clashes between the state and grassroots associations. As anticipated by the B-log organizers, their impressive ability to collect donations in their large online community got them into trouble with the police, who froze their bank accounts after seeing the unusual cash flow. The organizers decided to take a risky move: they called on more than twenty journalists from domestic and foreign media outlets and went to the City Police Bureau to demand the money back. Shinan, one of the organizers, described the process to me: "We went there with twenty-some journalists, mainly from the foreign media, with cameras, camcorders, and lighting devices. We actually frightened those boys in the City Police Bureau. Laoluo [owner of B-log] strode into their office—you know, he's a tall and big guy, a northeastern person, an imposing character—and began railing, 'You fucking [*tamade*] hooligans in uniform!'"[8] The police officers' faces, according to Shinan, suddenly turned pale, but they restrained their anger because of the journalists' presence. At the time of the earthquake, Chengdu was in the spotlight, and foreign and domestic journalists were able to report in an unprecedentedly free manner. Even a small issue involving the government would be reported widely. Therefore, all state sectors cautiously adjusted their performance in front of the camera so as not to damage the government's image. Moreover, B-log gathered many influential political bloggers and self-proclaimed "liberal intellectuals" whose criticisms of the Chinese government were often cited by foreign reporters. Consequently, the account was reinstated. Such an interaction would have been unthinkable during "normal" times.

In sum, despite the tragedy and devastation it caused, the Sichuan earthquake led to a consensus crisis that facilitated Chinese citizens' civic engagement through civic associations. It posed challenges to the Chinese state's disaster management system, and thus the state—particularly local governments—needed grassroots associations' social services to undertake the response tasks effectively, especially when GONGOs were quickly overwhelmed by the post-disaster need for aid. This urgent need significantly reduced the state's institutional restrictions on civic associations. It fit well with the imbalanced development of Chinese civil society in which social-service-delivering associations had grown more rapidly than other types of associations. At the same time, the Chinese state's moral image was at risk, particularly in the aftermath of several crises since the beginning of 2008, such as the snowstorm, the Tibetan riots, and the Olympic relay incidents. Moreover, the civic associations' spontaneous altruistic actions had some common ground with the state's official altruism, and were thus encouraged by the state. State and society also reached a consensus concerning the overarching importance of saving people's lives. This weakened the conflicts and differences between the state and society on some legally ambiguous issues, such as illegal donation collecting. All these features collectively created a favorable political context for large-scale civic engagement.

Comparative Cases

Why did such large-scale grassroots civic engagement not occur in previous disasters? To answer this question we must think in both structural and situational terms. A consensus crisis is a result of the interplay between structural state-civil society relations and the situation. It will not occur if the structural conditions do not provide citizens with channels and resources outside the state system to participate in large-scale public activities. For example, in 1976, when the Tangshan earthquake struck, civil society did not even exist. Therefore, although it was by far the deadliest earthquake in the history of the People's Republic of China, it did not lead to a large wave of grassroots volunteering.

Another comparable disaster was the 1998 floods of the Yangtze River, which broke riverbanks in multiple spots, caused heavy casualties, and overwhelmed the government's administrative capacity. Nevertheless, it did not lead to large-scale civic participation in disaster relief mainly because of the lack of structural readiness in the 1990s. The development of Chinese civic associations in the late 1990s remained nascent and was restricted by the state's regulations. In 1997, the central government launched a "clean-up and reorganization" campaign to tighten control over the registration of NGOs and other issues by updating "Regulations on Social Group Registration and Administration." The campaign lasted two years, until October 1999 (Wang 2011, 23). A direct result of this control was a decrease in the number of social organizations in the period from 1997 to 1999 (Watson 2008, 37).

Some disasters do not lead to a consensus crisis even when structural conditions are favorable. This is because situational features do not always turn structural conditions into opportunities for civic engagement. For example, the 2003 SARS epidemic broke out at a moment when China was experiencing an associational revolution in which civic associations mushroomed and endeavored to make a difference. The scale of the epidemic might have provided these associations with an opportunity to get involved. Yet SARS only led to sporadic volunteering (Geng and Hu 2011; Schwartz 2009). The absence of participation could be explained by the epidemic's nature and the state's corresponding quarantine. The infectiousness of the disease deterred large-scale human mobility and convergence. The state's quarantine further strengthened immobility, making convergence almost impossible. The Chinese state also exerted draconian control over transportation and the flow of people between and within cities. People who traveled to Hong Kong were quarantined, and inbound and outbound transportation to and from Beijing was shut down for a while (Kleinman and Watson 2006; Davis and Siu 2006). This centralized and top-down response strengthened the state's control over society instead of opening an opportunity for ordinary citizens

(Thornton 2009). Moreover, the response system was not overpowered; therefore, the epidemic did not lead to a nationwide consensus crisis.

A consensus crisis creates a situational opening for citizens to access the political opportunity structure, but whether they can seize the opportunity depends not only on their structural readiness but also on their interpretation of the political opportunity. Sometimes, like organizations involved in social movements, civic associations may misread the situation, underestimate their opportunities, and exaggerate structural constraints (Kriesi 2004). This is what occurred in the case of the snowstorm in late January and early February 2008, four months before the earthquake. The snowstorm hit many southern provinces in China, paralyzing the transportation system and causing the collapse of many power transmission towers. The timing of the snowstorm could not have been worse: it came during the Chinese New Year holiday, when millions of migrant workers yearned to go home to be with their families. Many were stranded in railway stations in major cities, as more people flooded into the stations to try their luck at buying tickets. The police and railway security barred their entrance. At several points, serious clashes broke out between outraged crowds and the police. Many passengers were injured in stampedes. The sub-tropical southern cities had no facilities to deal with this kind of severe weather and could do little but wait for the snowstorm to subside. In some cities, such as Chenzhou in Hunan, residents did not have any power or tap water for more than a week. Grievances with the government quickly mounted. Wen Jiabao went to several places to comfort stranded passengers, but his grandpa image did not help much. Public opinion was critical of the government's response to the crisis and questioned its management ability.

The snowstorm had the potential of becoming a consensus crisis. It affected most southern provinces, and the government's response was inadequate to the extensive and urgent need for various social services, such as delivering food and water to migrant workers stranded in railway stations as well as to peasants in remote villages. The state and civil society also had a general agreement on solving the practical problems in the crisis. For the government, its handling of the crisis was significant for its image during the Olympic year, and no evidence indicates that the government enforced restrictions on citizens' public participation. Therefore, the snowstorm generated an instant opening of access to the political opportunity structure. Nevertheless, except for a few actions in

Guangzhou and Guizhou in early February, most associations either did not react to the snowstorm at all or reacted slowly.

When the storm subsided in February, various media and NGO newsletters began to reflect on why civic associations failed to respond adequately when they should have and could have. Some attributed the failure to the NGOs' own incapacity, while others blamed the restrictive institutional conditions (Wang 2008). Neither explanation, however, is convincing since, four months later, when institutional conditions were not much improved, the same "incapable" associations played a much more significant role in the Sichuan earthquake relief work. One key reason was the associations' failure to interpret the snowstorm as an opportunity. The response to previous disasters was mostly monopolized by the state, and there had been no large-scale civil society response to previous disasters. When the snowstorm started, as an NGO manager confessed, most of NGOs remained "insensitive" because he believed "the grand narratives [about the snowstorm] in the mainstream media had nothing to do with grassroots people like me" (Sijia 2008). Thus, his organization did not take action until the end of January, when he heard that some small groups in Guangzhou had delivered food to people stranded in railway stations. This discussion about civic associations' failure, however, motivated them to take part in the relief effort after the Sichuan earthquake, even though their structural ability and institutional conditions were not significantly improved.

ENGAGEMENT AND ASSOCIATIONS

How did Chinese citizens in different kinds of grassroots associations take part in the large-scale relief activities? How did the consensus crisis affect their engagement on the ground?

Among the associations whose members I interviewed and contacted, there were some typical civil society organizations, such as formal NGOs dedicated to education, protection of the environment, and community services, and small civic groups dedicated to public and cultural causes, such as the preservation of ancient architecture. However, many more may resemble Putnam's favorite "bowling groups" (Putnam 2000): a marathoners' group, a car owners' club, a mountaineering group, and so on. A few others may even seem trivial and playful: for example, a Super

Girl (the Chinese equivalent of *American Idol*) fan club and an online discussion group on cosmetics. In other words, the post-earthquake engagement went beyond the "third sector" or "nonprofit sector," where serious-looking NGO practitioners used grand words to talk about big topics. All kinds of associations took advantage of the rare political opportunities brought by the consensus crisis in the wake of the earthquake and demonstrated their enthusiasm, creativity, and achievements in different ways.

Emergent NGO Networks

The New Operation Hump, the coalition network mentioned at the beginning of this chapter, the one that "shipped their stuff by plane," was formed by four registered NGOs and a magazine in Shanghai right after the earthquake to collect and transport supplies to the quake zone. The organizations that founded the network reflected on their failure to respond to the 2008 snowstorm and had a strong incentive to seize the next available opportunity for public participation. After deciding to take action, the coalition network set up a blog and used the Internet to collect donations and supplies.

When New Operation Hump started, numerous civic associations had already begun collecting money and materials, but they had difficulty in delivering them to the quake zone. Postal and commercial delivery services were too expensive to ship bulky and heavy supplies. Some small groups drove to the quake zone, but for most groups, this kind of direct action was unrealistic because of their jobs and family commitments. To avoid the hassle, some groups simply transferred their money to the Red Cross, but others hesitated because of the Red Cross's problematic management and lack of transparency.

In contrast, the New Operation Hump appeared a much better option. It outperformed many GONGOs in terms of cost, speed, and transparency. The network provided a free channel for delivering materials directly to the affected people. It had a constantly updated blog, on which the staff posted a list of materials received and scanned receipts of the donations from both the Shanghai and Mianyang warehouses. The network also collaborated with a private foundation, whose Sichuan staff picked up their materials from Mianyang Airport and delivered them directly to villages through their work stations and volunteers in the quake zone. Later, when the airline partner could no longer offer transportation, the network managed to find another private airline company, which ran a route between Shanghai and Mianyang, to transport their materials for free. During the whole process, the New Operation relied on the synergy of civic associations, corporations, and the media rather than on governmental resources.

Luqiong, my interviewee, who worked for one of the organizations in the network, described the delivery chain in the blog:

> For example, if an ordinary Shanghai resident donates a case of infant formula, he can deliver the case to our warehouse in Qibao [a town in Shanghai] or our office. He can get a Donation Receipt issued by the New Operation Hump and the five participating organizations. When the case of formula enters the warehouse, the Shanghai Charity Foundation's Pudong chapter [which owns the warehouse] can issue another receipt and a donation certificate. The case will be delivered by plane and then trucked to the quake zone, with help from the Amity Foundation. The affected local people will sign the receipt.

For donors dissatisfied with GONGOs' opaque operations, the New Operation Hump was a more reliable alternative because they were able to see where their donations went. At a later stage, when the network was widely reported on in the media, even the Shanghai Youth League asked the staff if they could help transport some of the league's donated materials. In other words, as Yufan, director of one of the organizations in New Operation Hump, pointed out, in that situation GONGOs were no longer able to control all the channels but had to join the competition for effective shipping methods. Consequently, materials flooded in, exceeding their capacity; fortunately, many volunteers, affiliated or unaffiliated with the participating organizations, also signed up to help. They worked long hours every day in the warehouse and the office, answering calls and receiving and dispatching materials.

The network's cooperative relations with the government partially explain its success. The Shanghai government tolerated, encouraged, and even helped this large coalition. Strictly speaking, the network's donation collecting was illegal, but no government agency seemed concerned about it. Instead, an officially sanctioned charity foundation provided it with a warehouse free of charge and issued official receipts for donors. Some high-ranking officials from the Municipal Bureau of Civil Affairs visited the warehouse. Instead of intervening in the volunteers' work, the officials asked if they needed any help. Although Yufan interpreted the visit as surveillance, it at least sent a welcoming signal.

One of the network's major organizations, a social work organization, was registered with and administered by the Civil Affairs Bureau of the Pudong District government. A typical example of "dependent autonomy" (Lu 2009), it relied on the Pudong District government as its principal funding source and client. However, the relatively liberal-minded officials in Pudong practiced a hands-off approach so that the organization had room to operate and develop. The organization identified itself as an NGO and regularly joined in all kinds of inter-organizational NGO activities. It shared with other NGOs the same anxiety about the general incompetence revealed in the snowstorm relief, as well as the same eagerness to take action when the big moment came. In New Operation Hump, the organization played a critical role in communicating with the municipal and district governments.

A similar network of NGOs but on a bigger scale, 5.12 Relief, was formed in Chengdu after the earthquake. The network consisted of about forty NGOs loosely connected to more than a hundred associations. When the network was launched, however, no NGO was willing to coordinate the activities, fearing possible suppression by the state. Finally, Gaoyan, director of the Chengdu Disaster Management Center (CDMC), stepped forward to shoulder the responsibility. This move should not be attributed to Gaoyan's bravery alone. The CDMC originated from the Youth League in Panzhihua, a city in Sichuan, and Gaoyan was a member of the municipal committee of the Chinese People's Political Consultative Conference in Panzhihua. Since none of the participating NGOs had any legal bank accounts because of restrictions on NGOs' fundraising, Gaoyan, his official status and governmental connections serving as a shield, used his personal bank account to raise funds.

As expected, 5.12 Relief was investigated by the police. Some Hong Kong media reported that the investigation brought the network to an end. Yet, in my interviews with Gaoyan and another director of the network, they denied this. The network was designed to run for seven days but had to be extended for another week because more supplies than expected were collected. When the network was investigated, it was about to end. The investigators quickly cleared the case, and the network ran for a few more days. None of the organizations in 5.12 Relief was further interrogated or punished. Instead, Gaoyan's CDMC received some requests from local governments in the quake zone to undertake more projects.

Both cases show an interesting pattern of registered NGOs' activities in disaster relief. Their eagerness to act converged with the state's need for social services in the earthquake's aftermath. The NGOs had initiated networks and actions, and the state tolerated, and even encouraged and assisted, their work. The state also suspended legal restrictions on fundraising, while keeping an eye out for fraud. Much of the state's tolerance can be attributed to the dependent-autonomous relations between the state and a few leading organizations—either semi-GONGOs or groups with good connections with the government. Facilitated by the state's tolerance and even encouragement, NGOs demonstrated creativity and capability in their synergetic activities. They made a difference. In addition to collecting numerous truckloads of materials, both networks made connections among groups and individuals who were otherwise detached from one another. They carefully and successfully managed and maintained their trust relationships with the small groups and the government by making their activities transparent. Through the coalition, otherwise relatively weak NGOs and isolated small groups were synergized into a confluence of material resources, personnel, compassion, and enthusiasm.

Gongyi (Public Welfare) Groups

My focus-group interview with the Taicang Group, a typical public welfare or philanthropic (gongyi) group, was held in a barbecue restaurant called Super-Hot Chicken Wings, owned by the group's leader, who went by his online ID of Emotionless. Four core members of the group were at the table. Our conversation was facilitated by chicken wings, which confirmed the accuracy of restaurant's name Super-Hot, and cold beer, which was much needed in early May in Taicang, a muggy city near Shanghai.

Taicang had twenty-some core members, mostly young people with middle-class and lower-middle-class jobs, such as shopkeepers or restaurateurs like Emotionless, office workers, journalists from local papers, and teachers. From its inception in 2007, Taicang had been devoted to various community services and charity activities, such as volunteering in nursing homes, providing food and hot water for migrant workers stranded in the local railway station, seeking financial assistance for students from low-income families, and the like. As the group gradually established a reputation in Taicang through these activities, it also developed from a casually organized and loosely connected small group to a semi-formal association. The group has its own bylaws, a formal division of labor, and a board with regular members. Emotionless did most of the day-to-day work, such as communicating with outside people and maintaining the website.

Emotionless said the group had not been attached to any GONGOs. The local Youth League tolerated the group's existence but had set up its own public welfare group to compete with the Taicang Group. The official group, however, soon dissolved because of its limited influence. Group members made a clear distinction between the "official" (*guanfang*) and the "civil" (*minjian*), identifying themselves as the latter. Emotionless said that, in normal times, the Taicang Group "absolutely wouldn't get close to the Red Cross or the Youth League." It was the Sichuan earthquake that provided both the Youth League and the Taicang Group with an opportunity to work together.

The group members met the day after the earthquake and decided to collect donations through local radio stations. The materials sometimes came in bulk––for example, five tons of plastic tarps, which evacuees could use to make temporary tents. More often the donations came in small amounts. I looked through their list and found numerous small items like three dozen pens donated by an elementary school student, a box of antibiotics by an office worker, and two tins of infant formula by a housewife. Group members worked for long hours every day to receive and process all these donations. Later, they decided to hold a charity sale in the central public square in Taicang to attract more donations. Despite their strong sense of independence from the government, they had to get support from the local Youth League, which secured a permit for them to use the square. The core members, wearing T-shirts with the Taicang logo, set up tables, umbrellas, and boxes on the sidewalks to raise funds. In the late afternoon, Emotionless told the other members to wrap up and go home, but most refused to leave. One still held a poster over his head, calling out repeatedly to passersby, "Please donate for the earthquake victims!" Emotionless said he couldn't forget the scene: the sunset cast its light on the young volunteer holding the poster high, standing fast in a crowded street.

Taicang then used the money to purchase materials, comparing prices at different local vendors in nearby towns. If the price difference was significant they would go to the vendor with the lowest price, even though this might involve a couple of hours of driving. The members bargained aggressively. Sometimes the unit-price difference seemed minor—only 10 fen (1.6 cents) for a pair of medical gloves or a mask, for example—but, since they usually bought in large quantities, the total difference might amount to a few thousand yuan, "a significant amount that can save someone's life." Sometimes they could get deep a discount or "zero-profit" prices when they told the vendor they were buying the materials for the quake victims. In the end, they collected materials with a value of about 400,000 yuan (approximately $60,000), a significant amount for a small local group. They then shipped bulky materials, such as tarps, to the New Operation Hump's warehouse in Shanghai. Later, after China Post provided free shipping for relief materials, they sent their small packages to the earthquake zone via the postal service.

The Taicang Group was one of the numerous *gongyi* groups that had been mushrooming in China and that were made visible by the earthquake. They ran openly and independently, without any official blessing, but their regular activities and structure prepared them for joining in a large-scale public activity. They had already enjoyed a certain degree of local publicity and credibility, but did not carry as much burden as the formal NGOs. They had no paid staff; members did all the work on a voluntary basis. The earthquake gave them an opportunity to demonstrate their capacity and transform the group's distant relations with the state into a cooperative one. Local authorities did not even investigate their "illegal" fundraising. The group accepted only material donations in the first days. Not until their public-square donation collecting was permitted and supported by the Youth League did they decide to accept money. They engaged in a silent competition with GONGOs by providing a more transparent, reliable, and swift method of donation. Group members talked proudly about their efforts to provide detailed status updates on their donations, scanned copies of receipts signed by the ultimate recipients and local authorities in the quake zone, and receipts for their purchases. For ordinary donors who distrusted the Red Cross, civic groups like Taicang, with a certain degree of credibility, were good alternatives.

Networked Groups

Another important type of group was what I term "networked groups." These relied on face-to-face interactions among their members, while at the same time being branches or chapters of a larger network. The Super Girl Club, the most interesting and surprising group I interviewed, was such a networked group.

The Super Girl (*Chaoji nüshen*) was one of the first interactive talent shows in China and caused a sensation among teenage girls, college students, and, later, people of all ages and classes in China. The 2005 Super Girl competition was a momentous event, attracting an unprecedented crowd of competitors and huge audiences. The three finalists of the 2005 competition emerged as superstars and had an extraordinary number of dedicated fans, who ran massive campaigns for their idols. After the 2005 competition, fans organized into nationwide networks based on the Internet. Fans in the same geographic area clustered together into a branch of the nationwide network.

The Super Girl Fan Club I studied was such a group, based in Sichuan as a branch of a nationwide fan network. Their regular activities were those that people would expect from fans of popular singers, such as buying their CDs to distribute, purchasing group tickets for concerts, taking trains or even flights to attend concerts, following every twist and turn in their idol's personal life, and sometimes engaging in debates with rival fan groups. Their popular image would seem to have had nothing to do with the big idea of civil society. They were the concert crowd screaming rapturously for their idols, rather than coffeehouse patrons—in Habermas's classical example—deliberating about the public good.

A lesser-known aspect of the fan club, however, was that it had been involved in various public welfare activities. After the 2005 competition, EE-Media, the company that ran the Super Girl program, worked with a few public welfare foundations to host a charity show in which the newly enthroned Super Girls performed and called for donations for children in poverty. Since then, the Super Girls have been engaged in all kinds of charitable activities. While these activities were mainly for PR purposes, fans endorsed and copied whatever their idols did, as well as endeavoring to outperform their rival fans.

Right after the earthquake, members of the local branch in Chengdu started to take action, driving two truckloads of supplies to Yinghua, one of the towns hard hit by the earthquake. The road to Yinghua was severely damaged by landslides and jammed with relief vehicles. Survivors walked out of the town, waving down vehicles and begging for food and water. The volunteers' supplies were quickly gone, so they felt a significant amount of supplies were needed there. They rushed back to Chengdu and communicated with other Super Girl fans online. Tens of thousands of yuan had already been raised by the nationwide network. As for how to use the money, opinions were divided. Some said that they should submit the money to the Red Cross in Chengdu and allow the official relief organization to handle the whole thing. Volunteers without special skills, they argued, could do very little on the ground.

Mood, a girl who went by her online ID, the head of the Sichuan branch, and other local fans strongly opposed this idea because they knew that the Red Cross was already overwhelmed. Some of them were volunteering for the Red Cross and were furious at its inefficient and chaotic management. Donated supplies were piled up in the Red Cross's warehouse, but there were not enough vehicles to deliver them. A truckload of *nan* (flatbread) donated and delivered from Xinjiang quickly went bad. When Mood and her friends told the Red Cross that they had money and vehicles to deliver food and water to wherever they were critically needed, the Red Cross told them that food and water were not needed and they should not worry about it. "You can simply leave your money with us," said the Red Cross, "and we'll handle it." Mood was infuriated, because they had witnessed the shortages of supplies in the affected places; at the same time, heaps of undelivered supplies sat in the Red Cross's warehouse. Mood said they then decided to use their own vehicle; the only thing they needed from the Red Cross was a permit to get through the checkpoints. The Red Cross issued them a permit but said, "Your safety is not our responsibility."

In this situation, the overwhelmed GONGO, though not intentionally, created an instant opportunity for groups like the Super Girl Fan Club to take action. Mood and her fellow fans then used the donation money to buy six truckloads of supplies, and took off at night for Pingwu, a devastated town, which had received little media coverage during the first few days after the earthquake. Mood and other young girls experienced a 5.0-magnitude aftershock, saw corpses on the roadside, and finally reached Pingwu. Through one of the members' friends, who happened to be a PLA officer working in Pingwu, they delivered supplies to the people and troops in the town. After returning from Pingwu, Mood found that money was flowing in like water. Thanks to the nationwide network, with its millions of fans, the main difficulty that Mood and other local members now faced was how to use up the money. This difficulty led to repeated deliveries and later various charity activities, such as sending gifts to child survivors on Children's Day (June 1). Eventually, they had to call a halt to donations, the sheer amount of which exceeded their capacity to handle them.

The Super Girl Fan Club was one of the numerous networked groups in Chinese society. One More, a nationwide online-based education assistance network, participated in earthquake relief in a similar fashion. The Sichuan branch played the role of warriors on the front, while members around the country raised money. A group of mountaineers followed the same pattern. They were self-mobilized from a national mountaineering network and got in touch with the Sichuan local group, which provided accommodations and guides. They found that urban areas already had received enough relief, so the group decided to deliver food and medicine to a remote, isolated village. Each member, carrying about 60 pounds of medicine, trekked across the mountains for about ten hours. Finally, they reached the village, collapsed on the ground, and unloaded the medicines, which the local doctors and residents desperately needed.

A classical civil society scholar might either dismiss the Super Girl Fan Club as a typical case of the market's "colonizing" of civil society, or ignore its new network feature. It is tempting to argue that the fans simply followed their idol, did what she did, and said what she said, without a conscious idea of enhancing the public good; and she, the idol, was clearly a product of the entertainment industry. Unlike the Taicang Group and NGOs, the fans' primary identity was not that of public-spirited civil society actors, and they only occasionally engaged in public welfare activities. In fact, they appeared content with their entertainment-based identity, loose structure, and self-serving goals. They had no intention of becoming a registered, formal NGO. Nor did they join in NGOs' professional discussions. They did not "talk big." Even when they took civic action, it was hard to tell whether their motivations were to help people, to follow in the footsteps of their idols, to impress their peers, to beat their rivals, or all of those.

Nevertheless, their public image of being recreational groups belied their advantages over formal NGOs. Their triviality was politically safe--they escaped political and institutional constraints. Since the consensus crisis after the Sichuan earthquake generated a need for social services and donations, those groups were handed the opportunity to demonstrate their public spirit. They bypassed the overwhelmed GONGOs and went directly to the quake zone. In terms of the donations they collected, many outperformed NGOs because they were able to mobilize resources from their nationwide networks. For example, the Guangzhou branch of the Super Girl Fans network alone raised about 180,000 yuan. This did not include the money directly donated by individual members to specific communities and schools in the quake zone. Mood said that their network was the "poorest" of the three major Super Girls fan networks and almost always lost the "charity competition." On a televised charity evening in Hunan, for example, the Hunan branch held a poster bearing big numbers that indicated the amount collected--50,000 yuan--but soon was embarrassed when a rival club held up their flashy poster showing the amount they had collected: 1,000,000 yuan. Their large-scale fundraising was usually conducted via personal accounts, and it was certainly illegal, even bordering on fraud. But they were never investigated. In this sense, although they believed they had nothing to do with government and politics, it was the state's latent and silent tolerance of such extensive fundraising that made their activities possible. Although there is no way to calculate how much money the networks collected, their calculating unit was usually 100,000, even a million. None of the donations collected by networked groups were included in Civil Affairs' official "private donations" statistics.

SMALL GROUPS

Compared to most of the associations I studied, the Shanghai Car Club's members were older and of higher socioeconomic status. Its initial and core members were middle- and upper-class people with stable jobs and high incomes because owning a car in China in the 1990s, when the group started, was still a luxury. For example, Lao Cai, head of the club, owned a motion-sensor factory. Maomao, another active member, was a certified accountant. Lao Xue, who went to Sichuan with Lao Cai, owned several enterprises. The club followed strict, egalitarian rules in organizing its activities. The members collectively discussed and voted on the destinations, schedules, and costs of their activities. They shared the costs equally among them. The club had a relatively low turnover rate: many members had been regularly participating in the club's activities since its inception. Thus, a sense of solidarity had developed among the core members. When I interviewed Lao Cai, his wife was hospitalized; we met at a café near the hospital where she was being treated. Some members of the car club helped Lao Cai find the right doctor and hospital; some made chicken soup, which Chinese believe can speed recovery, and brought it to the hospital. Lao Cai said that the car club members were "better than my relatives," who ritualistically said nice words but gave no substantive help.

The club's regular activities mostly involved long drives to tourist attractions. After sweeping almost all the major tourist spots in the areas adjacent to Shanghai, the members found the activities "repetitive and boring" and tried to find something "more meaningful." They began to engage in various volunteering activities, such as driving high school students to the college entrance exam, donating and delivering supplies to schools in remote and impoverished areas, and delivering blankets and clothes to migrant workers stranded in the railway stations during the 2008 snowstorm. Thus, unsurprisingly, with vehicles, relatively wealthy members, and previous experience in civic engagement, the group took immediate action after the earthquake.

A few hours after the earthquake, Lao Cai and Lao Xue packed their off-road SUV with medicines and food, and took off immediately. They drove nonstop for twenty hours, taking turns to eat and sleep. When they reached Sichuan and took a break in a highway rest area, a young man approached them and suddenly knelt down, begging them to deliver their medicines and supplies to a town in An County. The young man said many people had died there, and the survivors did not have enough medicine. He was sent by the local people to buy supplies because he owned a car, but he could not find many medicines. Lao Cai was a little suspicious about the young man and asked a policeman nearby, who knew the town and had heard that the situation there was dire. The young man gave Lao Cai his ID as a pledge and drove ahead of their car and led them to the town. Upon arrival, they were terrified by the tragic scene: many people, including some students, lying on the ground, barely alive or already dead. The local hospital doctor wailed when he saw them--the small hospital did not have enough medicine to help those who were still alive. Parents of the students wept and told them that local township officials concealed the casualties and devastation for fear that the bad situation would endanger their careers. Thus, the misinformed upper-level authorities had not sent enough relief materials and personnel.

The two men decided to drive to a big city where cell-phone service was still available. Upon reaching Mianyang, they called the car club and learned that a Shanghai military medical team was deployed nearby. They rushed there and brought two military ambulances and two small teams of doctors and nurses to the town. Lao Cai said that "all the people in the hospital burst into tears when they saw us, shouting 'the PLA is here!'" When he told me the story, he choked back tears. Later, he proudly recounted the hospital doctors' compliment: "You saved the lives of several thousand people!"

Lao Cai and Lao Xue helped the military doctors and soldiers set up surgery tents and coordinated the relief work. The local officials, who initially were arrogant and impatient, now begged him to introduce them to the head doctors, whose ranks were two levels higher than their own. Lao Cai said, "I didn't even bother to talk with those bastards." The local situation turned into a military takeover, aided by the car club volunteers. The local officials became of secondary importance and were even ignored. Other members of the club soon loaded another vehicle with supplies. Once they got messages about the location and situation from their two pioneers, they took off immediately.

Numerous small groups like the Shanghai Car Club participated in fundraising and relief work, although many of them did not go to Sichuan. Cidi, a group based on a Douban page,[9] was started by five young urban professionals to pursue their interest in ancient architecture. They held regular exhibits to enhance public awareness about endangered ancient Chinese architecture. The group had been around for several years and had earned a reputation among Shanghai yuppies interested in traditional Chinese culture, who followed their activities on their Douban page.

Compared to the Shanghai Car Club, the members of Cidi were much younger; most of them were in their late twenties and early thirties. All had white-collar jobs—architects, office workers in foreign-invested companies, etc.—so my meeting with them was, appropriately enough, at a Starbucks on West Nanjing Road, a main boulevard in Shanghai's glamorous central business district. After the earthquake, Cidi decided to collect donations by holding a charity sale in the coffeehouse where they usually held exhibits. Core members of the group made an announcement on their Douban group page, calling for people to donate items for the sale. Though the sale lasted for only a couple of hours, they raised about 33,650 yuan (approximately $5,000). Most donors had already arranged for their buyers, who came to the sale, paid, and picked up the items. They then embarked on an odyssey of purchasing materials from various places: supermarkets, small vendors, even a tent factory. After that, they transported the goods on the New Operation Hump's plane.

While the Shanghai Car Club and Cidi still fit into the image of civil society because of their clearly stated purpose of public welfare (*gongyi*), many groups had not engaged in any public welfare activities before the earthquake. Most of them were recreational. For example, a marathoner group I interviewed in Shanghai did not engage in any activities other than running, but decided to go to Qingchuan and, using their own money and labor, build a prefabricated school for a village.

Some groups emerged after the earthquake. The Boilers was one such group. The Boilers did not have clear boundaries. Anyone could claim affiliation by wearing a T-shirt with the words "Boiling Public Welfare" (*Feiteng gongyi*, the name of their group). Even Phoenix, the "big brother" (*laoda*) of the group, had no clear idea of the exact number of members, because people came and went from time to time. The members did not know each other before but through various trajectories finally converged in a small town in An County, which I call "Antown" here. Phoenix went first to the Red Cross and was assigned to a place with other volunteers but found nothing to do. He met some other volunteers and moved around in the quake zone, finally settling in Antown. Many buildings in the town and adjacent villages were damaged or even destroyed by the quake, although the casualties were not as severe as those in other towns in An County. Nevertheless, residents still had to leave their damaged houses and lived in tents set up in the yard of the township middle school. Moreover, residents and schools from an adjacent mountainous town, which had been devastated by tremors and landslides, were temporarily evacuated to Antown, with the result that the population in Antown suddenly doubled. Core members of the Boilers—a few college students and young office workers—stayed in Antown for several months. They were hardworking, educated assistants to the doctors. They taught summer school for free so that the children's parents could devote their time to reconstruction. They were particularly popular among the children, who were curious about their urban lifestyle and admired their youthful enthusiasm.

In areas close to the quake zone that largely remained intact, such as Chengdu and Mianyang, numerous "friend groups" emerged in the wake of the earthquake. Routine life in the two cities was halted after the earthquake. Supplies, vehicles, and all kinds of participants in the rescue and relief efforts flooded into the two cities and then quickly flooded out to the quake zone. Schools were closed for several days; companies asked their employees to stay home because of unpredictable aftershocks. Chengdu residents called on each other, arranged vehicles, rushed to supermarkets to buy supplies, and drove to the quake zone. Zihou, one of the earliest volunteers, went to Juyuan High School only a few hours after the quake. He and his friends were proud of their "heroic deeds" and swift response, but when they merged onto the highway to Dujiangyan, they found that numerous taxicabs and private cars, with emergency lights on, were already on their way to the quake zone. This scene was widely reported by the media and confirmed by another interviewee, Mr. Tang, who owned a café in Chengdu and also took off on the day of the earthquake. Zihou said that it was the most touching moment in his life. Many local groups in Chengdu got in touch with their acquaintances in the quake zone and therefore were able to make deliveries to specific places instead of randomly distributing supplies along the roads. During my fieldwork in Chengdu, whenever I talked with a Chengdu resident about my project, the first thing he or she mentioned was usually this wave of spontaneous volunteering in Chengdu. An interviewee said: "Back then, it seemed everybody was donating, and everybody was looking for vehicles to deliver supplies."[10]

A striking feature of these small groups was their tininess; they were what Gary Alan Fine terms "tiny publics," small groups that gather citizens and constitute a civil society (Fine 2012). The Cidi group had only five regular members and no explicit rules or regulations; the Boilers' core members were fewer than ten; Xiaoli's Caring Babies, mentioned earlier, was a "two-man NGO" as they jokingly called themselves. Friend groups had even fewer members, usually two or three. Their activities were embedded in their existing and emergent personal networks, which were relatively less influenced than formal NGOs by the political structure. Their resource mobilization hardly went beyond their immediate network and a single Douban online page. But they made a difference by raising a significant amount of money and giving people an opportunity for civic engagement. Except for a few cases which the government investigated for potential fraud, these small groups had no interaction with the state. On the contrary, the state took actions to facilitate small groups and individual donations. On May 23, China Post announced that parcels and remittances to donation-receiving agencies, such as the Red Cross, public foundations, and the governments in the quake zone, would be exempted from mailing and remittance fees. Many groups took advantage of the new policy and chose to mail their small parcels.

MULTIVOCAL COMPASSION, MULTIVOCAL SOLIDARITY

How did the different types of participants talk about the meanings of their volunteering? How did they talk about their interactions with the locals? How did they feel emotionally?

When asked to describe the atmosphere after the earthquake or their feelings about their volunteering, most of my interviewees used the words "goodness" (*shanyi*) and "solidarity" (*tuanjie*). They believed that the goodness of their hearts was "activated" (*jifa*) by the massive disaster, a national crisis, and that volunteering—a typical act of compassion—was a way to express their intrinsic but otherwise little discernible warm feelings. This colloquial understanding was consistent with Adam Smith's moral sentiments argument: our intrinsic moral nature—the "man within" us—demonstrates itself in a devastating disaster, such as the imagined earthquake that "swallowed up" China in Smith's book (Smith [1759] 2009).

This discourse of goodness and solidarity, however, was only the lowest common denominator of the various discourses about volunteering. What was more salient was the diversity and multivocality of meaning in their narratives.

The term *tuanjie* was central to the state's discourse about volunteering and altruism. The key to the official discourse of *tuanjie* was not volunteering per se but the party-state's leadership, under which the

Chinese people demonstrated their altruism and created an uplifting moral atmosphere. The moral community in the official discourse is the nation-state under the leadership of the party.

One might be tempted to argue that earthquake volunteers followed this official discourse when they used the word *tuanjie* to understand their volunteering, directly and indirectly lending support to the party's leadership. At a cursory glance, to an outside observer, this speculation might make sense, particularly against the background of a series of political incidents before the earthquake. The Tibetan riots in March provoked a strong wave of nationalistic reaction against what many Chinese believed to be anti-China attacks in Western countries (Brownell 2012). This upsurge of nationalism reached its peak when the Olympic torch relay was disrupted in almost every city outside of China it passed through. After a Chinese torchbearer--a disabled fencing athlete-- was physically attacked by pro-Tibet activists in Paris, young Chinese protested in front of the French Carrefour department stores in China. Technically savvy, English-speaking young Chinese made videos to show how the Western media distorted the image of China in their inaccurate and even biased reports.

From a different perspective, one might also be tempted to argue that the volunteers represented the rise of a civil society that gained power through post-earthquake volunteering and had the potential to become an independent and important force in China (Xu 2008). Nevertheless, the cultural sociology of civil life has taught us that participants of civic engagement do not robotically copy dominant discourses. They may form a particular communication style dramatically different from the dominant discourse in civil society and may even be "uncivil" (Eliasoph and Lichterman 2003). Sometimes, they face multiple and even conflicting cultural elements in the dominant discourses, and they may pick and choose, mix and combine those elements to understand the meaning of their volunteering (Swidler 1986; Sewell 1992). For example, American volunteers use individualism to understand their altruistic "acts of compassion" (Wuthnow 1991).

The Chinese volunteers after the Sichuan earthquake had the same variety of patterns of interpretation in their narratives about their volunteering. A few volunteers closely followed the official discourse of national solidarity and used the official language of nationalism to make sense of their volunteering. They wore military-style camouflage clothing and used military metaphors to describe their action: "I'm going to the front" (*shang qianxian*), which meant "I'm going to the quake zone"; when introducing their fellow volunteers, they said "these are my comrades-in-arms." Not surprisingly, most of them were male with a conspicuous air of self-importance. I met one of them in Chengdu in 2009. A thin but energetic man in his early thirties, he insisted that we called him Ironman (*tieren*) because, he claimed, he had the "iron willpower" to stay in the quake zone for a long time, while other, "nerdy" college-educated, volunteers only said nice words, distributed gifts, and left. A native of Hunan, Mao Zedong's home province, Ironman went to Sichuan immediately after the earthquake because, according to him, he thought he could be of help to the affected "masses" (*shouzai qunzhong*), an official term to describe people which I rarely heard from other volunteers. He was apparently proud of his ability to do various manual jobs, including building houses, making furniture, laboring in fields, and so on. He claimed even the ablest local handymen could not compete with him.

In F's hotel lounge, he spent a whole night telling his stories to a group of guests: that he survived the toughest physical challenges—lack of food and water—in the wake of the earthquake; that he enjoyed working for the affected people; that he did not charge local people any money as long as they provided him with accommodations and food. His heroic stories provoked suppressed giggles among the otherwise amazed audience; the guests looked at each other with suspicious but generous smiles on their faces. A Hunan-based foundation set up by national labor model Hong Zhanhui discovered this contemporary Lei Feng, a model of Communist altruism celebrated in the 1960s, and sent a cameraman to follow him on a subsequent trip in order to make his story part of a documentary on volunteers.

Clouding Ironman's Lei Feng–like story was his marginal socioeconomic status in Hunan and Sichuan: he did only odd manual jobs in Hunan, and was still doing odd jobs in Sichuan; he was unmarried; he had no education beyond high school. He tried to dodge, and was sometimes disturbed by, the audience's probing questions about his work and life and quickly switched the topic of conversation to another round of heroic stories. Ironman was one of the most conspicuous and impressive volunteers I have ever met, particularly against the background of Communism as a fading and even collapsing belief.

On the other end of the political spectrum were the so-called right-wing or liberal intellectuals and dissidents, who embraced the idea of individual liberty, constitutionalism, equality, and democracy. Many of them were engaged in the earthquake relief through their NGOs, with aspirations to make a difference in developing a civil society. Some liberal intellectuals were particularly surprised and delighted when even local officials used terms like "civic engagement" (*gongmin canyu*) and "civil society" (*gongmin shehui*) to praise their activities. Many of them also talked through the media about the prospect of China's civil society. Thus, they were both local bearers and public advocates of the prevailing "birth year of civil society" idea.

Some of those liberal intellectuals admitted that there was extraordinary national solidarity in the wake of the earthquake, but they made a distinction between the national solidarity they talked about and official nationalism. Shinan, a fairly famous dissident who was arrested by the police for his commemoration of the 1989 Tiananmen movement, believed that it would be incorrect to use the dark side, which gradually emerged later, to deny that there was national solidarity in the wake of the earthquake.[11] Many more, however, avoided the term "nation" in order to distance themselves from what they believed was the "grand narrative" of nationalism. They usually used the terms "humanity" (*renxin*) and "goodness" (*shanyi*), virtues intrinsic in human nature, to explain the upsurge of volunteering. One of the dissidents, who used his blog as a hub for associations to exchange information and publicize their activities, said that he was not "Lei Feng's relative"—in other words, he consciously stayed away from the official narrative that equated the post-earthquake volunteering with Lei Feng's spirit of "serving the people."

In between these two ends of the political spectrum were the vast majority of participants, who were much less flamboyant than Ironman and less articulate in talking about the political meanings of their engagement than the liberals. They drew on various ideas in their cultural repertoires—religious, philanthropic, individualistic, and national identities—to make sense of their actions. Sometimes they reconciled those different ideas, negotiating with the present reality to give meaning to their actions.

Some interviewees believed that the huge wave of volunteering was a sign of the Chinese people's national solidarity, which, although not salient, did exist in everyday life. It was the earthquake, a disaster, a national crisis, that "activated" the goodness and solidarity among Chinese. In this type of interpretation, the society imagined in civic engagement overlapped with the boundaries of the Chinese nation. Thus, the "goodness" activated by the earthquake and represented in volunteering was a sign of the nation's resilience and promising future. As Bojun, a law-firm partner in Chengdu, who organized a local volunteer community in Luoshui, a town ravaged in the earthquake, put it:

> We Chinese people are taught that a person should have a sense of social responsibility and make a contribution to society. But we have no opportunity to practice these ideals. I think the earthquake gave us this opportunity.[12]

Jiajun, a middle-aged manager of a state-owned enterprise (SOE), expressed a similar sentiment:

> I used to be somewhat pessimistic. But this time I felt China and the Chinese are promising. This time the whole Chinese nation, regardless of political views, regions, and everything, worked for the same goal selflessly, without expectation of a reward. This kind of mutual help and love is something that has not been lost in the thousands of years of history of our nation. This is the Chinese nation's contribution to humankind.[13]

Yang Shuang, a retiree in Chengdu and an amateur photographer, analogized the earthquake solidarity to the united front between the Chinese Communist Party (CCP) and the Nationalist Party during the Anti-Japanese War to substantiate his idea that the Chinese nation will unite and overcome internal differences and conflicts in the face of common challenges and crises. The challenges, according to Yang and other volunteers, included not only the earthquake but also the happenings before the earthquake—particularly the Tibetan uprising, or in the official vocabulary, the "Tibetan independence" (Zangdu) movement, and the protests against the Olympics—which were considered threats to the Chinese nation.[14]

Nevertheless, the volunteers who interpreted the outpouring of aid in terms of national solidarity also differed from Ironman in that they rarely used Maoist language and styles and never demonstrated unreserved support for the party. Instead, many criticized the government for local officials' corruption and stupidity. It was the consensus crisis—with its common threat, agreement on goals, and urgency—that activated the "banal nationalism" in their cultural repertoire and overshadowed their differences with the party-state (Billig 1995). This was consistent with the classic assertion in conflict theory that conflicts with other groups enhance in-group solidarity (Collins 1975; Coser 1956). Moreover, the volunteers who accepted this national solidarity interpretation did not have distinctive class or age features: they included older and younger volunteers—a retired SOE worker (Yang Shuang), an SOE middle-level manager (Jiajun), a lawyer (Bojun), college students, an accountant in a foreign-invested company, and so on.

Some volunteers, however, used a discourse of individualism to talk about their volunteering: "I volunteered because it made me feel good and satisfied." Xiaoli, the young man who set up Caring Babies, whose story has been presented earlier in this chapter, spent almost all his savings—about 140,000 yuan ($20,000)—on purchasing supplies in addition to donations he and his business partner collected. As a start-up company, that money was pretty much all they had. He described their financial situation this way: "If [before the earthquake] we still had two bricks, then the bricks were gone, and we had only cinders." But Xiaoli did not regret this.

> How many people would use money to do this kind of thing? Also, how many people can use this little money to do such as big thing? Yes, I spent around a hundred thousand yuan, but I collected relief materials worth more than three hundred thousand. From an economic perspective, I made a fortune! Although the materials didn't end up in my hands, it was more than a hundred percent profit! I believe any businessman who can make that kind of profit would be considered successful.[15]

He believed his goodness would pay off later in life. Also, he felt very satisfied when the survivors in the quake zone expressed their appreciation for his help. He felt like a hero. The purpose of volunteering, he said, was to satisfy himself "spiritually" (*jinshenshang*), which in Chinese means "psychologically": "It [volunteering] can't bring you anything. But at least, you're satisfied spiritually. Even if you have a lot of money you can't buy this satisfaction. Rich people aren't necessarily happy; poor people aren't necessarily unhappy. I feel what I did was to make myself happy. Who cares about other things?" Born in the 1980s, Xiaoli was a member of the so-called "the after-eighties generation" (*balinghou*). Unlike their parents, who suffered material scarcity in the 1960s, and the older "after-seventies generation," who bore some lingering impact of the era of scarcity, this generation had grown up in incredible material abundance, as well as with a more individualistic consciousness. They were believed to be intensely committed to their personal pleasure instead of to the public good. Their parents frowned on them; intellectuals lamented that they might be the tipping point toward the fading or even collapse of Chinese "traditional morality." Nevertheless, popular culture celebrated and even commercialized this new self-centered mentality. For example, advertisers catered to this Me generation in the slogans of Chinese brands targeting young consumers: "I'm the king of my zone!" (China Mobile); "I choose, I like" (Anta sports shoes); "Don't follow the normal path!" (Meters Bonwe jeans); "Anything is possible!" (Lining sportswear).

To some extent, Xiaoli's words reflect the common image of the after-eighties generation: he did not even use a single phrase like "we Chinese" to understand his volunteering. It was all about "me": "the volunteering was meaningful because it made me happy; it satisfied me, particularly when I was respected by the locals; oh, yes, I did lose some money, but see how much money I made!" Zhou Yin, a young woman in her twenties, another member of this generation, was an office worker who earned only a meager wage. Like Xiaoli, she also found the meaning of her volunteering in her own happiness, particularly the happiness that came from seeing the survivors' smiles because of her help.[16]

This individualistic interpretation of compassion and goodness is very similar to what Wuthnow describes in American volunteers: the seemingly paradoxical compatibility and even positive relations between self-oriented individualism and altruistic values and behaviors (Wuthnow 1991). In other words, while both individualism and altruism are legitimate values in the cultural framework for volunteers, individual volunteers have to find a way to reconcile the two to make sense of their actions and themselves. Both Xiaoli and Zhou Yin mentioned the popular image of the after-eighties generation—the selfish, one-child generation, etc.—and tried to refute this image through their actions. Nevertheless, they did not want to be Lei Feng–type volunteers, an image in the older generation's minds. Consequently, the individualistic interpretation was the best way to reconcile two conflicting aspects in their cultural framework: "I, an independent young man who started a business to pursue personal success, spent so much money on the donation collection and volunteering not because I'm stupid or duped by propaganda but because I feel satisfied and happy in doing this. It's about my own pleasure." Mr. Tang, who was born in the late 1970s (a few years before Xiaoli) and owned a café in Chengdu, also said that most volunteers, including himself, contributed to the relief to satisfy themselves. He did not mention the generation issue since the after-seventies generation image is ambiguous in public discourse and cannot be easily labeled. Whether his remark about "most volunteers" was true may be open to debate, but this discourse of "selfish altruism" was prevalent among volunteers even of his age. For example, at a gala hosted by an NGO in Shanghai, a woman in her late thirties or early forties used very polished PowerPoint slides to talk about how volunteering provided her with an opportunity to find meaning in life amid her mid-life crisis: it changed her materialism, made her devoted to meaningful goals, and so on, although her talk rarely addressed the struggles of the population her volunteering was supposed to help.

Moreover, in this discourse, complexity in local situations was simplified into a "me-survivor" relation. In fact, Tang encountered quite a few occasions on which young, strong male survivors waved down his vehicle and took his materials, even though he tried to stop them. He did not know whether his materials went to the neediest people or who those people were. Nevertheless, Tang did not interpret these encounters as robbery; he explained them away by his remarks on "human nature"—that hungry and desperate people would do whatever they had to do to survive—and simplified them into a narrative about "my happiness."

The individualistic interpretation often came from first-time, occasional volunteers, who were still struggling to find a proper rhetorical tool to understand their unusual actions and express their enthusiasm. Those with previous volunteering experience did not take such pains to reconcile different cultural discourses. They took volunteering for granted and used *gongyi* to talk about why they volunteered and how they felt. *Gongyi* is less ideological than the Lei Feng–type official discourse of socialist solidarity and less politically charged than the civil-society discourse. Therefore, it was a term widely used by civic associations to identify themselves: for example, instead of identifying themselves as "nongovernmental organizations" (*feizhengfu zuzhi*), which implied a potential confrontation between state and civil society, they called themselves *gongyi zuzhi* (public welfare organizations), which sounded apolitical and philanthropic.

When asked why they volunteered, people who had been involved in *gongyi* activities before the Sichuan earthquake usually said, "I've been active in *gongyi* activities, so it was natural for me to volunteer after the Sichuan earthquake." Most of them reacted immediately: joined the civic associations they had been involved in and called on friends to collect donations, and so on. But they rarely demonstrated the same level of excitement as first-time participants like Xiaoli and Zhou Yin. They often considered the earthquake volunteering as an extension of their previous civic engagement and did not feel the same tension as Xiaoli felt between individualism and volunteerism. Hang Wei, an accountant in Shanghai and a trained amateur psychiatrist, went to Sichuan through the civic association in which she had received training and been volunteering. She believed that it would be a pity if she had not gone to the quake zone since she had already learned skills that were needed: "It was like if a doctor didn't treat a patient."[17] Xiaomi, a young office worker in Chengdu, who had worked as a full-time teacher volunteering in a remote, mountainous area in Guizhou, also said engaging in disaster relief was her natural reaction.[18] Soil, an office worker in Shanghai, also felt it was "natural" to participate in *gongyi* activities after the earthquake––the earthquake was not a turning point or watershed event in her life.[19]

A few volunteers used religious terms to understand the suffering after the earthquake and their volunteering. Buddhism, with suffering and compassion as two major elements of its teaching, was a common item in the cultural frameworks for volunteers to understand their actions. Wenting, a self-identified lay Buddhist, volunteered in Pengzhou. She interpreted the massive deaths caused by the earthquake not as a direct result of the karma of the victims themselves but as a collective karma acting on all members of society. It was the victims who carried the burden and alerted us to our past wrongdoings. In this sense, she believed victims and survivors were morally superior to volunteers. When she volunteered in Pengzhou, she found out her team's volunteer driver was a local resident who had just lost fifteen relatives in Beichuan. But the driver neither wailed nor complained; instead he silently did all the driving, not revealing his tragedy until asked. Wenting was deeply moved by the driver and reflected on the meaning of her volunteering in

Buddhist terms: "I felt strongly that in all those processes, like Buddhist teachings say, they [the survivors] used their Buddhist light to purify us. In other words, when I help someone who had been a hundred percent cultivated in Buddhism [*fo hua*] and he accepted my help, then he transmitted three percent or five percent of that Buddhist cultivation to me." Wenting believed that volunteers as helpers in fact became those who received help: they learned much from the survivors, and their volunteering was also a process of purification. Unlike Xiaoli, who understood volunteering in unambiguously individualistic terms, Wenting criticized some volunteers for being too self-centric: "If I can be a little blunt or even mean, they [some volunteers] were satisfying themselves instead of helping the affected people. It is all about 'I': 'I' can help people or 'I' want to do something. They felt superior to others, even if they did not do much."[20]

For Feizhu, a young Christian who had just returned from Australia and tried to find a management position in Shanghai, volunteering showed that the most fundamental, truest aspect of human nature was manifested in a major crisis; that is, people showed love and compassion for others in misery. Why did it take a disaster to show this? Feizhu believed that it was because "we have too many desires and sins," which, in her terms, "hijacked" us in everyday life. The disaster destroyed or took away the things one desired and loved; it warned us that we should not be obsessed with material things and must try our best to help others in need. In other words, it is other people's suffering that sends us a warning signal that we have been trapped in our sins for too long. And now we must take action—as Good Samaritans—to help others and help ourselves, and to eliminate our own sins.[21]

This diversity in the meaning-making of volunteering must be understood within the macro-level social and political context, which shaped the volunteers' cultural repertoire. The official discourse of solidarity was politically dominant but mostly relied on the power of the state's propaganda machine to make itself ubiquitous. It had been seriously challenged by other cultural forces in China in recent decades: political apathy; distrust of the government; increasingly vocal individualism; Western ideas about individual liberty, equality, and democracy; and deep-rooted religions. The party-state's new ruling tool, nationalism, may have coexisted with these new cultural changes, but whether it was as effective as the public believed or whether it backfired remains

FIGURE 4. A volunteer teaches in a tent summer school in An County. June 19, 2008. Photo by Xiao Fengyi.

an open question (Weiss 2014; Qian, Xu, and Chen 2017). In short, the cultural frameworks available to volunteers were multiple, diverse, and conflicting.

Despite their multivocality, however, these diverse interpretations did share a common view that volunteering was a way to act out compassion. This commonality was reinforced by volunteers' actions: they transcended their particular group boundaries and devoted themselves to a large-scale public activity to alleviate other people's suffering. In this way, as Tocqueville says, "feelings and ideas are renewed, the heart enlarged, and understanding developed only by the reciprocal action of men one upon another" (Tocqueville 1969, 515).

Most of my informants clearly remembered the warm feeling among people in the first weeks after the quake. Jiajun, the Chengdu volunteer, gave several bottles of water to a local mother with a child, who only took two bottles, saying other people may have needed them. Chunlin, another Chengdu volunteer who went to Beichuan right after the quake, encountered a local family living in a tent, but the father had already gone to other places to volunteer. When Soil left the school she taught at for a few months, the students in her class stood up and sang a song in both the Qiang (an ethnic group in the quake zone) language and Mandarin as a farewell. When Lao Cai, one of the early volunteers from the Shanghai Car Club, was loading supplies into their car bound for Sichuan, a migrant worker nearby gave them 10 yuan and asked them to "buy something for the Sichuan people." Others reported that during the first several days in Sichuan, local people gave them free rides and free food. On my first day of fieldwork in Chengdu in 2009, a year after the earthquake, I interviewed a taxi driver on my way from the airport to downtown. The driver had gone to Dujiangyan to offer free rides to injured people. After I reached my destination, he refused payment—about 50 yuan, not an insignificant amount—even though I insisted, because, he said, "You're doing things for the Sichuan people."

The emotional atmosphere in the first weeks after the Sichuan earthquake was described as "touching," "surprising," "unprecedented," and, as Shinan, a self-identified liberal intellectual (someone who would be least likely to buy into official ideology) vividly put it, "boiling goodness," which was deeply "memorable."[22] Guangchuan, a businessman in his forties, made a surprising comparison between the Sichuan earthquake and the Tiananmen movement in 1989:

> You know, the situation after the Sichuan earthquake was pretty much the same as that during the Tiananmen movement. I was in Beijing in 1989. During the movement, the crime rate was very low. If you were a student arriving at the Beijing railway station to join the protest in Tiananmen Square, people would give you a free ride. The atmosphere was simply beautiful. The Sichuan earthquake was like that.[23]

The two events were so different: one a protest, and the other a disaster. Yet the comparison also made perfect sense in terms of the social and political conditions needed to bring them to life. Both needed political opportunities, resources, groups and organizations, and support from the rest of the population to emerge as large-scale collective actions. Both, in a deeper sense of civil society, turned otherwise isolated and self-serving groups into public-spirited ones, and pushed already public-spirited ones to the front. For instance, Beijing college students behaved very differently before the movement—playing bridge, studying for the TOEFL (Test of English as Foreign Language) to go abroad, and going to dance parties—and during the movement—enthusiastic, self-sacrificing, and heroic (Zhao 2001). Therefore, both shared the same euphoria, which sprang from their actions to address issues not directly related them and their pursuit of a goal higher than their individual interests.

The mechanism enabling this multivocal solidarity was the consensus crisis, a result of the disaster's interplay with the political and social conditions. The consensus crisis allowed different sectors of civil society, with different cultural frameworks, to interact with each other. The most important thing for them was the act of compassion and the state of being together.

This post-earthquake solidarity usually occurred among *strangers*—people who ran into, but did not know, each other. A common experience among volunteers—my own experience as a volunteer, too—was that they often did not know most of their fellow volunteers' real names, but only their online IDs or screen names. Organizations and groups interacted with many outside people every day to accomplish their tasks. They came and went, offering help for a day or a week; what mattered was not their names but their hands. Nevertheless, they were not lonely islands in a sea of ruins. They were connected to each other; they tended to act in groups and were mobilized by formal organizations. The groups and associations constituted a giant network that gathered an unbelievably large amount of materials and money and mobilized hundreds of thousands of people. In doing so, they sympathized with the unfortunate survivors, felt reciprocal kindness from them, and felt encouraged by strangers devoted to the same goal. My interviewee Luqiong used poetic language to describe the process:

> This social and public work [volunteering] is charged with a huge sense of responsibility and commitment. It has a power that connects you with the world. . . . You're a channel, or a node, that links many networks. Everyone is so important. Everyone is a humble but great node. It's a small version of an ideal society. Everyone is devoted to a single common task with convergent ideals and commitments.[24]

This network of associations was the social condition for solidarity among strangers. A few scholars have described a similar solidarity—such as a "brotherhood of pain"—in other disasters. They argue that social order breaks down in a massive disaster, giving rise to a state of "liminality" or "mechanical solidarity" (Oliver-Smith 1999; Turner

1967). This otherwise reasonable theoretical argument does not match reality in a modern society. The social order did not break down in the wake of the Sichuan earthquake. Instead, the social and political structure interacted with the features of the earthquake as a consensus crisis that made everything possible: its challenges to the state's administrative capacity, the need for public services from civic associations, a consensus on priorities and tasks, and the moralization of the response. These features amplified some enabling structures and weakened restrictive ones. This situational condition enabled civic associations to actively engage in relief work and demonstrate their creativity and capacity without being restricted by the authoritarian state, at least for the time being. Meanwhile, they self-organized into networks, which connected otherwise isolated groups and organizations. Through these networks, they built trust relations, brought their different cultural repertoires together, and found a rare solidarity. Compassion and solidarity were both widespread and multivocal.

CHAPTER 2

Mourning for the Ordinary

On May 19, seven days after the Sichuan earthquake, the Chinese government declared a three-day period of national mourning. At 2:28 p.m., all around the country the national flag flew at half-staff, and air-raid sirens blared. People observed three minutes of silence in squares, on sidewalks, in parks, in their offices, and in their homes. Foreign journalists reported that the whole nation "came to a standstill" (Barriaux 2008). During the night, people held vigils to commemorate the victims. In public discourses and personal narratives, people used the phrase *kongqian tuanjie* (unprecedented solidarity) to describe their feelings.

This observance of silence was the peak moment in the aftermath of the earthquake, a time of catharsis, solidarity, and effervescence. The commemoration was one of the very few moments, if not the only one, for which the Chinese state was almost unanimously praised. Public opinion applauded the state's decision to hold a national mourning rite for ordinary citizens and its effort to "respect people's lives and dignity." This praise came not only from the mainland Chinese media but also from some Hong Kong media, which mostly were not subject to political censorship from the central government and hence were normally critical of the Chinese government.

In one sense this mourning was not surprising. It confirmed Durkheim's classical theory of mourning rites: enfeeblement felt by a community over the loss of its members, especially when the casualties are heavy, motivates people to gather to mourn, and the mourning rite reconfirms and strengthens the community. According to Durkheim, "A shared misfortune . . . enlivens collective feelings, which lead individuals to seek one another out and come together" ([1912] 1995, 403). Similar rituals of public mourning are ubiquitous in modern societies: in the wake of various disasters, for example, many modern states fly the national flag at half-staff and hold days of commemoration for disaster victims (Eyre 2007; Post et al. 2003; Bin Xu 2013).

Nor was it surprising to some people, who interpreted this moment of mourning as another nationalistic show orchestrated by the government to shore up its legitimacy. For example, Luxin, a young businessman in Chengdu, who identified himself as a "liberal intellectual" (*ziyoupai zhishifenzi*), believed the mourning was just a "house performance" (*tanghui*), a term that originally referred to private opera performances given in dignitaries' homes. The mourning was *tanghui* because, according to Luxin, it was sanctioned and sponsored *by* the state and performed *for* the state. The crowds in public squares waved the national flag and shouted "China will never fall!," all of which seemed to substantiate such an idea.[1]

Nevertheless, neither view captures the political significance and complexity of the mourning. From a longer historical perspective, the Sichuan earthquake mourning was extraordinary. It was the first time in the history of the People's Republic of China that the state had held a large-scale public mourning for ordinary disaster victims. Previous state mourning rites had been held for state leaders, high-ranking officials, fallen soldiers, and other human embodiments of the state. For example, there have been four politically significant state funerals: Mao Zedong's and Zhou Enlai's funerals in 1976, Hu Yaobang's in 1989, and Deng Xiaoping's in 1997. The long morning period for Mao entailed typical practices of a leader's funeral in a totalitarian country, resembling Lenin's in many ways—state-organized rallies, identical rituals throughout the country, the preserved dead body, the long line of cadres paying their last respects, and so on (Wakeman 1985; Tumarkin 1983). A memorial service commenced on September 11 and culminated in a mass commemorative rally in Tiananmen Square on September 18. About one million people reportedly attended the rally (*Renmin ribao* 1976b). Every ritual conducted during the funeral confirmed the party's hierarchical order—from the sequence of the names of funeral committee members to the order in which people paid their final respects to Mao's corpse in the bier.

The other two important funerals, Zhou Enlai's in 1976 and Hu Yaobang's in 1989, however, gave people a rare opportunity to air their grievances about the authorities. The two funerals directly led to two of the biggest protests in the history of the People's Republic, both centered in Tiananmen Square: the April 5, 1976, protest, which was later reevaluated as a "patriotic movement," and the Tiananmen movement in 1989, which remains a taboo subject in China. Despite the unrest they brought about, they resembled Mao's funeral: leaders were at the center of a symbolic practice.

The other prevalent type of public mourning is war commemoration. War victims' death and suffering were woven into an official narrative that legitimized the state and the nation (Mitter 2000; He 2009; Jager and Mitter 2007). Thus, their ordinariness differed from that of the earthquake victims, who were not victims of state military and political actions.[2]

No public mourning had ever been held for victims of disasters until the Sichuan earthquake. China is prone to all kinds of disasters because of her complex geological features. The word "people" appears in China's official name—the People's Republic of China—and in other state institutions (e.g., the People's Bank of China). Nevertheless, state mourning services and related symbolic practices had never been held for the people unless they died for the state in wars and other military conflicts. For example, neither of the two recent deadliest disasters—the 1976 Tangshan earthquake, which killed about 240,000 people, and the 1998 Yangtze River flood, which killed about 3,600 and affected an area half the size of France—had led to state-held mourning. It was even more striking that after the 1998 floods, a mourning proposal was raised but received no response from the government.[3]

In shifting the symbolic focus from leaders and war victims to ordinary people who did not die as the consequence of a political action, the Sichuan earthquake mourning represented a type of mourning common elsewhere but entirely new to China. I term it "mourning for the ordinary": large-scale, state-sanctioned public mourning to honor ordinary citizens instead of human incarnations of the state. Its core significance hinged on the answer to a question with rich moral and political implications: "For *whom* does the bell toll?"

Moreover, contrary to cursory observations, the Sichuan earthquake national mourning was not a state-orchestrated event. Instead, as I will show in this chapter, it was the result of advocacy by public intellectuals and the liberal media, which articulated values typically sustaining the liberal view of civil society, including equality, individual dignity, and independence from the state. If civic engagement is defined as "coordinated action to improve some aspect of community life" (Lichterman and Eliasoph 2014), then advocacy of mourning is a form of engagement aimed to improve a symbolic aspect of civic life: to enhance public awareness of the value of ordinary people's lives. The mourning turned tears into public discourses and sympathy into a vocal demand for the state to demonstrate its compassion for the victims through a public ritual. The advocacy resonated with various cultural ideas about human life and suffering and even found common ground with the government, which desperately needed to repair its moral image in that particular context. Expressions of meaning from different sectors of society were thus diverse and multivocal. Only an in-depth, thick description instead of an outside, journalistic account can reveal the nuances.

In this chapter, I first ask: Why did mourning for the ordinary emerge after the Sichuan earthquake but not in previous disasters? Who advocated the mourning? I trace the trajectory of the development of the Chinese public sphere and examine the political context in the wake of the earthquake. The long-term development of civil society and the contextual conditions reinforced each other, leading to the mourning proposal and its acceptance. Such structural and situational conditions were absent or weak in two previous high-profile disasters—the Tangshan earthquake in 1976 and the 1998 Yangtze River floods; therefore, no mourning was held. The second part of the chapter is devoted to a thick description of how Chinese citizens took part in creating meanings and symbols in both the public sphere and the ritual practices on the ground during the mourning period. I ask: How did different people—for example, advocates of the mourning and ordinary participants of the ritual—interpret the meaning of the mourning in different ways? What can account for the variation in their meaning-making practices?

THE CHINESE PUBLIC SPHERE

The root of the mourning can be traced to the development of the Chinese public sphere since the economic reform. In the 1980s, the nascent Chinese public sphere consisted of a network of college-based intellectuals, salons, newspapers, magazines, think tanks, and book publishers. The public sphere was dominated by cultural elites—such as elite college students and establishment intellectuals—who claimed to represent the Chinese people but, in real political practice, particularly during the 1989 Tiananmen movement, alienated those from other ranks of society, such as workers (Walder and Gong 1993; Calhoun 1994, 188–212).

After the Tiananmen movement in 1989, Chinese civil society and the public sphere were brought to a halt but restarted soon after Deng Xiaoping's "Southern Tour" speeches in 1992, which called for a more comprehensive economic reform. Since then, the public sphere has developed hand in hand with a booming market economy. The ideal type of public sphere is a space autonomous from both the state *and* the market. Yet, in both its historical origin and contemporary version, the public sphere sometimes has an affinity with the market. Think, for example, of the emblematic coffeehouses in Habermas's public sphere: They were places for rational-critical thinking and discussion, but they were also *businesses* (Habermas 1989). Small bookstores and other nesting places for the East European public sphere under socialism were also *businesses* (Goldfarb 2006). The market in China in the 1990s constituted a space somewhat independent from the state. It also empowered the public sphere with a large and differentiated audience as well as providing an economic foundation (Zhao 2008).

Moreover, such commercialization was encouraged and even designed by the state. Without granting the media full freedom, the government bureaus dealing with journalism and propaganda aggressively undertook a market-oriented media reform in the 1990s. The reform aimed to meet multiple goals: to retain legitimacy in the face of an increasingly pluralistic society; to meet society's demand for information, entertainment, and the expression of opinions; to allow the government to reduce spending on media and propaganda while claiming its share of profits from the booming media industry (Stockmann 2013; Zhao 1998, 2008). Consequently, the media market expanded rapidly in the 1990s and continued to boom in the 2000s.

The state's decision to commercialize mass media, however, led to a significant unintended consequence: a greater space for news reporting and many influential non-state media outlets, who gained a wider audience by pursuing an alternative agenda. A few of the early ones derived from state media outlets, such as *Bingdian* (Freezing Point), a section of the *China Youth Daily*, the Youth League's official newspaper. They targeted a wider audience and thus were devoted to bold investigative journalism and more unorthodox cultural and social reporting. Some of them, such as *Southern Weekend* (*Nanfang zhoumou*) and the *Southern Metropolis Daily* (*Nanfang dushibao*), branded themselves as messengers of ordinary people's grievances and were generally believed to be more credible than the government's mouthpieces (Stockmann 2013, 161–79). They also gathered a regular group of columnists, mostly liberal-minded public intellectuals with well-articulated ideas about the dignity and value of independent individuals. Since the new millennium, those media, labeled "liberal media" (*ziyoupai meiti*), have constituted a significant force. The booming media market also boosted the emergence of New Left intellectuals, who used the journals *Dushu* and *Tianya* as their major venues to criticize the detrimental impact of global capitalism and neoliberalism on Chinese society.

The game between the public sphere and the state was transformed from one of "control vs. anti-control" to negotiation (Huang 2007). Using various "guerilla tactics" (Tong 2007), savvy media, like the *Southern Metropolis Daily*, repeatedly tested the boundaries of the state's restrictions—what Chinese media practitioners call the "red line." Consequently, "the nature of the game has changed. Chinese media are employing various strategies to advance their own agendas, uphold their professional principles and, of course, gain audiences" (Qian and Bandurski 2011, 71).

This change converged with two other important trends in the 2000s. First was the rapid development of the Internet. Internet service became affordable in China in the early 2000s, and the online space it provided constituted an alternative to traditional media for meeting various demands from society. Netizens were politically opinionated, critical of

China's political conditions, and supportive of democratic norms (Lei 2011). This can be explained by the social characteristics of the majority of Internet users—young, urban, and educated, but middle to lower in socioeconomic status—a socially progressive but economically disadvantaged population that represented an ideal audience for liberal ideas (Zhao 2008, 257). Various media and public intellectuals—including the New Left and the liberals—soon found allies in various online discussion forums. This new, Internet-based public sphere soon became the focal point of public opinion and a hotbed of online activism (Tang and Sampson 2012; Yang 2009).

The second was a dramatic increase in what official discourse termed "collective incidents" (*qunti shijian*): protests, demonstrations, riots, and other contentious actions against the state. This increase was largely a result of the widening gap between the rich and the poor and heightened tensions between government officials and the people. Collective incidents increased tenfold between 1993 and 2005, from approximately 8,700 a year to about 87,000 a year (Cai 2008; Fewsmith 2008, 231). Unlike the intellectual- and student-led movements in the late 1970s and 1980s, protests in the 1990s and 2000s were usually staged by ordinary, underprivileged people, such as laid-off urban workers, peasants, homeowners, aging war victims, and netizens (Hurst 2009; Lee 2007; O'Brien 2008; Cai 2010; O'Brien and Li 2006; Shi and Cai 2006; Xu and Pu 2010; Yang 2009). These collective actions differed from the student movements of the 1980s in that they focused on practical issues—jobs, benefits, displacement, local cadres' misconduct, and so on—instead of on democracy and freedom of speech.

In the late 1990s and early 2000s, some intellectuals published several investigative journalistic bestsellers about problems in rural areas, such as the intense pressure on local governments to collect taxes and implement the one-child policy; conflicts between peasants and local governments; peasants' poverty in the hinterlands; and other issues believed to threaten "social stability" (Cao 2003; Chen and Chun 2004; Li 2002). Even official research institutes expressed the same concern about structural inequality and the great divide between the urban and rural areas. As a result of these perceived grave social problems, in the early 2000s different forces of the public sphere converged to form the prevailing opinion that a "comprehensive crisis" was looming. Martin Whyte terms the perception a "myth of a social volcano," the idea that the Chinese's public outrage over alleged unjust structural inequality could accumulate and eventually threaten social stability (Whyte 2010, 5). Although Whyte's purpose is to debate this conventional wisdom and provide a more complicated picture of Chinese perceptions of social inequality, he admits—other scholars suggest too—that this "social volcano" view was accepted by the new Hu-Wen administration and directly led to some policy adjustments (Zhang 2012).

All these factors resulted in a transformation of the public sphere. In the 1980s, the public sphere was dominated by elite circles of semi-official reformists and pro-democracy liberals, which closed their doors to rank-and-file people who lacked the requisite sophisticated scholarly knowledge and exotic vocabulary. In the 2000s, intellectuals and media of various political stances relied more on the market, competed for ordinary audiences, and turned themselves into actors engaged in advocacy and activism. Consequently, the main topics changed from grand narratives about "China's future" in the 1980s—represented in River Elegy, a highly influential political documentary in 1988, and topics of scholarly books—to ordinary people's everyday grievances and demands. The major figures in civil society were journalists, rights lawyers, and public intellectuals, people whose professions required and enabled them to bring awareness and critiques of social problems from otherwise voiceless ordinary people to the public sphere, sometimes influencing state policies. The new public sphere gained momentum in several landmark events of civic engagement in the 2000s, such as the Sun Zhigang incident (Zhao 2008). This incident started with the media's investigation of torture by the authorities in a detention center. Liberal-minded columnists soon commented on the issue and criticized the government, and their voices quickly converged with netizens' remarks to spark public outrage that forced the state to modify its policies and practices.[4]

This rapidly developing public sphere, however, had its weaknesses. The state still directly or indirectly controlled most media outlets, including the bolder ones. Despite their intrepid investigative journalism and commentaries, the liberal media were still supervised and monitored by the party's propaganda system. How far they could go largely depended on some contingent factors: the people involved (for example, a relatively liberal-minded official in a provincial propaganda department might allow more space for criticism); the political sensitivity of the issue, which was sometimes determined by entrenched interest groups lobbying the Propaganda Department; timing (for example, not report-ing negative issues around the time of an important party congress), and so on. Reports were sometimes removed from the pages of newspapers and journals or edited by propaganda officials. Journalists and editors in the liberal media were occasionally fired and even sentenced to years in prison under non-political charges. It would be overly pessimistic and inaccurate to declare that the Chinese public sphere was entirely stifled by the authoritarian state. But it would be equally wrong to claim it was independent without acknowledging its intrinsic weaknesses.

THE OPEN PUBLIC SPHERE IN THE WAKE OF THE EARTHQUAKE

The multifaceted structural nature of the public sphere cannot easily explain the emergence of the mourning since it harbored both con-straints and opportunities. It had to be combined with other factors in the immediate context to lead to advocacy of a moment of national mourning. The most important contextual factor was the relatively open public sphere in the wake of the earthquake.

Before the Sichuan earthquake, the Chinese state usually heavily restricted reporting disasters for fear that the devastation and tragedy would reveal its weak disaster response capacity and shake people's ideo-logical beliefs about human beings' power over nature. In the first report about the Tangshan earthquake in 1976, the *People's Daily* used only one short sentence to describe the devastation: "The epicenter area sustains losses in varying degrees" (*Renmin ribao* 1976a). Photographs in the *People's Daily* showed no dead bodies, no collapsed buildings, and no crying children. The death toll was not released until three years later, announced by the Chinese Seismological Association at a professional conference. Even during the 1998 flooding of the Yangtze River, news-papers reported on the devastation in a restricted manner, providing a rhetorical background for the army's and government officials' heroic devotion.

In the wake of the Sichuan earthquake, however, all kinds of media—including the core official media, such as China Central Television (CCTV) and the Xinhua News Agency—reported on the disaster in an astonishingly bold, direct way. This change came about in two different ways. Right after the earthquake, the core official media received an order from the Politburo about the official reporting: reports must be "timely, accurate, open, and transparent" instead of covering the disaster with a "positive" spin, as was the case in previous disasters (Peng and Feng 2009).

At the same time, some non-state media outlets received a verbal warning from the Propaganda Department that they should not go to Sichuan. This warning apparently contradicted the Politburo's message. Yet, without knowing the Politburo's decision, some media decided to go anyway since, according to Zhuang Shenzhi, editor-in-chief of the *Southern Metropolis Daily*, everything else was unimportant compared to the heavy casualties. He also believed that the worst scenario would be that the reports were written but not allowed to be published. Even in that case, the only loss would be the expense of sending journalists, which was minimal compared to the potential gains (Nan 2009, 33–34).

Even after almost every major media outlet's journalists set foot in Sichuan, they still did not receive further word from the Propaganda Department, whose warning was made moot by the Politburo's unambiguously welcoming attitude. Journalists from domestic and foreign media also found the local governments mostly cooperative and friendly. On some occasions, they were even allowed to follow the military. Foreign media journalists, who were seen by the Chinese government as having an "anti-China" bias only months before, began to praise the government's openness (Nan 2009).

Scholars and commentators have speculated on the reasons for this opening, although no one knows for sure the behind-the-scenes decision-making process. The most plausible reason might be the interplay between the disaster's features and the contextual conditions. For the Chinese state, 2008 was a year of image building. The Beijing Olympics, scheduled for August, presented an opportunity for the Chinese state to demonstrate and maintain a respectable image under the spotlight of international attention. Yet, this image-making effort encountered its first challenge after the Tibetan uprising in March, which was a wake-up call for the Chinese government. The government blocked the foreign media's access to Tibet and, consequently, infuriated the foreign media, who mostly relied on Tibetan exiles as their source of information.

The state's concern with its image was further strengthened by the earthquake, an event that highlighted the state's moral responsibility for its citizens' lives. The Chinese state demonstrated its ability to adjust its performance to the situation by mobilizing resources from the whole country to respond to the disaster in a laudably swift manner. In addition, leaders, particularly Premier Wen Jiabao, "Grandpa Wen," quickly made appearances in the most dangerous places, worked around the clock, and comforted children and victims (Xu 2012). In this atmosphere, blocking access to the quake zone made little sense because it would reverse all the efforts the state had made to repair and enhance its image.

Moreover, disasters differ from riots and other contentions in that they are management crises. Their direct causes can be identified as uncontrollable natural hazards engendered by mother nature—at least temporarily. Reporting on devastation and tragedies is relatively less risky than riots and protests, and coverage of the government's effective response can bring about positive public relations effects. From a broader historical perspective, 2008 was not 1998, let alone 1976. A disaster that affected millions of people's lives was impossible to cover up in an age of electronic communications. Before the state's decision to allow media access, people in the quake zone had already taken pictures with their cameras and cellphones and uploaded them to social media. In some sense, the state followed changes in society instead of initiating those changes.

Consequently, all kinds of media flooded into Sichuan after the earthquake, enjoying the unprecedented freedom and competing with each other to produce sensational reports. Even the core state media also joined the crowd. In Xinhua and CCTV, the two state-run media outlets, there were many old propaganda-style reports about heroes, government officials' selfless devotion, and the government's efficient management (Zhou 2008). On the other hand, new things did appear in the state media, including reports on the devastation, deaths, injuries, lack of food and supplies, and, more importantly, people's sorrow, which were new to the Chinese official media and the national audience. In the first two days, audiences saw reports and pictures from Xinhua that depicted the tragedy at several devastated spots: students buried and killed by the collapse of schools, parents' grief, towns utterly devastated by landslides, desperate and hungry refugees hiking across the mountains to escape their destroyed hometowns, and survivors' lack of food and water. Seeing the core state media's move, the non-state media went even further, using all their pages and primetime programs to cover the earthquake. Their reports created a saddening emotional atmosphere, which highlighted issues of life, death, and appropriate symbolic practices to express compassion.

PROPOSAL AND ACCEPTANCE

A key symbolic question soon emerged in this emotive context: In addition to the state's emergency response, what kind of symbolic gesture toward people's suffering should the Chinese state make? As early as May 13, the day after the earthquake, some online commentators suggested lowering the national flag to half-staff to mourn the victims. This suggestion was overshadowed by the ongoing rescue efforts for a few days, until May 15 and 16, when there was only a faint hope of rescuing those who had been under the rubble for more than three days. Then public intellectuals and columnists openly raised the proposal and articulated the meaning of such a ritual; they claimed that previous national mourning rituals had been held for leaders, but now it was time to pay respect to ordinary people. Ge Jianxiong, a professor at Fudan University, one of the first public intellectuals to propose the mourning, articulated its intended meaning: "First, to show the government's respect for citizens' lives and its willingness to shoulder responsibility for citizens; second, citizens need a ritual to express their grief over their relatives and friends; third, the ongoing Olympic torch relay is inappropriate and must be stopped, as well as other public activities and entertainments."[5] He also proposed some details of the rituals: flying the national flag at half-staff, having air raid sirens blare for one minute, asking all citizens to observe one minute of silence and religious groups to mourn and pray for the victims. He proposed a date, May 19, seven days after the earthquake, in accordance with the Chinese custom that the first seven days after a death (*touqi*) should be devoted to mourning.

After coming up with the idea, Ge thought about petitioning the State Council or the People's Congress but finally decided to send a short essay via email to *Southern Metropolis Daily* (*SMD*). This was not only because he was a contracted columnist for the newspaper, but also because he believed *SMD* could publicize the idea faster than any of the state organs. His thinking proved true. Soon the idea was enthusiastically spread by the newspaper's readers and echoed in online comments. His logic of action was consistent with other social advocacy in recent years, such as that surrounding the Sun Zhigang incident: while the institutional way—communicating with the legislature or other state organs—does not guarantee a satisfactory response, pressuring the state through public opinion is sometimes more effective.

Other articles in opinion-leading newspapers emerged at about the same time, emphasizing that the state must "respect the lives of its own citizens" as "humans" regardless of their social status (Shu 2008). Some commentators cited other countries' mourning practices, such as the 9/11 mourning, and interpreted them as an "international convention" to justify their claims. Other commentators stressed that flying the flag at half-staff for victims of natural disasters is required by the National Flag Law, although the practice had never been followed. The National Flag Law was introduced in 1990. Article 14 states that "when unfortunate events or serious natural disasters happen and lead to extraordinarily heavy casualties, the national flag may be lowered to half-staff as a way of mourning." The law was part of the ideological movement after the Tiananmen incident in 1989, aiming to propagate patriotism to defend against the "Western capitalist countries' conspiracy of peaceful evolution." Many articles cited this regulation and urged the government to put it into practice. An article in *Xinmin Evening News* (*Xinmin wanbao*) bluntly said that the Five-Star Red, China's national flag, had never been lowered for ordinary citizens, but, "now, it is the time!" (Li 2008). Similarly, an article in the *China Youth Daily* repeated an urgent message: "Let us set up a mourning date for the unfortunate victims in the Wenchuan earthquake! Let us set up a mourning date for the unfortunate victims in the Wenchuan earthquake!" Most of the proposals were raised in commercialized evening papers or youth papers or influential liberal newspapers, instead of the state-controlled daily papers.

Meanwhile, because of the newly open public sphere, images of collapsed schools and child victims buried under the rubble were widely circulated on all kinds of media and in online forums. Such images even appeared frequently in the core official media, such as Xinhua and CCTV, but were used to convey a different political message. In early footage and pictures of Premier Wen's visit to schools in Dujiangyan, Wen tearfully watched rescuers digging out elementary school students who had suffocated to death under the rubble. Much other footage depicted rescuers' around-the-clock efforts to pull students from the ruins. The purpose was to demonstrate the leader's compassion and the rescuers' devotion, but the media images unintentionally triggered a series of poignant questions about causes of the collapse of schools. Some of the most aggressive liberal media, including *SMD*, insistently raised the question. On May 15, *SMD* published a report about Beichuan High School, asking: Why had only the new building collapsed while the other, older buildings were still standing? Local residents and outside volunteers also took pictures of the devastation and uploaded them to the Internet. The pictures highlighted the thin steel girders in the rubble, suggesting the problem was substandard construction. Netizens' comments on the pictures pointedly indicated a scenario familiar to many Chinese: corruption involved in the contracting process may have been such that the contractor had to use low-quality materials to defray the cost of paying bribes.

Consequently, several days after the earthquake, from around May 15 to May 18, the issue of holding a state-sanctioned mourning rite—and its political implications—attracted tremendous public attention amid sorrow and outrage. If the state did care about people's lives, as demonstrated in Wen's tears and the state rescuers' sweat, why not have a state mourning observance for the unfortunate victims, particularly the children?

At that moment, the Chinese state's options were limited by the flow of events and structural conditions. As the state opened up the public sphere, responded to the disaster swiftly, and endeavored to construct an image of being moral, empathetic, and responsible, it would have been impossible to reverse the changes by not accepting this reasonable proposal. Furthermore, mounting grievances about the collapse of schools made keeping silent on the proposal impossible. At the same time, accepting the proposal could buttress the state's moral image and possibly apply a symbolic Band-Aid to the wound caused by the collapse of schools.

An additional situational factor expedited the acceptance. On May 17, the public learned that Peru had declared May 19 as a mourning day for the Chinese victims.[6] This news put moral pressure on the Chinese government, as it appeared to lag behind other countries in mourning its own citizens. Many newspaper articles urged the state to do the same as soon as possible; online writers had already become outraged.

As a result, an official announcement was made on May 18, designating a three-day mourning period starting on May 19. The state ordered that, at 2:28 pm on the nineteenth, the national flag be flown at half-staff, air raid sirens sound, vehicles honk, and people observe three minutes of silence. In addition, the Beijing Olympic torch relay, a competing state ritual with a different emotional tone, was suspended for three days. All these ritual elements closely followed the course that public opinion had suggested. The Chinese state was unlikely to have had a conscious plan right after the earthquake.[7] A more plausible scenario is that the decision was a response to the strong public demand.

ABSENCE OF MOURNING IN PREVIOUS DISASTERS

Why did mourning for the ordinary not occur in previous deadly and destructive disasters, for example, in two landmark disasters—the Tangshan earthquake in 1976 and the Yangtze River floods in 1998?

The Tangshan earthquake lacked almost all structural and situational conditions necessary for such mourning. Civil society and the public sphere did not exist. Consequently, there was no effective channel for moral sentiments about ordinary people's lives to turn into public action. Moreover, in the prevalent moral imagination and official political culture, the "people" were undifferentiated "masses" (qunzhong), subordinates of the regime rather than individual citizens. Casualties and devastation were mostly covered up in order to conceal the state's weak capacity to respond. The strictly controlled media were filled with reports about the heroic devotion of rescuers, PLA soldiers, and the Tangshan residents. The atmosphere was full of self-congratulation in official discourse and the fear of aftershocks in private conversations.

In December 1998, several months after the historic Yangtze River floods, an article in the China Youth Daily asked a poignant question in its title, "For Whom Are the Flags Lowered?" The author, Guo Guangdong, a law school student in Shanghai, boldly stated that, despite the regulations in the National Flag Law, flags had been lowered only once, in 1998--for President Yang Shangkun, who died that year, but not for the victims of the floods. He used the examples of disaster commemorations from other countries to support his call for a state-sponsored commemoration. The article was published in the *Freezing Point* (*Bingdian*) section of the paper, a new social and political section famous for its in-depth reports and op-eds. The moral idea contained in the *Freezing Point* article was no different than that expressed in the Sichuan mourning proposal. Why then did the proposal fail to lead to any response from the state?

The answer rested in both the micro-level human actions in this situation and macro-level state-society relations. Timing was an important factor. When there was no mourning by October, Guo first decided to write a petition letter to the premier. More than ten days passed, but he received no response. He then revised the letter into an article, sent it to two newspapers, and, again got no reply. Finally, he sent it to the new but influential "Freezing Point Comments" (*Bingdian shiping*), a column in *Freezing Point*, and it was accepted by the column's adventurous editor, Li Datong. It was published in December, two months after he came up with the idea and three months after the floods—too late for the government to do anything, given that such mourning usually happens shortly after a disaster. Certainly, Guo's action strategies can be partially blamed for the delay. He chose to petition the State Council first, a move that would have been unlikely to receive a response even in 2008. But was this delay an individual strategic mistake owing to his lack of experience?

Maybe, but it was more likely to have been the result of macro-level structures that constrained Guo's options for action at the time he decided to publicize his idea. The public sphere in 1998 developed rapidly and enthusiastically. Many pioneers within and outside the official media, including *Freezing Point*, *Focus* (*Jiaodian fangtan*, on CCTV), and *Southern Weekend*, combined resources from the official media and the market with their own ideas about making news reports bolder, more readable, and closer to ordinary people's lives. Yet these early reformists focused more on investigative journalism and in-depth reports than op-eds. Open advocacy and direct challenges to state policy were still seen as high-risk actions that might invite suppression. *Freezing Point* was the first influential op-ed section, but it did not exist until November. After the article on mourning was published, Li Datong was still worrying about possible criticism from the government and his superiors, because not many other newspapers had dared to do what he had done (Li 2005, 290). In other words, Guo's delay was more likely the result of the fact that the forums allowing a citizen to directly advocate a change in state policy and practice simply were weak and uninfluential. By contrast, in 2008, when Ge Jianxiong chose *SMD* as his first venue to raise his proposal, public-opinion leaders' advocacy through media was already common. Guo's delay involved a small, individual action--one which, however, revealed the difference in state-society relations in the two situations.

More broadly, the macro-level political context was not conducive to such a proposal. In the second half of the 1990s the Chinese state tended to build its legitimacy on a comprehensive, at-all-costs plan of economic development. Jiang Zemin, then China's president, decided to recruit "new social strata" into the party, including private entrepreneurs, a practice that contradicted the fundamental ideological base of the party as the vanguard of the proletariat. The state clearly adapted itself to the changing environment by opening access to the power system, but this access was granted to only the social and economic elite, not to ordinary people. "Ordinary people" were not on this new agenda of market authoritarianism. Numerous laid-off workers in formerly state-owned enterprises received only meager pensions, limited benefits, or no compensation at all (Hurst 2009). In addition, the state noted the fading of Communist ideology and a subsequent vacuum of belief after Tiananmen. As a substitute, it turned to nationalism (Gries 2004), evident in a wave of anti-Japanese and anti-American actions in the late 1990s. In this legitimacy link between the state and society, the "Chinese nation" and "new social strata" that represented the "advanced productive forces" left little room for ordinary people.

The situation and flow of events also mattered. The floods were far from minor, but they were mainly a domestic matter and attracted only sporadic international attention. A search of reports in four major newspapers and agencies (*New York Times, Washington Post, Associated Press, Financial Times*) from June 1 to October 31, 1998, yields 106 results (with key terms "China" and "flood"). A search with key terms "China" and "earthquake" in the same media from May 12 to October 11, 2008, yields 1,259 results. China was not in the spotlight, and the government did not feel the same pressure as in 2008 to repair its image. There was no indication of large-scale, self-organized volunteering. Thus, the disaster response was a state-dominated affair without substantive participation by civil society. It did not provide adequate state-society interactions that could possibly lead to mourning for ordinary citizens. All these factors together led to the absence of mourning for the ordinary, even though such mourning was proposed.

MULTIVOCAL SOLIDARITY IN THE PUBLIC SPHERE

The official announcement of the mourning had only 134 Chinese words and was devoid of an elaborate discourse. This simple announcement, however, did not prevent the public sphere from bursting forth with numerous discourses, symbols, and narratives about the various meanings of the mourning. The advocates of the mourning—public intellectuals and the liberal media—celebrated *their* successful proposal and reaffirmed *their* intended meanings: individuals as members of society, regardless of their rank, political views, status, and achievements, are worthy of society's respect through a publicly held death rite. The mourning, as they argued, shifted the sacred object from modern nation-states, or their human incarnations, to ordinary citizens, extolling the sacredness of the ordinary as well as the dignity of humans. It presented a symbolic model of state-society relations opposed to the traditional, state-centered one. It also represented some of the key moral ideas of civil society: individual dignity, civility through compassion, equality, and symbolic independence from the state (Cohen and Arato 1992).

They also praised the government for its *shunying minyi* (compliance with public opinion). Even this praise, however, did not come without reservations. First, public opinion was the active subject in the discourse, whereas the state, being the passive subject, "followed" the public and made a correct move along the direction pointed out by the public. Second, they implied that ordinary people had been blatantly neglected until this event. An editorial titled "The Mourning Days: Let the State Get Closer to Human Feeling and Power Walk toward Humanity" in *Southern Metropolis Daily* declared:

> This [mourning] is progress at the cost of enormous sorrow. When the state is trying to express human feelings, and power is trying to get close to humanity, the flame of humanity shines against the dark background. . . . When the country is suffering and millions of people are sharing the pain, politics is not something detached from our hearts;

power is not confined inside of palace gates to be revered only from a distance.... This is the first time the state will lower the flag and pay its final respects to ordinary citizen victims. Through these national mourning days, cold political terms begin to be charged with our feelings, and the towering state structure begins to connect to the hearts of the ordinary, like you and me. (*Southern Metropolis Daily* 2008b)

Again, this passage assigned an active discursive role to citizens and *shengming* (life) and *renxin* (humanity). The state could only "get close" to people's basic feelings instead of playing a paternalistic role in "caring for people," as in official discourses.

Hong Kong media that were not supported by the Chinese government cautiously praised the decision, but stressed that the mourning should be a "new start" for the Chinese government. An editorial in *Apple Daily*, a Hong Kong newspaper famous for its criticism of the Chinese government, stated:

This [decision] at least shows the Chinese government is attempting to "be in line with international society" and to show it is not a regime that callously disregards human life.... We wish this mourning decision for the earthquake victims were made because the Chinese government knows that "people are more important than emperors." We hope that they realize people's suffering deserves more respect and mourning. If the Chinese government does think in this way, then the mourning days starting from today will have extraordinary historical significance. (Lu 2008)

The official media also joined the chorus but described the mourning as a symbolic vehicle for the state to show its sympathy with citizens in sorrow and respect for people's lives. Meanings about life and rights expressed in public opinion were incorporated into the old-style Communist rhetoric about "the people" (for example, China's official name, the People's Republic of China). A piece printed in *People's Daily*, "The National Flag Demonstrates the Dignity of Life," said:

When the republic's national flag is lowered for ordinary citizens, when hundreds of millions of people share this sorrow, it [national mourning] uses a solemn ceremony and distinct symbols to manifest the flesh-and-blood connection between the government and the people [*renmin*], to demonstrate the nation's respect for life, and to incarnate the ruling party's principle that "all power belongs to the people." (He 2008)

Most regional official media followed the lead of core state media, affirming that the government's leadership was strong and its decisions were correct, using nationalistic language to interpret life and humanity and to reaffirm "solidarity among the Chinese people" (Yu Yuhua 2008). None of the articles, however, referred to the child victims. Instead, broad and vague terms like "the people" (*renmin*) or "ordinary citizens" (*putong gongmin*) were adopted to forge an image of an empathic and responsible state.

Between the paternalistic official discourse, which suggested the state should take care of "ordinary people," and the liberal discourse suggesting the state should "comply with" and "get closer to" people, the common ground was the use of the word "people." This rare consensus between the government and the public, however, did not mean that the intended official meaning was received perfectly. The consensus was in fact more discursive than substantive, and the moral and political implications of the terms were articulated differently. Multivocality and ambiguity about the terms—who "the people" are and whether they should take an active or passive role—still remained.

Nevertheless, it was this multivocality and ambiguity that gave considerable room for many other actors to express the meanings they attached to the mourning and talk about issues related to life and death. In most reports and public discourses in the media, these two different lines of interpretation—the official and the liberal—were often mixed, but *no* commentators addressed this difference. Instead, they expressed compassion through various symbolic representations. For example, some influential websites set up pages where people could pay respect to the victims by sending virtual flowers and lighting virtual candles. Many Internet users changed their status on MSN Messenger (an instant messaging program) to "offline" during the three-minute silence. This collective action was organized neither by the state nor by Microsoft (*Southern Metropolis Daily* 2008a). Online users produced numerous artistic and literary works on influential public forums. One of the most visible genres was poetry. Most commemorative poems that emerged in the wake of the earthquake were written by amateurs in a highly emotional state, and the literary value of the poems varied widely. The poems might remind people of the Tiananmen poetry in the mourning for Zhou Enlai in 1976, but they differed in that they were rarely charged with political implications. The major themes of the poems in the Sichuan earthquake mourning focused on the child-mother relationship, mourning victims, and encouraging survivors.

Numerous newspapers also reduced the color on their front pages to mainly black and white––appropriate colors for mourning. Words and symbols on the black-and-white front pages were also a mixture of national solidarity—"the republic is wailing"—and ambiguous words of mourning. In some influential forums, many online users reportedly called on others to wear black and white on the mourning days and for women not to wear much make-up. This call appeared not only on large public websites but also on community-based forums (Gu et al. 2008). The actual percentage of people who wore black and white might not be researchable, but the call for action itself was a highly visible symbolic practice that helped create the overall emotional atmosphere.

ACTIONS AND MEANINGS ON THE GROUND

What did ordinary people who participated in the mourning do? How did they talk about the meaning of their actions? How did political conditions shape their actions and the meaning they attached to those actions?

To examine their actions and meanings at the micro-level, we start from the macro-level structural and situational conditions in which they acted. In most previous Chinese state rituals, the state played a central role in setting up procedures: it arranged spaces and time, organized and mobilized participants, and demarcated the spatial center and its periphery. In the Sichuan earthquake mourning, the state retreated from the symbolic/spatial center (central squares or memorial sites, for instance), opened the commemoration's boundaries, and avoided organizing large-scale official gatherings in central ceremonial places. For example, state leaders lined up and bowed in a relatively small public space outside the Zhongnanhai compound, the headquarters of the CCP and the State Council, instead of in Tiananmen Square in Beijing. Commemorations in provincial capitals followed the same pattern, and therefore avoided putting the state at the center of attention. The official three minutes of silence was organized in state-owned companies and government bureaus but not in public spaces. State rituals that created an incompatible emotional atmosphere, such as the Olympic torch relay, were paused during the mourning period. Entertainment programs on TV and performances were also rescheduled to later days or simply cancelled. In other words, the state cleared the stage for the mourning.

The state's retreat and opening to unofficial rituals seemingly contradicted its usual logic of action whereby it banned unauthorized rituals and even strictly controlled participation in state rituals, because, as Pfaff and Yang point out, such large-scale rituals could provide people with opportunities to stage protests. This tendency is undoubtedly true, but Pfaff and Yang's analysis presumes that before the ritual, "discontents are generalized and dissenting subcultures have formed but regime surveillance and repression have prevented the formation of an opposition movement or organized parties" (Pfaff and Yang 2001, 549). This was not the case during the Sichuan earthquake mourning.

Before the mourning, angry voices were certainly heard. Even during the mourning period, the liberal media used big-character headlines and emotional language to continue their reports on the school collapse issue. Nevertheless, the government promised a thorough investigation of the issue and severe punishment for the culprits. Despite the mounting anger, many people believed this official assurance. Shinan, one of my interviewees, a dissident intellectual who would have been one of the least likely people to believe official discourses, told me that back then "almost everyone believed" the government's promise. The reason, according to him, was that the causes were so obvious, and solutions seemed straightforward—"just some bad officials in the local governments. Go get them and put them in jail—done." It would also be unreasonable to expect the investigation to be completed only one week after the quake.[8] On May 21, the last day of the mourning period, desperate parents staged the first protest, but it was small. The local government responded through dialogue instead of suppression.

Thus, the grievances did not lead to a generalized discontent articulated by a devoted group of dissidents. The double-edged effect of the official ritual did not take place, mainly because the state responded quickly to the grievances by openly making reasonable promises. The anger did not disappear but instead led to even stronger sorrow over the child victims, which could be publicly expressed in the mourning without leading to any large protests in urban centers. Photos of the mourning rites taken by my informants in various public spaces showed that many message cards and banners were dedicated to the "poor children."

All kinds of media used images of children in their special reports on the mourning, adding more emotional power to the ritual. Moreover, children were the representative figures of the "ordinary" to whom the ritual was dedicated; the state media also propagated the image of state leaders kissing and hugging child survivors to show their compassion for the "people." The otherwise empty term "people" (*renmin*), which appeared everywhere in the state's propaganda, was incarnated in the children who suffered from the earthquake.

Around 2:28 p.m. on May 19, 2008, the designated time for the three minutes of silence, many people gathered in central squares in the main cities. That night, even more people gathered to hold vigils for the victims. Videos on Youku (a video-sharing website, the Chinese equivalent of Youtube), media reports, and interviews showed that, in at least nineteen major cities' central squares, there were large rallies around the three-minute silence or nighttime vigils.[9] Videos show that those squares were fairly crowded at the time of the silence and at the vigils as well; my interviewees estimated that the number of attendees ranged from several thousand in smaller cities to twenty thousand in Chengdu and Shanghai. No adequate evidence exists to indicate who organized these gatherings in central squares in so many cities. On May 18, some informants in Shanghai and Chengdu received text messages and emails indicating there would be a mourning ceremony in Tianfu Square in Chengdu and Renmin Square in Shanghai. Some of them forwarded these messages to their friends, but they admitted that they had already expected that there would be some activities in the squares. The government was unlikely to have been the organizer. Since most attendees were college students and young professionals, I contacted two informants who worked, respectively, for the Education Bureau of Shanghai and a university. Both confirmed that it would have been impossible for either the Education Bureau or the university to have organized such events. As one of them said, the government had "an instinctive" caution about "collective gatherings" and therefore would not encourage them. The other, who was responsible for directing students' "political and thought education" at a Shanghai university, said that the university encouraged students to stay on campus instead of commemorate in public places.[10] Either these signals did not reach the students or they ignored them. But the state did not make much effort to control the gatherings. One interviewee was surprised by the scarcity of police officers, considering the large crowd in Shanghai's Renmin Square; other interviewees said that there were police officers, but they did not intervene. In Tiananmen Square, a politically sensitive public space, police presence was heavier around the time of silence on the first mourning day, but there is no indication that people were not allowed to gather there, at least on the first day.[11]

This open boundary to ceremonial spaces led to a high density of participants' bodily co-presence, and, hence, it raised the possibility of highly intense emotions, as depicted in media reports and videos. Hardly any situation could be a better example of Durkheimian mourning and collective effervescence than the commemorative gatherings on May 19 in Tianfu Square in downtown Chengdu. Chengdu was the metropolis closest to the affected areas. Although the city remained mostly intact, many residents experienced the terrifying shocks and took part in rescue and relief efforts. Before the silence, people had laid flowers and wreaths, which soon piled up like a small hill. On personal message cards attached to the flowers, people wrote prayers for the victims, especially the children. By the time of the three-minute silence, there were already about ten thousand people in the square; when the air-raid sirens wailed, many people began sobbing. Strangers held hands, crying for those whom they had never met. The crying was soon transformed into rhythmic chants of "*Xiongqi!*" accompanied by arm-waving. Some people began to sing the Chinese national anthem and the song "Power Comes from Solidarity."[12] Tears turned to cheers, sorrow to solidarity.

This is a picture we are familiar with and take for granted as an example of collective effervescence. It was witnessed by hundreds of thousands and imprinted in China's national memory. It undoubtedly created a strong wave of emotional power, which, said my interviewees, *zhenhan* (moved) the participants deeply. But social analysis must go beyond the point of "where there's a crowd, there's effervescence." As Randall Collins argues, even at the most elated moments, not everyone will be equally involved in symbolic practices. Some people, whom Collins terms "active minorities," are the most vocal and aggressive, followed by sympathetic others, creating a wave that sweeps over those who are reluctant or hesitant (Collins 2004).

This theoretical point enables us to turn the undifferentiated "long shot" of effervescence into a "close-up" image in high definition. For example, contrary to what we might imagine and unlike the pictures in the media, most central squares were not fully packed with a single

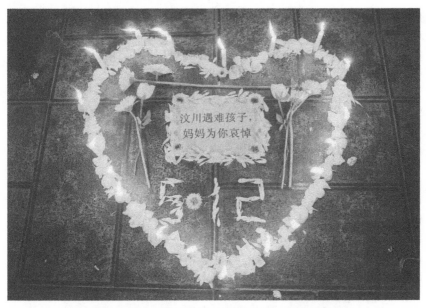

FIGURE 5. Candles and flowers are placed in the shape of a heart during a candle-lit vigil at a square in Guiyang, Guizhou Province. May 20, 2008. The Chinese characters read "Mothers mourn for the children who died in the Wenchuan earthquake." Reuters/China Daily.

crowd but instead with many clusters.[13] In the middle of these clusters were certain groups that usually led the symbolic practices. Some were apparently members of preexisting groups. They were more willing to display their deep feelings, brought symbolic materials (candles, flowers, etc.), distributed them to others, and promptly led chants and waves. A video on Youku shows about forty young people, wearing similar white T-shirts reading "China will tough this out!" holding hands as they lined up along Tiananmen Square. Their line soon became the focus of attention, surrounded by people taking photos and videos. Some groups were emergent. Amid the huge crowds, the loudest chants were usually from clusters of young people who waved their hands and flags emotionally. In vigils, this phenomenon of ritual group enclaves was even more visible. Crowds consisting of numerous clusters surrounded candles on the ground. The candles usually were brought by active minorities and arranged in symbolic shapes or words: hearts, 5.12 (the date of the earthquake), and Sichuan. Videos showed that it was usually a small group of people instead of the whole crowd that led the chants and singing amid the candles. Interviews also suggest that many netizen groups or "QQ groups" (groups organized via QQ, a popular instant-messaging service in China) started their commemorations in public squares even before the mourning days.[14] Only on very few occasions, such as collecting donations at the time of mourning, were formal organizations such as the Red Cross involved.

In the ubiquitous observance of the three-minute silence, active minorities performed the same functions. They behaved more conspicuously, occupied critical positions in the physical setting, and were more likely to lead the observance by becoming the focus of attention, creating situational pressure on others. Videos show that these people usually took action in small groups instead of individually. Clip S-77 (Baoding) from Youku shows members of a car club (QQ Candy Club, named after a compact car model) parking and arranging their vehicles in a circle in a shopping area, and honking simultaneously at the silent time. One member even held a flag with the club's name on it. Other car owners nearby echoed the honking. Another clip (S-78, Caozhou) shows a group of about thirty young motorcyclists, stopped in a street, each wearing a white or black T-shirt and holding white chrysanthemums, the mourning flower in China. A young man announced to the cars behind the motorcycles that at 2:28 p.m. they would honk their horns. Another member distributed chrysanthemums to pedestrians and drivers who stopped to watch or join them. In fact, they blocked the whole street, but there were no discernible complaints about this intentionally created a traffic jam. Some other groups were not members of civil associations, but were instead embedded in their own work organizations. Employees in small roadside shops, for example, were organized by their employers to line up on sidewalks (clips S-8, S-22, S-23, S-30). Their well-organized and conspicuous observance put pressure on many neighboring shops, whose employees joined them (e.g., clip S-30, Xi'an). Certainly not all people observed the silence so faithfully. Some posed in a more casual manner, and some cars did not stop, with a legitimate concern about safety. Nevertheless, the variation in minuscule details did not reduce the ritualistic efficacy of most scenes, in which massive numbers of cars and people who stopped were accompanied by blaring sirens and honking.

Those small groups did not act in a political vacuum. Instead, interviews with the tiny publics and examination of their "tiny texts," such as blogs, forums, and so on, show that they interpreted the meanings of their participation against the larger political context. They joined the crowds not at the behest of the state, but for their fellow citizens and for themselves. In this way, their small activities acted out the moral implications of mourning *for* the ordinary—for people "like you and me"— and the collective actions *by* people like you and me.

My interview with members of one of the groups attending the mourning in Tianfu Square in Chengdu demonstrated this politics-in-miniature. Hanling, a young man who had studied in Europe and the United States, organized a Returnee Club for those who had studied abroad but had come back to work in Chengdu. The club held regular activities (twenty-six in 2008, fifteen in 2009), such as dinners, hikes, movie viewings, and so forth, none of which had anything to do with politics. Before the mourning ritual, he sent text messages asking members to gather at a department store close to Tianfu Square to attend vigils there. About twenty club members made it. The club called on people to donate their extra candles for the affected people who had no electricity. In a picture, one of their group members held a poster high above his head that read, "Please leave your candles here. The affected people need them. Thank you!" The club ultimately collected more than ten boxes of candles. Hanling described the silent observance organized by the state-owned company where he works as "boring" and "sort of a political task." The vigil was "different" because, he said, "it was *our own* [activity]."

In addition to joining the crowds, small groups held "their own" small commemorative rituals in social spaces far away from central squares, such as in parks, on school campuses, and within small public spaces in residential areas. One of my interviewees held a small vigil with his friends at a place in Chengdu called Hejiangting, where two rivers converged. They arranged candles in the shape of a heart with the number 5.12 in the middle. The police came to see what they were doing but did not ask them to leave. Similar vigils were held in numerous places that night. In Chongqing, a metropolis that formerly belonged to Sichuan Province, a group of young people—my informants as well—placed candles on paper boats and set them afloat on a river, to let the current carry the boats and flames away. Some commemorations were held within state-owned spaces, such as universities, but were organized by students. At a prestigious university in Nanjing, students called on each other on an Internet forum to gather in a little square on campus to hold a vigil. My interviewee was one of the organizers, but he did not know the other organizers' real names; they simply communicated with each other online and showed up in the place they chose. Several thousand students came to the vigil, and everyone bowed three times before the candles. The whole ritual was extremely quiet. University authorities at first tried to dissuade them, but later gave up and even joined them. Administrators from the university also appeared at the ritual and observed the silence.

In addition to using phrases like *"our own* activities," they described their activities and other people's participation as *zifa* (spontaneous). People *spontaneously* gathered in small public spaces; bystanders *spontaneously* joined them in arranging candles and handing out flowers; participants *spontaneously* brought candles to the gathering; after the activities, they *spontaneously* stayed to clean up the candle wax on the ground. They spoke of the spontaneity as warm, moving, and touching. Yet, this spontaneity did not originate in a vacuum. People organized themselves through preexisting networks and had a primitive division of labor about who would bring what to the gathering. In many cases, they were well versed in what Tocqueville terms "the art of association." For example, the boat-candle group in Chongqing was, in fact, an anti-Japanese "patriotic" group that held regular symbolic activities, including commemorations of victims of the Great Chongqing Bombing during China's war with Japan during World War II. I had observed their activities for another research project. They had a young man as their leader, several core and enthusiastic members, and a set of regulations about how to behave in public activities. As with their other activities, before they lit their candles and released their boats, the leader gave a brief speech about the meaning of people's lives and their love for their compatriots.

What does the narrative of spontaneity tell us about the politics of mourning? In her study of 1960s black student sit-ins, Francesca Polletta showed that the spontaneity narrative "denoted not a lack of prior coordination but independence from adult leadership, urgency, local initiative, and action from moral imperative rather than bureaucratic planning" (Polletta 1998, 137). In the Sichuan earthquake national mourning, this narrative played a similar role but denoted independence from the state. In the official Chinese political vocabulary, "spontaneity" (*zifa*) was

usually used by organs of the party-state to suggest that certain collective actions--such as the anti-American demonstrations in 1999, after
NATO bombed the Chinese embassy in Belgrade--had not been orchestrated by the state. This expression, however, was borrowed by citizens to
suggest that they were not organized by the state or state organizations
but by themselves. When they used the word *zifa*, it was usually in opposition to *guanfang* (official) instead of "organized." It denoted the same
thing as Hanling's declaration that "It was our own!"

At the same time, the clear distinction between the state and their
own groups did not necessarily mean that their interpretation was based
on the classical idea of civil society as in neo-Tocquevillianism. For
Hanling's returnee club, their rhetorical independence from the state
was more of a matter of political apathy than opposing the state. For the
Chongqing group and many other groups, their rhetorical independence
from the state was often combined with a feeling of national solidarity.
Many participants of the mourning believed they mourned because the
deceased were their compatriots, and mourning itself was not a simple
expression of sympathy but a powerful demonstration of the Chinese
nation's solidarity. Some members of the Chongqing group frequently
criticized the government for being too soft on the Japanese. Yet, their
national solidarity or political apathy was shared with public intellectuals and liberal media who believed that ordinary people's lives should be
honored.

To a cursory observer, the national mourning could be easily interpreted as another state-orchestrated show or *tanghui*. A fine-grained
analysis of the texts, words, and actions of the advocates and participants, however, shows that this interpretation is simplistic. The story of
the national mourning was a story of civic engagement. Prominent intellectuals and ordinary citizens proposed a rite by which the state could
change its approach to symbolic practices and society could recognize
individuals' dignity and value. Their advocacy was enabled by the long-
term development of the public sphere, the relatively open public sphere
in the wake of the earthquake, and other political factors in the context.
The state accepted the proposal to repair its image and shore up its legitimacy in the face of the political challenges in 2008.

The mourning period was also a rare opportunity for Chinese citizens to articulate various meanings about life and death and to demonstrate their compassion through symbolic practices in public spaces.

The meaning of the mourning that the public intellectuals and liberal media expressed was close to the classical civil society notion of equality and the individual's value, but they resonated with other participants not by those abstract civil society ideas but by their rhetorical emphasis on ordinary people's lives. Nationalism had a strong presence in the expressions of meaning, and the "people" were considered as members of a national community. Most participants, however, even including those with a strong sense of national identity, attempted to demonstrate a symbolic distance from the state. With the open public sphere in the wake of the calamity, their commonality triumphed, although they sang the same requiem in a multivocal way.

CHAPTER 3

Civic Engagement in the Recovery Period

On June 4, three weeks after the earthquake, the State Council released a document titled *Wenchuan Earthquake Recovery and Reconstruction Regulations*, which marked the end of the emergency response period and the beginning of the recovery period, roughly from June 2008 to May 2010, the second anniversary of the earthquake, by which time major recovery projects had been finished. Search and rescue work stopped. As the survivors were still living in tents and prefabricated houses, heavy machinery had already been dispatched to remove the ruins and level the ground to rebuild the affected towns and villages.

In early July, when I arrived in Dujiangyan as a volunteer, the town's vitality had already been restored. Shops were open; traffic was busy again; buses were running. Young, female receptionists in *qipao* gowns bowed to incoming customers at the doors of hotpot restaurants. Three-wheeled motorcycles, which operated as unlicensed taxis, cruised the streets for passengers. The town appeared no different than it had before the earthquake--except for the x-shaped cracks on building walls and the piles of rubble that stood in busy streets, reminding people of the shocks they had experienced just a couple of months earlier. In the village where I stayed, peasants were tearing down half-collapsed houses and clearing the rubble, while those who had been displaced searched for temporary jobs in transportation and construction. Outside volunteers like me were teaching and entertaining children in tents at summer camps. Like people in many other places in the earthquake area, the villagers were struggling to get back on track, despite the emotional and physical scars.

Many associations stayed in the quake zone, and more continued to arrive, in the hope that the demanding recovery tasks would create opportunities for them to launch projects, obtain funding, and make a difference. Nevertheless, the consensus crisis that the disaster generated eventually and inevitably faded as differences in the interests of the parties involved emerged and the general agreement on priorities and goals disappeared. The remaining volunteers and associations encountered more difficulties and dilemmas than during the effervescent emergency response period. The political context changed; so did the room for further engagement.

How then did volunteers and associations deal with the changing context? What were the long-term effects of their civic engagement? As the school collapse issue emerged as a focal point of public debates, how did volunteers, most of whom were helping children and survivors in places close to the collapsed schools, talk about—or not talk about—the ethical and political meaning of their action?

THE STATE-BUSINESS ALLIANCE

The post-earthquake drama changed in the recovery period. A state-business alliance emerged among the central government, local governments, GONGOs, and big corporations. This alliance invested billions of yuan, monopolizing major recovery plans and leaving limited room for grassroots civic associations. State-business alliances are ubiquitous in post-disaster contexts, in which states practice a neo-liberal strategy to work with corporations to benefit from the devastation and tragedy caused by disasters. For example, corporations and states sometimes wipe out everything on the sites of disasters to rebuild a brave new world. The more devastated a disaster-hit place is, the easier it is for such an alliance to form (Klein 2007). The post-Sichuan recovery was an instance of this "market of sorrow" (Adams 2013).

After the emergency period, local governments in Sichuan still faced a series of daunting recovery tasks. The issue of permanent housing loomed large in survivors' minds and was a major concern of the local governments. Some towns and villages were too devastated to remain habitable, and a few villages at the bottom of valleys simply disappeared in the torrents of landslides and floods. Those places, including their infrastructure and administrative units, had to be redesigned and relocated. For instance, the Beichuan County seat, which had been utterly destroyed by the quake and landslides from the surrounding mountains, was relocated to Yongchang, a new town which incorporated several places in An County. This involved negotiations between the two counties, fiscal rearrangements between the provincial and county governments, and the migration of tens of thousands of people.

Nevertheless, despite these difficulties, the problems had now become manageable, falling within the scope of the state's comprehensive recovery plan. The scale of the problems did not overpower the state system, which determinedly used its authoritarian command structure to mobilize resources throughout the country. In other words, the earthquake's aftermath no longer consisted of a crisis but various large-scale, state-funded recovery projects, from restoring infrastructure to accommodating the displaced population, from erecting prefabricated houses to providing financial assistance. Those massive projects, as a document from the Ministry of Housing and Urban-Rural Development emphasized, had to be and were already led by the party and government (Ministry of Housing and Urban-Rural Development 2008). As Christian Sorace's study shows, the central, provincial, and local governments made decisions, and used their Leninist work style, to implement massive reconstruction plans without listening to the local residents about their needs and grievances (Sorace 2014).

The central government allocated a significant amount of funds to the recovery. In 2008, it allocated 38.437 billion yuan to the affected provinces for disaster relief and 69.870 billion for recovery and rebuilding. In 2009, it allocated another 97 billion for further recovery (Liu 2010, 49). Also, most donations collected through government and local state organizations, which I will explain soon, were also transferred to the governments in the affected provinces. This amounted to about 57.8 billion.

The central government also employed the traditional "one-on-one support" (*duikou zhiyuan*) mechanism to mobilize resources from other provincial governments. Each county was paired with an unaffected province, which invested a certain proportion of its annual revenue in the county's recovery and reconstruction. The actual investment from the supporting provinces was about 68 billion yuan, almost the same as the relief funds from the central government in 2008 (Liu 2010). With this large amount of money, the central and local governments were able to provide the affected people, most of whom did not have hazard or homeowner's insurance, with comprehensive subsidies and assistance. Every family whose house had been destroyed by the quake received a cash subsidy of 16,000 to 25,000 yuan ($2,500–$4,000), depending on the family's size, financial situation, and location, to defray their rebuilding costs (Sichuan Provincial Government 2008). Seriously injured survivors received free medical care from state-run hospitals, which were subsidized by the government for the services they provided.

GONGOs resumed their status as a major force of recovery mainly because of their monopoly in managing the donations through official channels, which amounted to 65 billion yuan. The complex flow of the donations is beyond this book's scope, but the complexity boiled down to a simple fact: the government and GONGOs received and used all the *legal* donations. Approximately 42 percent of total recorded donations were collected through public foundations, most commonly (about 36 percent) through China Red Cross and China Charity and their foundations and local chapters. A distinctive feature of the system is that the GONGOs' local chapters transferred their money directly to the local governments in their area, instead of to their national headquarters. Even so, national GONGOs were still able to use the 7.411 billion yuan in donations, and the Red Cross alone had 5.271 billion yuan (Deng 2009, 89). Comparisons might make more sense than abstract numbers. Donations to national GONGOs and public foundations (7.411 billion, not including their local chapters) were greater than the 2007 GDP of the three most devastated counties combined, about 5.5 billion, including Wenchuan (2.9 billion), Beichuan (1.3 billion), and Qingchuan (1.3 billion).[1]

The GONGOs allocated the money to their local chapters in Sichuan and then to the local governments, which used them in various projects. In other words, the final and actual users were local governments. Only a few public foundations, such as the China Foundation for Poverty Alleviation (CFPA), set up their own offices and work stations in the quake area to run their projects. Thus, the local governments welcomed the GONGOs for their ample funds and official status. Their strong presence in the quake zone squeezed out grassroots organizations; moreover, they consolidated their dominance over civic associations by monopolizing donations. The China Red Cross Foundation, for the first time in history, set up a special fund of 20 million yuan to support NGOs' recovery-related projects. Compared to the donations the organization received--5.271 billion--20 million was only a tiny proportion (0.38 percent). Even this small proportion, however, excited many NGOs. In sum, the upsurge of funds did not alter but instead reinforced the imbalanced power structure between foundations and grassroots associations by increasing the associations' dependence on the foundations.

Local governments in Sichuan had their own priorities, which focused on attracting outside investments and programs. The earthquake brought about a loss of 200 billion yuan to Sichuan, which lowered the province's growth rate from 13.7 percent in 2007 to 9 percent in the first half of 2008. Although this number would look impressive elsewhere, it was below China's national average (*Sichuan Daily* 2008d). To recover from the devastation, Sichuan needed about 1.67 trillion yuan, but as of September 2008 only a quarter of that amount was available (*Sichuan Daily* 2008a). To make things worse, a few months after the earthquake, the global financial crisis hurt the province's export economy as well as the capacity of potential outside investors. The official media in Sichuan, which usually promoted a positive image, used words like "pressure" (*yali*) or "difficulties" (*kunnan*) or even "severe situation" (*yanjun xingshi*) to describe the economy.

Facing this situation, provincial leaders and officials made frequent trips to other provinces, holding exhibits and business conferences to woo big investors. Sometimes they invited potential investors to tour Sichuan, to see for themselves how lucrative the post-earthquake market was. The official media desperately reassured readers that investors remained confident in Sichuan's future (*Sichuan Daily* 2008c). At the top of their preference list were big projects with huge investments, which could do the most to boost the GDP number and create jobs. An editorial in *Sichuan Daily*, the official organ of the provincial government, unambiguously stated this intention in its title: "To Attract Investment and Boost Development [We] Need Big Projects" (*Sichuan Daily* 2008e).

Lower-level government officials shared the same hunger for investments, projects, and donations. Some township officials made well-designed laminated pamphlets that selectively presented images of devastation and tragedy. They welcomed civic associations and corporations with resources to invest in local communities and schools. One of my interviewees, Luxin, accompanied a Hong Kong NGO to a town in An County to discuss the possibility of spending the donations the NGO had collected on a local school rebuilding project. Local officials gave them a building cost quote of 1,800 yuan per square meter––several times the original cost and almost equal to the average cost of commercial real estate in Chengdu. Local officials claimed that the provincial government had set the cost and they could do nothing about it. But soon they decided to offer the Hong Kong NGO a better "price" at 1,200 yuan. Luxin felt this was like haggling at a flea market instead of talking about donations. His more experienced Hong Kong colleagues warned that since the cost was negotiable, the school project might not have been in the provincial rebuilding plan. Several months after the project was launched, the construction quality superintendent hired by the Hong Kong NGO declared that he would quit, because he was unable to control local officials and contractors, who used cheaper and substandard materials in construction.

Money mattered. Most recovery projects needed a massive investment and ample institutional resources and connections, which most civic associations lacked. For example, before the earthquake, the highest construction cost of a school in the affected area was 800 to 900 yuan per square meter (*Southern Metropolis Daily* 2008c). But after the earthquake, the cost increased significantly. For example, a three-story elementary school building (4,980 square meters) in Gaochuan, a remote township in An County, where I visited, cost 7.09 million yuan, a large budget for an elementary school in that location. The cost per square meter was 1,423 yuan. Some high-profile schools, such as the new Beichuan High School, even cost almost two hundred million (*Guangming Daily* 2012). Some schools' futuristic designs and expensive equipment, such as advanced projectors and super-large-screen LED TVs––equipment often not even available in many American universities––made them appear surreal in their rural, mountainous environments. From the perspective of civic associations that struggled to survive on a budget of several hundred thousand yuan a year, or small groups with no money, any of the rebuilding budgets was astronomical. Thus, their opportunity to participate in these big infrastructure projects was close to zero. Only those with ample funds—most of which were public foundations and overseas NGOs—were able to enter the game.

The biggest investments usually came from supporting provinces under the one-on-one supporting mechanism. Everywhere in the quake zone during the recovery period one ran across banners that expressed the solidarity between the supporting province and the receiving county (e.g., "Zhejiang and Qingchuan: Heart to Heart!"). Beneath this altruistic discourse, however, were material considerations. First, not all funds in the one-on-one projects were paid by the supporting governments. As mentioned earlier, supporting governments used donations to local public foundations and counted them as part of their aid. This amounted to about 20 billion yuan, almost a third of the one-on-one aid (Deng 2009). Second, the supporting provinces usually gave the projects to companies from their own provinces, even though local companies were capable of doing the same work. A close look at the billboards at construction sites showed that this phenomenon was ubiquitous in the quake zone. Some connections were obvious—a construction company from Zhejiang worked in Qingchuan, the province's *duikou* county; others might need familiarity with China's convoluted state-owned-enterprise system to decipher. For example, China Railway 14th Construction Bureau Co., Ltd, a major developer that was undertaking several large projects in Pingwu but did not seem to be connected to any province, was based in Jilin, Pingwu's *duikou* province.

Third, and probably more importantly, for the supporting provinces, the "support" was in fact investment. They cooperated with the receiving counties to create various industrial parks, which enabled corporations from their own provinces to set up factories. Some business-savvy provincial-level governments like Shanghai also invested in distinctive local industries, such as tourism in Dujiangyan, Shanghai's *duikou* county-level municipality. Some hoped to build long-term collaborative relations with the receiving counties, to develop exclusive markets or supply bases for them (Jiang 2008). The central government tolerated and even encouraged these profit-driven collaborations to keep the provinces motivated (Liu 2010).

Corporations, whose role was less central during the emergency period, became major players at the recovery stage. During and after the emergency period, some online forums constantly updated their round-ups of corporation donations, praising the larger givers as "companies with a conscience" and condemning those that gave less. These opinions compelled corporations to compete to make larger donations to recover their reputation. Real estate giants were among the most visible donors: Shimao pledged 100 million yuan to about a hundred hospitals in the earthquake zone; China Oceanwide pledged even more--224 million in two rounds. Public opinion usually blamed real estate developers for the housing bubble that had existed in China since the early 2000s. Thus, making donations in a spotlight moment was a strategy to change their moral image from greedy profiteers to "socially responsible cor-porations." Many of their donations, however, were realized in projects instead of cash. For example, the real estate developer Vanke invested a large proportion of its 100 million donations in a major recovery and redevelopment project in Mianzhu, including building temporary hous-ing and rebuilding schools and hospitals. Other real estate companies aggressively sought numerous and lucrative reconstruction contracts. Some economists warned against incorporating real estate developers into recovery projects because their hunger for profits might raise costs and lower quality (Zhang Meng 2008). Nevertheless, this feeble warning was submerged by a flood of corporate self-congratulations, expressed in advertorials in the media, and ignored by the local governments, which continued to sign contracts with real estate developers on a series of school and public facility projects.

MAINTAINING SOCIAL STABILITY

After the national mourning period, the school collapse issue became the most important public topic concerning the Sichuan earthquake. The first several places that Wen Jiabao visited happened to be schools with heavy casualties: Juyuan Middle School, Xinjian Elementary School, Beichuan High School, Longju School in Shifang, and Muyu School in Qingchuan. The tragic scene of devastated schools served as the stage for Wen's performance but almost immediately provoked angry questions about the construction quality of the school buildings.

The liberal media quickly acted on the issue and published influential investigative reports on the causes of the shoddy construction. In the first two to three weeks after the earthquake, the liberal media set the agenda and refocused public attention from the enthusiasm of public participation to the school collapse issue. For example, *Caijing*, a leading liberal financial magazine, carried one of the most important reports on the school collapse problem in its June 9 issue (Yang et al. 2008). According to the report, most collapsed buildings were built in the 1980s and 1990s, when school building construction codes were either unavailable or ignored. Moreover, this was before the agricultural tax reform, when township- and village-level governments were responsible for providing funds for constructing and maintaining school buildings. Local governments' education funds came from the fees rural residents paid. In some impoverished areas, such funds were often inadequate. As a result, many local education bureaus used unlicensed, cheap contractors, copied other schools' blueprints, and made unsafe changes to the blueprints to reduce costs—for example, a 4-story building constructed on a 2-story foundation. Contractors used substandard materials to lower their costs and increase their profits. Consequently, many buildings became unsafe almost immediately after they were built. In the late 1990s and 2000s, the central government introduced stricter regulations on school buildings, but local education bureaus did not take the regulations seriously. They cursorily conducted required inspections and inadequately shored up unsafe buildings. Some schools reported the unsafe conditions of their buildings to the education bureaus, while others did not. Therefore, the school collapse issue involved the collective wrongdoing of many parties—the state's lack of regulations and funds, schools' negligence, contractors' substandard construction, and education bureaus' irresponsibility.

The investigative report was widely cited and circulated in news portal websites, provoking a new round of intense criticism from both within and outside mainland China. Some investigative reports were written in such an emotional tone that they read like calls for action. For example, in a report about the parents of child victims in *21st Century Business Herald* (*21 shiji jingji baodao*), the journalist wrote:

> As of May 26, 1,990,000 square meters of school buildings collapsed, 4,737 students died, and 16,000 were injured—so many youths were disappearing.
> Why schools?
> Why children?
> Don't use tears to answer me. (Tan Hao 2008)

Local residents and outside volunteers also took pictures and uploaded them to various forums. Some pictures showed ultra-thin steel rebar and sand-like concrete in the rubble, suggesting substandard construction. This round of intensive public anger reached its peak around the time of Children's Day, when the earthquake children became sacred objects; any contamination of the sacred object became intolerable.

In late May, Lin Qiang, an education official in the Sichuan provincial government, demanded that he be allowed to quit his role as an Olympic torch carrier, which was usually seen as a high honor. The reason for his surprising decision, as he said in an interview with *Southern Weekend*, was that "as an education official, I felt guilty" about the collapsed schools and child victims. Therefore, he saw his resignation as an act of atonement. Lin went to Beichuan High School right after the earthquake and witnessed the devastation and the parents' grief. He also saw another building only 700 to 800 meters away from the collapsed one standing intact.

> Since that moment, I can't tolerate any evasion of responsibility for the tragic loss of life. We see so many children's deaths and so many broken families. If the lives can't override latent rules of politics, if we officials still protect each other—"you're good, I'm good, and all of us are good"—we have no conscience and are too shameless. (Chen 2008)

Even more strikingly, Lin was a model party member. He had been honored by the party's Central Committee and the government for his twenty years of contributions to the development of impoverished areas. He was a typical "good comrade," who would have supported the government's efforts to maintain social stability. His open criticisms and defiance were welcomed by many netizens and liberal intellectuals.

In the quake zone, grieving parents staged a few small protests. On May 25, only ten days after the earthquake, some parents of the student victims in Mianzhu marched along a highway to take their complaints about school construction quality to upper-level authorities in Chengdu, the provincial capital. Holding portraits of their children, wailing and chanting, the parents were stopped by local officials, who tried to dissuade them from petitioning. Jiang Guohua, party secretary of Mianzhu County, even knelt down several times to beg them not to walk further. The kneeling was extraordinary because county secretaries were usually seen as local "emperors." Even more extraordinary, however, was that the

FIGURE 6. Parents holding portraits of their dead children attend a memorial and air their grievances. The front banner reads, "Natural disasters are unavoidable; man-made catastrophes are despicable." Reuters/Jason Lee.

parents used derogatory words to scold him, and kept going. The petition ended when prefecture-level officials persuaded the parents to go home by promising an impartial investigation.

After the Mianzhu petition, there were protests and petitioning in several places where student casualties were heavy. On June 3, parents from Juyuan School gathered in front of the courthouse in Dujiangyan City, trying to file a lawsuit against the local officials and contractors who were allegedly responsible for the school's collapse. With children's portraits in hand, tears in their eyes, sorrow and anger on their faces, they shoved their way through the line of police, trying to break into the courthouse. "Why can't we sue? Tell us the truth!" chanted the parents. Some knelt down; some collided with the police. The police finally cracked down on the protest by detaining some of the parents. Three Associated Press reporters and two Japanese reporters were dragged by the arms to a room in the courthouse and were detained and questioned for about half an hour before being let go (Anna 2008).

The June 3 confrontation was the first time since the earthquake that the government had used force to deal with protests. It also signified that the government was returning to its normal track of harassing and detaining foreign reporters. Given that the Beijing Olympics were around the corner, the state obviously worried that the protests might trigger a chain reaction among parents and other people with grievances and damage the government's moral image. Right after the collision in Dujiangyan, from June 5 to 9, Zhou Yongkang, who then was a member of the Standing Committee of the Politburo and the head of law enforcement system, visited the quake zone. He urged the armed police and other law enforcement personnel to "maintain social stability" (*weihu shehui wending*), including resolving disputes and dealing with "collective actions" (*quntixin shijian*), which, in the Chinese political vocabulary, refers to protests (*Renmin ribao* 2008). After Zhou's visit, parents who continued to protest were treated more harshly than before. Some were bullied by local officials into silence and detained by the police when they gathered (Zhang Xiaozhong 2008a). The government also began to arrest activists working on the school collapse issue, such as Huang Qi. In addition, the domestic media received an unambiguous order from the Central Propaganda Department that reports on the school collapse issue and the protests would be banned. American, French, and Malaysian journalists reported that they were denied access to anyone involved in the parents' protests (*Sin Chew Daily* 2008; Martin 2008; Ang 2008).

The central and local governments kept a particularly close eye on civic associations that worked closely with affected families and had the potential of assisting the parents and even getting involved in the protests. A few volunteers did help parents to petition the higher levels of government and spread information about the shoddy schools to the outside. In this sense, volunteers transformed themselves into activists. For example, Wang Xiaodong, a volunteer-turned-activist, managed to obtain the blueprint for Beichuan High School; he submitted it to someone who he believed was an official from the Discipline Department of the Party Central. While this person's true identity could not be verified, Wang was interviewed by various Hong Kong newspapers and helped spread information to the outside. This involvement unnerved the local government, and Wang was placed under close surveillance by the Sichuan government. Tan Zuoren, whose story will be detailed in Chapter 4, was also a volunteer before he decided to investigate the school collapse issue.

The local governments were also cautious about people with a religious background, or any other background that could be interpreted as political. One of my interviewees, Feizhu, who worked for a Christian organization, was told not to stay overnight in the quake zone. Her fellow volunteers strongly opposed this restriction, but the director decided to comply in order to carry out their project.[2] Whether an NGO's project was politically sensitive or not largely depended on whether the local government interpreted its activities as being related to high-profile political issues. The Aiyi Cultural Development Center, a legally registered NGO based in the province of Shandong, went to Qingchuan after the earthquake to start a project to provide financial assistance for students disabled in the earthquake. The organization carefully arranged one-on-one assistance without involving itself in any cash transactions. Instead of collecting donations from the public, it paired donors with disabled students, allowing money to be donated directly to the student's family. Kou Yanding, the director of the center, assumed that the activity was politically safe, but the local government vetoed the project because of its concern with "stability." Aiyi entered Qingchuan at the time when internationally acclaimed artist Ai Weiwei was mobilizing volunteers to investigate the child victims. The local government believed the disabled students were also child victims of the collapsed schools, and thus somehow related to the school collapse issue. Although Aiyi later tried a different strategy and managed to carry out the project in Qingchuan, the difficulties it encountered when dealing with the local government were typical among grassroots associations (*China Development Brief* 2009).

Other obstacles stemmed from local governments' caution about associations' involvement in local politics and society. College-educated, idealistic volunteers without much knowledge about local politics sometimes constituted uncomfortable outsiders in the eyes of local officials. Many civic associations also received much media coverage. For local governments, this meant that negative information about their conduct could be leaked to the outside world, including mismanagement of donated materials and money, potential corruption in the recovery process, and disputes between residents and the government. Thus, many of the volunteers' activities even marginally related to these local issues could be defined by local governments as ones that "harmed social stability" (Li 2011). For example, the Boilers, whose story was presented in Chapter 1, worked in Antown for a few months. According to the central government's regulations, local state-owned clinics were to provide free services and medications for people whose injuries or illnesses were caused by the earthquake. The clinic in Antown, however, ignored these regulations and continued to charge local patients. Local residents in Antown asked for help from the Boilers, who then went to the clinic with them and demanded that it honor the government's promise. The clinic waived the charges, but only for residents accompanied by the Boilers and not for anyone who visited alone. Later, under pressure from the local government and the school they stayed in, the Boilers had to leave Antown.

SHRINKING ROOM

In the wake of the earthquake, various kinds of associations and volunteers, exuberantly and with high hopes, had flooded into the quake zone, set up work stations, launched projects, wrote reports and online posts to share their experience, and applied for funds. Only one year later, many stations had closed, projects had ended, and funds were used up; even in the stations that remained in the quake zone, staff were living below the poverty line. Meanwhile, the quake areas went back to their normal state—normal in the sense that the political nexus between the authoritarian state and corporations remained intact. Whether this "market authoritarianism" has helped improve the state's resilience and governance is still hotly debated (Nathan 2003; Yang 2004; Li 2012). In the case of the post-earthquake civic engagement, however, the combined force of the market and state gradually squeezed civic associations out of the quake area.

For formal NGOs, their relationship with the local governments reverted to the normal mode of "contingent symbiosis," in which, according to Anthony Spires, NGOs addressed some social welfare needs but refrained from challenging the state and thus could be tolerated and even used by the government (Spires 2011). The cost of their survival was their compliance with the local authorities, who had the upper hand in this unequal relationship.

Most formal NGOs that managed to stay in the quake zone practiced self-censorship and stayed away from "stability-harming" issues, including why schools collapsed. S&R, an NGO in Chengdu with a few work stations in affected areas, explicitly required its employees and volunteers, as representatives of a "third party," not to "get involved in the conflicts within the community." Even when local residents wanted to air grievances through S&R's work stations, the volunteers and staff members first had to report to the managers. The managers usually ordered the staff at the work stations not to respond to the demands because they did not want to damage their good relations with the local government, which allowed them to stay in the quake zone.[3] The director defined this "non-involvement" strategy as one of their principles of community work.

CDMC practiced the same strategy. Its daily work in the town of Hanwang in Mianzhu included operating libraries for children, showing movies, and teaching women knitting. None of these had anything to do with the more important issues in Hanwang that had made headlines around the country, such as parents' protests about shoddy school construction. Gradually, CDMC developed into a relatively large and effective association. This development, according to the CDMC's director, was attributable to the organization's conscious effort to define its role as an "interpreter" of government policies, instead of acting on behalf of the people. The CDMC's major principle was, "Don't make trouble, don't increase pressure, and be a good assistant to the government."[4]

Both S&R and CDMC, to remind the reader, were leading organizations of the high-profile 5.12 Relief network, which effectively made connections among NGOs and small groups. Nevertheless, during the recovery period, both associations practiced the same strategy of self-censorship, either through "non-involvement" in thorny issues or through "being a good assistant to the government."

In some cases, such compliance was explicitly required by the local government. Hua-dan Studio, a Hong Kong–based organization with expertise in psychological therapy through drama performance, had to sign a document promising that it would not say anything that "damaged the nation's image" and agreeing that the local government had the right to supervise and manage its activities. "If there is any inappropriate behavior," the document reads, "the studio will stop all activities" (Deng 2009, 63). In most cases, civic associations with work stations in the quake zone did not sign such documents; they did, however, have tacit agreements with the government not to get involved in any "rights protection" (*weiquan*) issues.

It was not breaking news that Chinese NGOs chose to be obedient to the government to acquire resources and opportunities (Hildebrandt 2013; Teets 2014). Nevertheless, the situation in the quake zone was not normal. NGOs were operating in places with heavy casualties and mounting grievances: in addition to the school collapse issue, disputes between local residents and the government on reconstruction and relocation issues were not uncommon in the quake zone (Sorace 2014). The volunteers and NGO employees worked right by the devastated schools, heard the parents' complaints, and knew all the local problems but were required to keep quiet and take no action. Most NGOs had zero contact with dissidents like Tan Zuoren or Ai Weiwei. Their reports and many Chinese-language books on earthquakes and civil society told us that their involvement in the earthquake recovery not only helped people rebuild their local community but also contributed to a civil society. Nonetheless, their laudable contributions and well-intentioned activities may have helped to develop civil society only in their own narrow sector—the NGO sector—without being connected to the rest of civil society. When both central and local governments tightened their political control, the rare political opportunity for public participation was significantly narrowed to that of quiet, nonpolitical service delivery.

In many cases, even staying away from politically sensitive issues was not sufficient for survival. An NGO had to develop good *guanxi* with the local government to address social needs on which the local government was unwilling to spend resources and time, and communicate with the government in a style favored by officials. In other words, if the local government did not have a critical need for civic associations' services, as in most cases, their ability to stay and operate in the quake zone sometimes depended on purely situational and even interpersonal factors. Gaoyan, CDMC's director, seemed quite proud of his association's good *guanxi* with the local government in Mianzhu, where the center's station was located. He attributed his success to his former role as a government official, because he knew more than the other, somewhat bookish NGO managers about how to interact with the government.

Even NGOs that managed to stay in the quake area had to live on the margins. Compared to the ample media attention they had attracted after the earthquake, their pay and living and working conditions were embarrassingly poor. Many NGO staff members in the quake zone lived on a monthly salary of 1,000–1,500 yuan (in 2009), with no, or very few, benefits. The income was almost below the poverty line. Many lived in prefabricated makeshift housing in remote villages for months or even a year. Even CDMC's "successful" program provided its staff with only meager salaries and a makeshift house, which functioned as a collective dormitory. Living conditions were even worse in remote areas. In Qingchuan, I visited an NGO workstation that worked to build low-cost and earthquake-resistant houses for peasants. Several staff members living there had to share a big bed in an earthen house. This was worse than the typical housing in the village, where peasants mostly lived in brick houses. Most of them were young college graduates with idealistic notions of changing the village. During my visit, however, a staff member had a mild quarrel with his girlfriend, another volunteer, who could not bear the filth, mice, and bugs in the place she lived, and was threatening to leave. The meager compensation and miserable living conditions were not conducive to long-term work in the quake zone, especially when the idealism faded as soon as realistic, day-to-day concerns emerged.

As described in Chapter 1, many coalitions emerged from the disaster relief, gathered together different kinds of associations, and collected a tremendous amount of materials. In the recovery period, most of them dissolved. Only a few, which evolved into coalitions made up of civic associations, local governments, and corporations, existed for a longer period. They intrigued and encouraged civil society scholars and practitioners, because they were believed to carry the hope that the NGOs' existence in the quake zone could be sustainable. Nevertheless, their cooperation with the local authorities and corporations was fragile and vulnerable to changes in the situation.

Probably no story better illustrates the vulnerability of cooperation than that of the Zundao coalition formed among NGOs, corporations, and the government in Zundao, a town in Mianzhu. The coalition was started as the Zundao Volunteers Coordinating Office, which managed volunteers from various NGOs and small groups, and Vanke, a real estate company that had started its own project in the town. The office achieved immediate success. Volunteers distributed supplies to affected people, set up a community center near the prefabricated house, held shelter-safety education workshops for the evacuees, and taught summer courses at local schools. The office gained the trust of the local community because of its transparent and fair work style. The town government also found the office useful in managing volunteers in the town and assisting them with various relief tasks. The office even received an award from the Mianzhu government acknowledging its contribution to the earthquake relief work. Zundao's story soon attracted the attention of scholars, NGOs, and the media, all of whom believed this coalition among volunteers, corporations, and the government might be the right method to solve many problems with China's NGOs.

A closer examination of this coalition, however, reveals that its success was temporary and precarious (Zhu, Wang, and Hu 2009, 138–49). The Coordinating Office got off the ground mostly thanks to a set of factors pertaining to the "consensus crisis" in the wake of the earthquake. The town government desperately needed social services and resources from outside volunteers. Also, Vanke, having decided to launch various rebuilding projects in Mianzhu, sent in its own corporate volunteers. In addition, numerous volunteers from about twenty other corporations and civic associations flooded in. Thus, the government, the corporations, and the volunteers all needed an organization to coordinate the volunteering work.

Nevertheless, the coalition would not have been possible if its leading volunteers had not deliberately kept a low profile. They claimed that they had only come to help and did not want to make trouble. "Whatever the government demands," they said, "we must get it done." This proved an effective strategy to gain the government's trust. Nevertheless, the relationship depended on the civic associations' submission, which was consciously practiced in exchange for the government's tolerance and cooperation.

This foundation began to dissolve when the emergency period ended and the consensus crisis features consequently changed. Rebuilding housing and economic recovery took priority, while the social services at which volunteers excelled became less urgent. The government needed a large amount of social and economic resources for recovery projects, and only corporations like Vanke could make a truly significant contribution. In October 2008, the Coordinating Office was taken over and transformed by the township government into a new unit, the Social Resources Coordinating Office, which was led by a "leading group" consisting of township officials and volunteers. The new name showed what the government expected of volunteers: to, through their outside connections, bring in more "social resources," which in that context meant money and institutional connections. Wang Yueyun, one of the major volunteers in the office, commented retrospectively that these expectations already exceeded the volunteers' capabilities and the office's responsibility. Besides, in a few meetings and interviews with the volunteers, the government made it clear that volunteers should not "make trouble" (*tianluan*). New volunteers had to be more carefully vetted and let go more freely. The volunteer office had to operate strictly in accordance with the regulations. It was required to inform the government of any sensitive matters (Wang 2009, 30). The message from the government was clear: Do not make trouble if you want to stay; feel free to go if you want to.

The "please leave" message was officially sent in April 2009, when the Mianzhu Youth League issued an announcement about "reorganizing" (*zhengdun*) the volunteers. The announcement required volunteers to register with the Youth League or be "persuaded to leave" (*quantui*). The purpose of this "reorganization" was to "prevent some people with special intentions from using their identity as volunteers to undertake activities that harm social stability" (Wang 2009, 29). The office disbanded soon after the announcement, while Vanke stayed and finished several large projects in Mianzhu.

The rise and fall of the Zundao volunteer office provoked a wave of discussion among NGOs and scholars. The high expectations for the coalition in the wake of the earthquake proved overly optimistic. The main reason for its failure was the local government's unwillingness to cooperate with civic associations with no resources but with a high possibility of "harming stability." In contrast, the government was more than willing to work with Vanke, which invested in Mianzhu on a huge scale.

What about the small groups that enthusiastically participated in earthquake relief? Most of their members understandably left Sichuan to return to work and study. Groups that had emerged in the wake of the earthquake, such as the Caring Babies group, dissolved as soon as their mission ended. Those that decided to stay in Sichuan barely survived. The Chinese Young Volunteer League, a group with a name much bigger than itself, started as a QQ group of about a thousand zealous and flamboyant members but ended up with only five young men staying in Chengdu. As donations gradually decreased and finally came to a halt, they had to make a living by selling cherries. They soon realized they could not compete with experienced vendors, who put wet paper at the bottoms of the cherry boxes to add weight. When I visited them, they had just finished a cherry-selling trip, which, according to them, was an "extraordinary success," since it could cover three months' rent (3,600 yuan [$580]).

A more common model was one in which group members dispersed and returned to their home cities, while continuing to work as a "public welfare" group engaged in all kinds of charitable activities pertaining to Sichuan. The Boilers, mentioned in Chapter 1, was such a group.

I met the Boilers in Chengdu in 2009 and joined them in establishing a school library for Antown Middle School. I was one of six volunteers who helped organize donated books and then load them on a truck bound for Antown. Another purpose of the Antown trip was to revisit the students' families, whom the Boilers had connected to donors to receive financial assistance for education. The Boilers and local teachers collected information about students from needy families and reported this information on their blog or through their personal networks. An interested donor would be paired with a student and would provide a moderate amount of money (about 1,200 yuan [$180] every year) to help defray the student's expenses at school. This one-on-one model required outside and local volunteers to revisit the families every year. Group members collected information about the families' financial situation, the parents' jobs, and the students' performance at school. Their reports were sent to donors, who could decide whether they would provide further assistance. Most families (21 out of 24) that the group visited had already received subsidies from the government and rebuilt their simple houses, but they suffered from parents' unemployment, disabilities, and disease. Added to these problems was the debt they owed for rebuilding their houses. In some cases, one or both parents had to migrate to coastal cities in search of higher wages to pay their debts. The students thus lived with their grandparents, and sometimes needed to do housework and work in the fields after school.

Members of the Boilers were quite homogeneous. Most were young and college-educated, and worked in lower-middle-class or middle-class jobs paying moderate salaries. A few were still in college. To save money, they came to Sichuan by the regular, slow train instead of by airplane. A few were engaged in other grassroots projects in addition to the Boilers' activities. For example, Yuyu, a college teacher in Jiangyou, ran another educational assistance program in Beichuan. Another member,

FIGURE 7. Volunteers revisit a family who received education assistance. Photo by the author.

Tanflower, later found a job in a nonprofit organization focused on providing financial assistance for children with chronic diseases. Xiaodong was an undergraduate student from Xi'an who also took part in a public-welfare program. He joined our Antown trip after returning from Liangshan, an impoverished ethnic region, where he had worked as a volunteer, investigating educational problems. This homogeneity in social characteristics, and even personalities, helped maintain ties among the members. Most were scattered around the country and rarely met each other. They communicated through email, phone calls, and instant messaging services. But, in their words, the Boilers felt like brothers and sisters because of their common ideals and interests. When two volunteers in the group got married in 2011, the other group members sent them videotaped blessings and congratulations.

At the same time, this homogeneity was their weakness. They shunned the media and other potential opportunities of publicizing themselves because they believed "those kinds of things are too showy and too opportunistic." Because of a lack of publicity, their resources were quite limited. Before they revisited Antown, a big corporation in Guangdong failed to honor its pledge to donate 30,000 yuan because, as the company bluntly put it, "We don't trust you!" In other words, the Boilers did not have an official status that would convince a corporation to invest its money. The Boilers replied to this remark by saying "You insult us by trashing our ideals," but could do nothing more.

Consequently, trust was maintained through personal connections instead of institutional relations. This in fact increased the cost of every member's devotion, especially for local volunteers. To revisit the families, volunteers had to travel from outside of Sichuan or Chengdu to Antown, and did so annually. Sister Deng, the only local volunteer, played an indispensable role in various ways: leading the visits, handing money to families, calling for a three-wheeled vehicle, walking with the volunteers so that they would not get lost in the convoluted village roads, and even putting up outside volunteers in her home. In the summer of 2009, six Boilers, including me, crowded her house; I had to sleep in a warehouse across the alley. The night I arrived, I was awakened first by some rats who welcomed their new guest by running around and sometimes jumping onto my bed to make my acquaintance. Then, after I managed to sleep for a few hours, I was awakened at midnight when a faucet suddenly broke and released a torrent of water. In the morning, Sister Deng had her husband fix it.

The school library that the group helped launch in 2009 also risked being closed because of a lack of books and funds. In 2010, despite their apathy toward the media, the group accepted an offer from a Guangdong newspaper of a small fund to keep the library open.

Many other groups like the Boilers encountered similar difficulties. Yuyu, who regularly participated in the Boilers' activities, organized her own education-assistance program with her friends. After the Antown trip, Phoenix, the Boilers' leader, and I accompanied her on a trip to Chenjiaba, a town in Beichuan that was seriously damaged by the quake. The trip started in the morning, from her hometown of Jiangyou. After a two-hour bus ride on a mountainous road, we reached the one-street town, famous for its homemade tofu. Like the Boilers, Yuyu had a kind-hearted local contact, Mr. Chen, who phoned the families to arrange our visits. Most roads in Chenjiaba were muddy and rugged and not suitable for driving. On the first day, I hired a minivan with a local driver to save time and energy, but we quickly got stuck in the mud. Fortunately we were rescued by passersby. We decided we'd walk during the remainder of our visit—two more days. Walking on rugged roads for two whole days was not easy, but Yuyu said she made trips like this about twice a month, to Chenjiaba and elsewhere, for the education assistance program. Yuyu's role resembled Sister Deng's in the Boilers.

Groups like the Boilers remained in the quake zone like stubborn grass in barren soil, but others had died out before being noticed. Those groups were apolitical and did not claim to be part of civil society or aspire to be NGOs. Thus, their relationships with local authorities were relatively less complex. They usually cooperated with local schools and families, who accepted them for the assistance they provided. But they lacked resources to deal with financially demanding cases and relied heavily on one or two devoted local volunteers. Therefore, despite their solidarity and high level of mutual trust, what they could achieve was constrained by their intrinsic weaknesses.

LONG-TERM EFFECTS

In 2013, after an earthquake in Lushan, Sichuan, earlier that year, *China Development Brief* (*Zhongguo fazhan jianbao*), an important online newsletter for Chinese NGOs, interviewed NGO practitioners and researchers to discuss and reflect upon the development of NGOs since the Sichuan earthquake. The points made in the discussions were consistent with the present analysis and revealed the long-term dilemmas of civic associations. Guo Hong, a scholar at the Sichuan Academy of Social Sciences, described the trajectory of civic associations since the earthquake. In the wake of the earthquake, about five hundred civic associations entered the quake zone. But this number quickly decreased to about fifty in the second half of 2009, for some of the reasons I have already discussed here: the volunteers left for study and work; the government dominated the recovery plan; and the government told the volunteers and associations to leave. Given that the earthquake affected 45 million residents, who still need a multitude of social services, this number was not impressive. Guo also argued that the Sichuan earthquake did not bring about many changes to the conditions of the NGOs, which still lacked resources and could not pay their employees decently.

The newsletter, however, carried a few somewhat upbeat stories of successful NGOs, those that acquired enough resources to stay in the quake zone. Their resources came either from state-controlled public foundations or from the government's purchase of services. One of the most successful associations discussed, the Wenchuan Datong Social Work Service Center, managed to persuade the Wenchuan County government to spend 1.2 million yuan—an unusually large amount—on purchasing its services. Datong carefully managed its relations with the local government by setting up a party branch in its organization, and consequently gained the government's trust. This strategy corroborated what Patricia Thornton observed in Shanghai (Thornton 2013). As Thornton pointed out, NGOs' "party building" (*dangjian*) raised the question of the organizations' autonomy at a deeper level because it could enable the party-state's control over the organizations through more permeating and direct ways than regulation restrictions. At this moment--as Thornton also pointed out--we do not have evidence about whether the party's penetration will bring about stricter control, but, in Datong's case, we certainly cannot celebrate its success without reservations. One wonders if Datong was indeed an NGO or merely an extension of the state.

Overall, NGO practitioners and scholars have corroborated my observation that the Sichuan earthquake relief work did not bring about the expected changes in structural state-society relations. Evidence has shown that, while civic associations gained some opportunities to provide social services in the quake zone, their development was quite limited. An NGO director said to *China Development Brief* that the master discourse of the public welfare sector (*gongyi hangye*) had already changed the term "civil society" to "social service"—or even "doing good things" (*haoren haoshi*), a phrase used in state propaganda to promote Lei Feng–type altruism. Many projects stopped after only a few years of (mostly unsuccessful) operation. In the long run, the best outcome may be that the social service sector of civil society will gain more opportunities than will other sectors. This development in fact will reinforce the already imbalanced structure of Chinese civil society: most civic associations are service providers, while advocacy associations and activism are seriously restricted. The consensus crisis after the earthquake enabled all kinds of civil society groups to enter the quake zone, but this access to the political opportunity structure gradually narrowed and, for those focused on advocacy and activism, vanished altogether.

COMPASSION AND APATHY

In discussing how a responsible citizen reacts to "distant suffering"—the injustice and tragedies that happen afar—Luc Boltanski upholds the value of talking about public issues in the private and public sphere: "Speech here is affected and it is especially by means of *emotions* that we can conceive of the coordination of spectators—each of whom is also a speaker—and consequently the transition from individual speech and concern to collective commitment" (Boltanski 1999, xv [emphasis in the original]). Therefore, talking about injustice that causes suffering in the public sphere, or even "clickactivism" on the Internet, is a legitimate form of civic engagement, although spectators do not actually leave their cozy living room to do something to reduce people's suffering.

In reality, however, people do not always engage in public-spirited talk even when they are participating in civic engagement. Nina Eliasoph's *Avoiding Politics* (Eliasoph 1998) shows that people take pains to keep up a "can-do" spirit, cautiously limit themselves to "doable" problems—raising funds for a local school, for instance—and maintain an upbeat appearance, without addressing even more serious issues—for example, poverty in the community that results in a shortage of funds for schools. Consequently, many civic groups in the United States develop a "speech norm" of avoiding talking about politics publicly or even using individualistic language to talk about their public-spirited activities, although they do talk about political issues privately. In other words, civically engaged people make an effort to create an appearance of political apathy.

In my interactions with the Sichuan earthquake volunteers, I found a similar phenomenon of avoiding politics—particularly the school collapse issue—but with interesting variations. While Eliasoph's American volunteers avoided talking about politics in group communications in order not to let political discussions crush the members' interaction and upbeat feelings, my Sichuan earthquake volunteers were reluctant to talk about the school collapse issue even in private conversations. Before I got in touch with the volunteers, I did not expect many of them to be engaged in the activism on the school collapse issue or publicly talk about it. They had legitimate reasons not to do so. In a repressive political context like China, activism could mean losing one's job, being harassed by the police, and putting one's family in jeopardy. Nevertheless, I did expect public-spirited volunteers to have serious private conversations about the bigger issues that led to the collapse of schools and their moral-political implications.

To my surprise, even in private settings, such as casual conversations and interviews, I heard less about the school collapse issue than I had expected. Most of the time, volunteers talked about their volunteering with great verve, without being pressed. In contrast, when I asked them their opinions about the school collapse issue, either in interviews or during casual conversations, they appeared uncomfortable, switched to another topic if they could, and when they could not, took pains to mobilize various rhetorical devices to deal with the thorny issue.

For example, Guangchuan, the middle-aged businessman in Chengdu who compared Sichuan to Tiananmen (see Chapter 1), represented a group of people who were completely aware of the school collapse issue but attempted to rationalize it as a common and pervasive phenomenon. Twenty years earlier, he was among the college students who went to Beijing to join the protest. Now Guangchuan owns a nightclub and a hotel in Chengdu and, as one of my interviewees put it, he is a "successful entrepreneur with a kind heart."

Guangchuan's wife grew up in Hanwang and graduated from Dongqi High School; in the earthquake, the main building in the high school collapsed and killed many students. After hearing this distressing news, he drove to the quake zone several times, delivering supplies and assisting local relief work; later, he helped a British relief organization, providing lodging for volunteers who came from outside of Sichuan. The amount of money he donated and spent on the earthquake volunteering was incalculable, in addition to his efforts.

When asked his opinion about the school collapse issue, however, he said:

> Those things are very normal, I think. You know I'm very Chinese. I mean, my way of thinking [is very Chinese]. I believe it's unrealistic to condemn them [those who constructed the schools] from a moral high ground because such a big earthquake didn't happen before. When they were doing that, they didn't know the school buildings would collapse and believed they would pass [the inspection]. Everybody can make profits on that. Now China is at the so-called primary stage of socialism [shehuizhuyi chujijieduan] or "capitalism without welfare"—the most primitive and brutal stage. In this situation, everybody makes

some money for themselves. In other words, if you could get through [an inspection], nobody would [strengthen the construction]. Even the affected people think in that way. Now the houses were damaged because they didn't build strong houses. So it's quite normal that, in order to save money and make more money, people do such things at this stage of development in China.[5]

Guangchuan attributed the collapse to the moral degradation in the society and rationalized the issue as a *normal* pathology of the present society, which looked ugly but which he certainly could accept. He clearly knew the reason for the collapse was not the earthquake but the substandard materials used in the school's construction. One of his friends, Liu Han, a local tycoon, had built many schools in the quake zone, but none of them collapsed because Liu had strictly followed good practices. Guangchuan was not a pro-government person. In fact he did not even try to conceal his disdain for the government. He told quite a few stories about how he quarreled with slacking local officials when he volunteered after the quake. The stories, however, usually ended with the comment: "That's China! What can I do about it?" Take action on it? No, that was not an option for a successful entrepreneur like him, whose business still largely depended on his symbiotic relations (*guanxi*) with the government.

Guangchuan had never heard of Tan Zuoren, who resided in the same city and was also a member of the Tiananmen generation. The interview was held in June 2009, three months after Tan was arrested. I told him that Tan was an activist for the school collapse issue and a writer. He then said, "A writer? Okay, those people do not adjust to society well. He still lives in his circle, and his thoughts haven't changed much." After I described Tan's activism and arrest, he said that arresting Tan Zuoren was "very bad" and "intolerable." But he seemed to accept it as part of the ugly reality to which one must "adjust."

Guangchuan's pragmatic attitude was a way to reconcile the uneasy feeling about the school collapse issue with his inability—and unwillingness—to change the bigger situation. Similar issues were pervasive in society, and he was embedded in the complex business-state nexus that resulted in those issues. Consequently, rationalizing the collapse of schools as a "normal" phenomenon is a variation of "avoiding politics." Similar thinking is reflected in a remark common in everyday conversations in China: "That's a feature of China [*guoqing*]!" *Guoqing* is not something to brag about but something one is expected to adjust to. When someone makes angry comments about the injustice underlying a problem, he or she would be openly mocked as "too young, too naïve," or "too non-Chinese."

Greentea, a young volunteer who went by his online ID, did not rationalize the school collapse issue as a normal thing. Instead, he mentally walked away from it. Right after the earthquake, he went to Mianzhu with a group of other volunteers to set up mobile libraries for the children in evacuee centers and later in schools. At the time he arrived in Mianzhu, about seven days after the earthquake, the county was at the center of a nationwide controversy. The earthquake utterly destroyed the Eastern Turbine Factory, one of the largest turbine companies in the country, which was located in Hanwang. Moreover, two schools in Mianzhu, Dongqi High School and Fuxin Second Elementary School, collapsed in the earthquake, killing hundreds of students. As mentioned earlier in this chapter, the parents of the Fuxin students later marched to Deyang and Chengdu to petition higher levels of government.

When Greentea went to Mianzhu, the parents already had started a sit-in by the rubble at the school and complained about the shoddy construction practices: "Along the main boulevard in Fuxin, there were mourning banners hung up. We actually hadn't known what happened until then, but we saw parents quietly sitting by the school. Since we carried cameras and camcorders, they thought we were journalists and then talked to us . . . kept talking to us. Back then I felt I could do nothing." Greentea and his fellow volunteers took notes of the parents' words but did not upload these notes—especially the parents' complaints, not to mention the pictures—to his online space. When asked why, he replied:

> I couldn't present all the truth, because the two words "truth" [zhenshi, two words in Chinese] are not something that everyone can accept. So I can only present them in a limited and appropriate way.[6]

So, what stories did he present? In his blog and on the online forum where he was an active member, he reported his team's volunteering on a daily basis. His reports were responded to by other members, who complimented the team on their "loving hearts" (aixin) and sent warm wishes. During the interview, he also told me many stories of his fellow volunteers' devotion and hard work, which moved him. Therefore, philanthropic compassion or a "loving heart" was the "truth" he felt appropriate to present to the public. The ruins of the school, the parents' tears, and the protesting banners seemed to be too fraught to be discussed.

Greentea, however, kept getting a dose of reality in the quake zone. Greentea and his volunteers assisted some psychiatrists in conducting surveys and interviews with the earthquake survivors in Dujiangyan. The psychiatrists required them only to listen and record, but not to comment. The survivors' attitudes toward those young college students varied, but many of them found the students to be good listeners to their grievances about the local government.

During my interview with him, I pressed him about how they dealt with the interviewees' grievances. Greentea said they were trained to listen with nodding and brief comments like "Yes, I understand" without commenting on the issue. The psychiatrists trained the volunteers not to focus on the issue but on emotions. "If you let them vent their grievances," said the psychiatrists, "you've already succeeded." There was nothing wrong with the psychiatrists' guidelines, but I imagine it would be hard for idealistic young volunteers to avoid crossing the fine line between a simple psychiatric interview and a heated conversation about local politics. I asked Greentea if his team's own mood was influenced by that of the interviewees. He confessed he had nightmares after seeing and hearing about the tragedies, as did his peers. But they talked about those in group chats, a therapy-like method. After "talking away the negative feelings," they felt refreshed and motivated, leaving the saddening topic behind. The newly acquired professionalism provided by psychiatry was Greentea's method to prevent bloody reality's "negative" impact on his emotional state.

While Guangchuan clearly attributed the school collapse issue to the fault of the people involved, Greentea carefully claimed that he was unable to comment on the issue without much evidence. Greentea was not the only person who shied away from the issue by using various items in his cultural repertoire to reconcile philanthropic compassion with the apparently bigger issues that caused the suffering. Their "negative feelings" manifested in the tension between witnessing suffering and the feeling of being unable to do anything about it. But they usually ended their accounts with words that added up to "I can't do much about that" and a helpless sigh, and switched to more upbeat things, such as their love for the children and the meaning of life they found in Sichuan.

For some volunteers, who did not directly witness much suffering, it was even easier or simply natural to stay in the comfort zone of volunteering without even noticing the bigger problems, which were probably not "one kilometer down the road," but not very far. For example, Siyi, a young volunteer from Guangdong in her twenties, who taught in a school in Pingwu for several months, softly said "What made me stay for such a long time was the children." She once had a student, a 10-year-old boy, who constantly fought with other children. Siyi attempted to talk with him, but the boy refused to say a word. Strangely, he followed her everywhere she went. When she asked why he followed her, he ran away without a word. This pattern was repeated several times until one day the boy suddenly hugged her and wept. It turned out he was an orphan who had lost his parents and grandparents in the earthquake. After that, the boy slept in Siyi's tent with another child. The boy called Siyi "Mom," although Siyi had never had children before. At one point, in mid-June, Siyi wanted to leave due to the physical hardship in the devastated town and her job in Guangdong. The local government also began to drive volunteers out of town because of the central government's decision to tighten control over outsiders. Having heard the news, the children threw stones to break the windows of school administrators' offices, crying and shouting angrily, "You're all bad guys! You're driving away our teacher!" The school responded by allowing Siyi to stay for another month.

Asked whether the volunteering experience changed her views and life, Siyi said it "enriched my experiences" and changed some of her views. For example, she is not as obsessed with "material things" as before and became more sympathetic to people who were suffering. This was a common sentiment expressed among volunteers. Lao Cai, the middle-aged man of the Shanghai Car Club discussed in Chapter 1, felt that his heart became "softer" after the earthquake volunteering and that he cried more often when he saw touching things. For most of them, volunteering involved suspending their routine and everyday identity and engaging in simple interactions with the victims, an experience they found memorable and beautiful. Siyi said that the most memorable thing in Pingwu was the stars. "The stars over the rubble, in the night sky of the quake zone, were unique," she said. "That's something you'll never see in cities. They're so beautiful."

This somewhat deceptive simplicity and beauty made many volunteers, including myself, wish to stay in the village forever. It was deceptive because during their brief stay the volunteers could temporarily leave behind all the complexities and challenges in their normal life: no rent to pay; no traffic to fight; no boss to hate. All human relations were reduced to the "helper-helped" connection, and, probably more importantly, a volunteer took the role of helper, a moral high ground imbued with a somewhat condescending feeling of being needed and loved. Thus, it did not come as a surprise that the volunteers consciously or unconsciously endeavor to protect the comfort zone of nice and warm volunteering.

Toward the end of our interview, I deliberately asked her if she had ever heard of Ai Weiwei's activism. To my surprise, she did not even know his name. This interview was held in 2010, more than a year after Ai started his investigation. After hearing my description of Ai Weiwei and his activities, she said:

> No, I've never heard of that [his activism], because I didn't pay attention to that kind of thing; I was able to handle the things that happened around me, within my capacity. I rarely pay attention to what other people are doing or what the government is doing or what celebrities are doing. I'm just an ordinary person. I don't have a huge capacity or strong backup. I don't. I'm just an ordinary person who happened to be there, accompanying the kids to see the stars. The kids could learn something; so did I. That's it.[7]

Like Eliasoph's American volunteers, a significant number of Sichuan volunteers like Siyi only cared about the things "within their capacity." Unlike Guangchuan, whose career and life were deeply embedded in "ugly reality," they were not concerned about the ugliness. This does not mean they did not see or hear anything. Not everything was beautiful in Pingwu. Siyi witnessed the unfair distribution of relief materials and the government's expulsion of volunteers in order to maintain "stability." But those things occupied a minor place in her narrative. The Shanghai Car Club saw more—for example, the fact that local officials had concealed the extent of the casualties and devastation. Lao Cai said that some dying people's bodies were still "soft" instead of stiff. With timely and proper medical attention, said Lao Cai, they could have survived. Nevertheless, such a thing was too uncomfortable to talk about.

He briefly mentioned it and then attempted to block it from bursting the "sunny" and "beautiful" bubble of compassion in their stories.

Siyi's unawareness of Ai Weiwei was telling in another sense. For a person outside of China who had regularly read English-language media or for a self-identified liberal intellectual in China, Ai's activism was well-known and even taken for granted as a natural part of the earthquake's political aftermath (see Chapter 4). However, what about an average person, who was not particularly interested in politics and did not try to cross over the "Great Firewall," the Chinese government's Internet filtering system? According to my search on Wisenews, a comprehensive Chinese-language news database, since Ai Weiwei's arrest on April 3, 2011, the domestic media in the mainland apparently had been restricted from reporting on him. The number of reports containing mentions of Ai decreased from 128 in the year before his arrest (April 3, 2010, to April 2, 2011) to 27 in the year after his arrest (April 3, 2011, to April 2, 2012)--and have remained around that level since then. Even before his arrest, most reports were in arts sections and did not mention his activism. Tan Zuoren had been largely unknown to people outside of the liberal and oppositional sectors. The number of reports mentioning his name has been zero since 2008 except for a few mentions in 2010. In short, their influence on the wider public in mainland China remain quite limited. This absence of media coverage and censorship explain Siyi's and other volunteers' unawareness of Ai Weiwei.

In other words, between Siyi's beautiful zone in which volunteers comfortably and enthusiastically worked and the ugly reality that activists attempted to change was a "great firewall," a high-tech-aided part of state censorship. It blocked the other side of reality, making alternative information unavailable to volunteers--most of whom were not particularly enthusiastic about obtaining information through alternative channels in the first place. In addition, the younger generation, like Siyi and Xiaoli, who made up the majority of the earthquake volunteers, found the volunteering experience was most meaningful for "me": "my" emotional satisfaction through helping the victims. Their compassion for the local people—especially for children—could easily overshadow disturbing problems that did not fit into their me-centered narratives.

Jiajun, the middle-aged volunteer whose story was briefly presented in Chapter 1, gave another kind of answer to my question "What do you think of the school collapse issue?" He paused for a few seconds and then said that if I were not from the United States, he would have talked more about it. Even after I assured him that I was 100 percent Chinese, that my interest was purely academic, that I had no political agenda, and that he was protected by a pseudonym, his comments remained cautious and ambivalent:

> It's better not to touch on that issue . . . because it's already . . . I mean, it'll become another issue if you touch on it. I saw a lot . . . because I was in the construction business for a while, and I know it. But this kind of thing—the children already had died—everybody knows what kind of thing it is. So even if I didn't talk about it, everybody knows it, right? As I've said, if there's a problem, it will be publicized when the time is ripe, right? So it would be necessary to strengthen preventive measures. So the lives of the children, the thousands of children's lives are the cost of safety for the children in the future. Some of the people involved in the issue probably are already dead; or, they are still intact. Punish them? Maybe it's not the time. [Xu: "Why isn't it the time?"] I don't know how to put it. Now this is the way things are. How can you punish them? This thing is so obvious, right? So I don't have anything more to say.[8]

His ambiguous, baffling words boiled down to two things: everybody knew what the issue was all about; therefore, it was impossible and unnecessary to confront it. His caution regarding my "American" identity certainly mattered. He was a person with a strong sense of pride in the nation; he praised the government a few times for leading the response, and the Chinese people for their impressive "national solidarity." His hesitancy in talking about the issue could be explained by his worry that his words—through me, a person with an ambiguous (in-between "American" and "Chinese") identity—could be used by "anti-China" foreigners for political purposes. I encountered that attitude from time to time in my fieldwork experience, in this and other projects. "Outside" people's comments on problems in China were usually considered a vicious attack on the nation. It hurt the feelings of those with a strong, sometimes exclusive national identity, one based on a clear-cut boundary between Chinese and foreigners but a less clear boundary between the people and the government. This concern impacted his narratives in a setting that involved a person from outside of China.

On the other hand, like Guangchuan, Jiajun accepted the situation as one that was already there and about which he could do nothing. Since the new preventive measures had been put in place, people tended to think that "thousands of students' lives are the cost of safety for future students." Let bygones be bygones. This future-looking narrative in fact was fairly consistent with the official narrative that "Sichuan's future will be more beautiful," which mostly referred to the anticipated economic development in the devastated places. In this narrative, later development justified silencing the past. However, a reality check would show that this seemingly positive message broke down. The new preventive measures could not replace a thorough investigation to determine responsibility for the collapse of the schools. In such a future-looking view, the cost of misconduct was minimum, which encouraged a further violation of regulations, especially when such regulations were not always faithfully implemented.

The most impressive achievement of civic associations during the emergency period was not how many tents and instant noodles they delivered to the quake zone but, as I described in Chapter 1, their transcendence of their particular interests and group boundaries, and the expansion of their circle of concern to people they had never met. Nevertheless, many of them stopped short of expanding this circle to include people suffering from the deepest sorrow, those who lost their children. All the volunteers were clearly aware of the school collapse issue, and some, like Greentea, even witnessed the parents' grief. But only some of them had heard of Tan's and Ai's activism; even fewer explicitly expressed their outrage through words and action. Formal NGOs refrained from talking about and being involved in this issue in order to stay in the quake zone to continue their projects. Their quiescence and self-censorship become part of their survival skill set. Volunteers also shied away from or rationalized the issue by seeing it as a "normal" thing, something they were unable to change and unwilling to talk about. While it may have been natural for them to choose "nice and warm" volunteering over "angry and dangerous" activism, the absence of serious private conversations among the volunteers was striking. This avoidance of talking about politically sensitive issues not only occurred during my interviews, when I pushed interviewees to respond to uncomfortable questions, but also in natural settings of interaction. For example, in the week I spent with the Boilers, the members of the group talked about the school collapse issue a few times in casual conversations--but these conversations quickly faded into silence and sighs, and they switched to another topic.

What can explain this apathy? There have been three common explanations for political-moral apathy (Eliasoph 1998). The first attributes apathy to narrow-mindedness, uncivil attitudes, and lack of knowledge; in Eliasoph's terms, people are "either too dumb or narrow-minded to be good citizens" (Eliasoph 1998, 231). This explanation does not stand in this case. Most of the volunteers were public-spirited and spent much money and time in their long-distance volunteering; some even lost their jobs and ran into financial difficulties. The second explanation presented in Eliasoph's work is based on group processes that produce a speech norm among civic group members of avoiding talking about politics when they collectively feel helpless in solving bigger issues (Eliasoph 1998). Therefore, avoidance of talking about politics is a collective communicative device to maintain the interaction order among the volunteers and to reduce the perceived uneasiness derived from the groups' inability to deal with political problems or bigger issues. This explanation makes much sense. The origin of the avoidance of political discussion of the school collapse issue was the volunteers' inability to deal with bigger issues.

Yet, we still have to ask a bigger question: What forces made the volunteers feel helpless? As I will detail in Chapter 4, the state's repression made the cost of activism and political discussion so high that everyone in China knew the possibility of getting into trouble if they spoke out. This is consistent with James Scott's idea that deprivation sometimes comes from being denied access to public forums (Scott 1990). In a subtle way, the state's political constraints created an inability to talk about political issues, which contributed to an acquiescence (Gaventa 1980). Volunteers like Greentea directly interacted with people with grievances but avoided bigger issues because they chose to convince themselves not to care about things outside of their immediate responsibility. Others, who were more deeply involved in the power structure, such as Guangchuan the businessman--whose business relied on good *guanxi* with the government--may have already internalized some of the ideas propagated by the state, and thus considered the collapse issue a "normal" phenomenon in the "primary stage of socialism." Volunteers like Siyi were unaware of activism because media censorship split activism from volunteering. People like Jiajun were more concerned with the nation's image than with the injustice involved in the issue of the collapse of schools. Moreover, his future-oriented attitude justified a forgetting of the causes of past suffering.

This observation certainly does not mean that the volunteers avoided talking about politics in general. In fact, they talked a lot about political problems that were remote: rampant corruption, stupid propaganda, and officials' misconduct. There also was much online discussion about the school collapse issue. Nevertheless, it is one thing to vent your anger about something you are not part of, say corruption; but it is quite another to talk about problems close to you, "one kilometer down the road," something that quietly bites your conscience. A random online user had nothing to lose and little to worry about. It was much more difficult for a volunteer to say anything about the injustice he or she witnessed but could do little to change due to political restrictions. A realistic option to cope with the dilemma, as Eliasoph says, was to make an effort to create apathy.

CHAPTER 4

Forgetting, Remembering, and Activism

Those students had their parents and relatives, dreams and laughter, and names of their own. Their names belonged to them. After three, or five, or eighteen, or nineteen years, the names are all that can be remembered about them.

Resist forgetting, resist lies.

We started this "citizens' investigation" to remember the deceased, care about the living, and shoulder the responsibility to bring happiness to the living. We look for every child's name and remember them.

These words are from a blog post written by artist Ai Weiwei on March 20, 2009, about the purpose of a small-scale activism he led to collect the names of the students who died in the Sichuan earthquake.[1] From January to June 2009, Ai sent forty-four volunteers in four groups to the quake zone to obtain information about the student victims from school administrators, local government officials, and parents. Twenty-two of them were detained and interrogated by the local police; their recorders, notebooks, and other personal items were confiscated.

This name-collecting activism was one of the ways some Chinese citizens took action to address the causes of the collapse of schools. They also created artistic objects, produced independent documentaries, and wrote letters to representatives in People's Congresses and government bureaus. In contrast to the politically apathetic volunteers described in Chapter 3, they transcended not only their group boundaries but also the boundary between volunteering and activism, two fundamental forms of civic engagement. Their activism revolved around commemorating the student victims in order to enhance public awareness of the school collapse issue, to uncover the causes of the collapses, and, as Ai Weiwei's blog states, to resist the forcibly imposed "forgetting."

Such engagement was not easy. During the period of recovery from the Sichuan earthquake, the state endeavored to reshape the memory of the earthquake by constructing official narratives, organizing commemorative rituals, establishing memorials, and even reshaping the topography of the most devastated places. Thus, the state's commemorations created a "covert silence" or "cacophonous silence," which differed from "overt silence," the literal absence of sound. It was a type of silence "covered and veiled by much mnemonic talk and representation." It was systematically designed to lead people to remember and forget at the same time: to remember the things that fit into the state's narrative of strong leadership with suffering and death as its background, and to forget those things that contradicted this neatly arranged narrative (Vinitzky-Seroussi and Teeger 2010, 1104). The covert silence and forgetting were bolstered by the state-business alliance through political and commercial investments in those commemorations. From form to content, the official commemorations were "big": large-scale anniversary rituals, huge memorials, massive projects that reshaped the topography of the most devastated places, and totalizing narratives of the "people." This bigness not only signified the Chinese state's impressive power but also induce forgetting by using big things to exclude and cover up small things: small schools and little children.

In contrast, the activists formed a "tiny public" (Fine and Harrington 2004), a small network of dissidents, intellectuals, volunteers, netizens, and the liberal media devoted to the school collapse issue. They lacked the resources to build big things, but they produced small and meaningful things and took small actions. They upheld the value of smallness— particularly ordinary little children and their names—and conveyed a clear message about the dignity of individual life and the pursuit of justice. They treated the school collapse issue as a bigger problem of injustice instead of something that could be fixed locally by helping individuals or simply by "doing nice things." They further transcended their limitations and conquered their fear by taking the issue of injustice to the level of generality. In this sense, their actions, and their articulations of the meaning of those actions, were close to the idea intrinsic in the neo-Tocquevillian or East European notion that civil society is and should be independent from—even opposed to—the centralized and authoritarian state. Nevertheless, the reader of this book already knows that these David-versus-Goliath struggles were rare in post-earthquake civic engagement. We should not take for granted that this idea naturally exists and prevails in a civil society with a quite different "moral ecology" than Western or Euro-American ones (Madsen 1998). Instead, this idea needs structural, situational, and cultural conditions to survive and develop.

This chapter explores how the post-earthquake activism developed, what social and political conditions enabled and constrained it, and how the activists talked about the meaning of their actions.

A NATURAL DISASTER (*TIANZAI*) OR A MAN-MADE CATASTROPHE (*RENHUO*)?

The post-earthquake activism started as a reaction to the state's denial—direct or indirect—of responsibility for the collapse of thousands of schools. At a press conference on May 14, two days after the earthquake, an official from the Ministry of Civil Affairs responded to the criticisms of the quality of school construction by claiming that schools were not the only buildings that collapsed. "The government's buildings, such as the building of Civil Affairs in Beichuan, also collapsed," said the official. Others blamed the media for over-focusing on the rescue of students. As a result, they claimed, public opinion tended to assume that a disproportionate number of students had died (*Chengdu Business Daily* 2008).

This rhetorical denial stirred up a storm of criticism. Official denial was then quickly replaced by a rhetorical admission of responsibility and a promise to investigate. On May 17, an official from the Ministry of Education and another from the Ministry of Housing and Rural-Urban Development admitted that substandard construction *might* have contributed to the collapse of buildings, and a thorough investigation was needed (Yu Wei 2008). The highest-ranking official responding to the school collapse issue was Jiang Weixin, the Minister of Housing and Rural-Urban Development, who did not explicitly admit there was a problem with construction but promised severe punishment, *if* problems and culprits could be identified (Jia 2008). For its part, the provincial government in Sichuan sent two investigation teams to the quake zone to examine the school construction problem (Zhang Xiaozhong 2008b). Local officials also claimed that samples and documents of the school buildings had been preserved and stored for future examination (Lai and Guo 2008). In a few places, such as Shifang, local prosecutors were involved in the investigation (Qi 2008).

In late May and early June, as discussed in Chapter 2, those responses convinced the public that there would be a speedy and uncomplicated resolution of this fairly local and clear-cut issue. Nevertheless, the "if" and "later" in the officials' statements left considerable wiggle room for the government later to deny there were problems. Two sophisticated methods of denial were practiced. First, *procrastination*, as the word "later" implies. In the emergency period, various official statements stressed that a careful and thorough investigation would take a long time, and thus "it is too early to draw a conclusion now." They then urged parents and the public to "be patient." At the same time, official discourses stressed that the emergency response itself, not blaming, was the top priority.

Second was *interpretive denial*, or *denial of responsibility*: "To attribute responsibility to forces—named or unnamed—that supposedly have nothing to do with the government and are beyond its control. Yes, something bad happened, but don't blame us" (Cohen 2001, 109). In a natural disaster, it is easy to find a culprit—in this case, an earthquake, an act of nature. This rhetorical device was not new. The state euphemized the Great Leap Forward famine, which lasted from the late 1950s to the early 1960s, as a "three-year natural disaster," although the consensus among historians is that policy mistakes and political struggles within the party caused that catastrophe (Yang 2012; Zhou 2012). Immediately after the Sichuan earthquake, some officials blamed the "intensity of the earthquake" for the collapse of buildings. This response was confirmed by Wei Hong, first vice-governor of Sichuan, who made that claim at a press conference on November 21, 2008, six months after the earthquake (China News Service 2008), and then, four months later, at a press conference held by the Sichuan provincial government during the annual meeting of the National People's Congress.

OFFICIAL COMMEMORATIONS

An even more sophisticated technique of controlling perceptions of the past was to construct loud and affirmative commemorative narratives to cover voices of trauma and resentment. This started with material "construction"—rearranging and rebuilding the most devastated sites to make them habitable and even profitable, and converting them into "sites of memory," including memorials, museums, and the preservation of ruins (Winter 1995).

On the second day of the mourning period, an editorial titled "Silent Observance; We Also Need a Monument to Express Our Sorrow" in *Southern Metropolis Daily* proposed setting up monuments and memorials for the earthquake victims (Shi 2008). These sites of memory, the editorial argued, embodied sorrow and demonstrated "the state's and the public's care for individual lives." The author expressed his hope that such monuments and memorials would manifest traces of the victims— their last smiles, their last letters, their suffering, and their struggle for life—instead of presenting grand narratives that raised their status or diluted the sorrow, because "life itself deserves the greatest awe!" An editorial in another liberal news outlet, *Beijing News* (*Xin jing bao*), echoed the proposal for an earthquake monument but went even further by proposing to inscribe every victim's name on the monument. The editorial argued that commemoration is a social responsibility. A monument with all the victims' names could show respect for each individual's life and dignity and make the memory of the disaster "specific and real." The editorial used as examples the 9/11 commemoration and other cases from the West, in which individuals' names were highlighted in commemorative rituals and monuments, to justify its proposal (*Beijing News* 2008a).

On May 22, only two days after the proposal in *SMD*, when Premier Wen Jiabao revisited Beichuan and inspected recovery work, he suggested that the devastated Beichuan county seat become a "ruins memorial" and that the local government choose another place to build a new county seat. There is no evidence about whether Wen followed public opinion or came up with this proposal by himself. Nevertheless, this issue did not matter much because the central and local governments soon played a much more dominant and even exclusive role in planning and undertaking the ambitious construction project of earthquake ruins and memorials. Relevant bureaus in the central, provincial, and local governments began inviting experts to inspect and assess various sites in the quake zone as early as two weeks after Wen's proposal. Meanwhile, the government called for donating earthquake-related items for the memorials.

The state did not try to conceal its practical goal: the memorials and ruins sites would become tourist attractions, and hence promote the recovery and development of the local economy. In early July, the National Tourism Bureau unveiled a draft recovery plan for the tourism industry in the quake zone. The plan provided tourism companies with tax subsidies and also designed a new "earthquake itinerary," which included the most devastated places (Zuo 2008). Local tourism bureaus in the most devastated places quickly embarked on their own recovery plans. By the end of July 2008, only two and half months after the earthquake, the Mianyang government had already released a formal tourism recovery plan, which aimed to develop a "Beichuan Earthquake Commemoration and Tourism Zone," centered on the old devastated county seat and Tangjiashan Quake Lake, a landslide-dam-created lake which formed after the quake. The zone was designed to become a World Natural Heritage Site as well as a 5-A level Tourism Spot, the highest level designated by the central government (*West China Metropolis Daily* 2008a, b). Other counties unveiled equally ambitious plans, all of which, it was claimed, would create sites that could compete for designation as UN World Heritage sites and National 5-A level tourism destinations. In quick order a national plan was adopted, designating four places as earthquake preservation sites: Beichuan, Yingxiu, Hanwang, and Hongkou.

Behind this swiftly executed plan was a fusion of economic motives and political considerations. The sites not only served as tourists' attractions that would generate revenue for the local governments and create jobs for the residents but also were carefully designed and constructed to fit into the state's narrative about the earthquake. The key issue was which sites were to be preserved, displayed, and covered, and how.

For example, Beichuan's old county seat, which was destroyed by the earthquake, was preserved as a ruins site for sightseeing and commemoration. A shuttle line connects the town to a memorial in Ren-jiaping, a Qiang-style village with restaurants and resorts, and a shopping street in downtown Beichuan, all of which constitute the Beichuan Qiang-Ethnicity Tourism Zone. On the site of the old county seat, ruins of stores, government bureaus, residential buildings, and schools have been carefully preserved and presented with concise introductions on marble plates. Even school ruins have been preserved and presented instead of removed, and plates on the sites of the schools give details about the number of student casualties. Signs and banners carry the words "Deep Mourning for the Compatriots Killed in the Wenchuan Earthquake."

At first glance, this site is unsurprising because preservation of ruins is a common commemorative practice. Nevertheless, it is surprising in its political context because the ruins of schools may remind visitors of the high-profile controversy over the issue of the quality of school construction and could fuel debate. The local government and tourism bureaus certainly had an obvious economic incentive, but how did they reconcile that with the potential political risk of demonstrating too much devastation?

Political subtlety hid in spatial arrangements. The old county seat was located in a narrow valley surrounded by mountains. When the earthquake hit, the ensuing landslides and boulders that fell from the mountains indiscriminately destroyed most buildings in the town, including government offices, police stations, and schools. Thus, the quality of the construction of the two schools in the town—Qushan and Maoba—was less a concern and had provoked fewer controversies and disputes than the collapse of Beichuan High School. Therefore, it was politically safe to transform the old county seat into a site of mourning with a display of relatively detailed information about casualties.

The earthquake memorial, only one shuttle bus stop away from the old town, however, follows a dramatically different narrative pattern represented in both the memorial's exhibit and in the topographical arrangement of the site. The exhibit in the Beichuan memorial starts with a giant column, on which President Hu Jintao's words "No difficulty can overwhelm the heroic Chinese people!" are inscribed. According to the exhibit's introduction, in both Chinese and awkwardly translated English, the exhibit "records the great earthquake relief and reconstruction process from May 12, 2008 to September 30, 2011, and mainly displays the catastrophic effects of the earthquake and revives the hugely successful post-earthquake relief and reconstruction work. The strength of the CPC [Communist Party of China] and the Chinese people is demonstrated and the incomparable superiority of the socialist system is highlighted."

This theme is elaborated by the plot line of the exhibit. It starts with panels about devastation and tragedies immediately after the earthquake but quickly moves to detailed and self-congratulating descriptions of fast and effective responses from leaders, the armed forces, and various state agencies. This long section is followed by panels about the impressive solidarity among people all over the country, who donated money and volunteered their services. A narrative about reconstruction plans and the benefits of the disaster dominates the last part of the exhibit. In an introductory panel, the earthquake is described as "a big step forward," which "turned [the] crisis into [an] opportunity" for the economic development of the affected areas, especially for a great improvement in infrastructure, which benefited from the ground that was cleared after the earthquake. The "ascending story" ends in a grandiose slogan: "Uphold the greatest spirit of battling the disaster; endeavor to write the Sichuan chapter of the China dream."

Only a few panels carry some poems dedicated to the child victims, expressing sorrow and sympathy for their death, but the whole exhibit remains silent on the causes of their death. In addition to this overt silence, the exhibit also imposes a covert silence. For example, a bright-colored picture depicts students laughing and running on the track field in their lavish new school, with a slogan on the top: "The Safest [Place] Is School" (Figure 8). An inattentive cursory visitor may take the narrative and image at face value and fail to explore the controversies to which the picture implicitly and silently responds. This picture, like other, similar ones, becomes an empty signifier and conceals the children's broken arms, their crushed bodies, and their parents' desperation and anger.

This high-profile memorial also physically conceals the sorrow, desperation, and anger provoked by the collapse of schools. It is built right on the campus of Beichuan High School, in which more than a thousand students died because of the shoddily constructed school buildings. Most of the ruins were removed to make room for the memorial, but because of resistance from parents, the local government did not remove the ruins of the main building, under which students' corpses are still

FIGURE 8. An exhibit panel in the earthquake memorial in Beichuan. The words on the top of the panel read, "The safest [place] is school." Photo by the author.

buried. Instead, the government covered the ruins with a grassy mound, which, together with other mounds, constitutes the major part of the memorial's external landscape. An inconspicuous banner on a square-shaped, low-profile wall indicates that this is where the students and teachers of Beichuan High died, without details about their death, let alone the causes.

The location of the mound also matters for commemoration. As studies of the material aspect of cultural objects suggest, a visitor's meaning-making experience when visiting a site is shaped by three mechanisms in the relationship between object and audience: distance, legibility, and orientation (Griswold, Mangione, and McDonnell 2013). The memorial building is located on the south side of the memorial park zone, right by a shuttle bus stop, while the mound is on the far north side of the park, about 300 meters from the memorial. Visitors usually enter the memorial via the square and entrance on the south side, and most of them do not even bother to walk to the mound on the north side. Their view is blocked by a labyrinth of irregular-shaped, maroon-color walls, which are designed to represent "cracks" on the ground after the earthquake. Even if they walk out from the maroon walls, from afar they see "nothing over there" but a grassy mound with a banner, on which the characters can barely be seen. If they happen to wander to the mound and see the sign, they may have a vague impression of the school's name, but neither the sign nor their memory provides them with details. After a sympathetic sigh, they may leave quickly to catch the next shuttle bus.

The memorial and the old town constitute a typical topography of forgetting: the loud voice of official memory in the main memorial is complemented and reinforced by the silence of its external landscape. This forgetting is not designed to achieve a dead, overt silence: "nothing happened here"; "no one died." Instead, it is subtly designed to be combined with the limited presentation of devastation in the old town, where landslides are blamed for indiscriminate destruction.

This pattern was repeated in Yingxiu, the epicenter town. The town has been carefully redesigned as a tourist attraction with hotels, department stores, restaurants, shops, and a convention center. It appears no different from any other small tourist town in China except for the commemoration site built around the ruins of Xuankou High School, where Hu Jintao delivered his speech in the first-anniversary ceremony. Xuankou High did not fall in the first tremor, so most students managed to escape and survive (Yang 2011). It was then hit by aftershocks and finally fell, but it broke into a few huge blocks of concrete instead of pieces. One of the school's buildings still stands today. The remaining ruins show a fair number of standard rebars in every concrete column. All these indicate at least acceptable construction quality, given the strong seismic waves in the epicenter of a 7.9-magnitude earthquake. The information panel in front of the ruins states that 43 of 1,527 students died in the earthquake. Casualties were thus 2.8 percent of all students, a low rate compared to that of many other schools.

In contrast, Yingxiu Elementary School, another school in the town, collapsed into pieces within several minutes after the earthquake. Two hundred and twenty-two of its 473 students were killed. The number of casualties was four times that of Xuankou: about 46 percent of all students, almost seventeen times that of Xuankou (*Beijing News* 2008b). The heavy casualties in Yingxiu Elementary immediately provoked controversy. In contrast, the Xuankou School administrators were even praised by the state media for their effective and fast response. After the earthquake, Yingxiu Elementary moved from its original site to a temporary spot on the other side of the Yuzixi River. The ruins were completely removed, and other buildings were erected on the site. Later, a new and modern-looking Yingxiu Elementary School was built near Xuankou High School, by the Ming River. The pattern of topographical changes in Beichuan was repeated in Yingxiu: politically controversial ruins were quickly removed, while politically less sensitive ruins were kept in place as a sign of devastation by natural forces instead of human actions.

In addition to sites like these, the official commemorations also included a series of anniversary commemorations after 2008. In May 2009, the Chinese government held multiple large anniversary commemorations for the earthquake victims in the most devastated spots in Sichuan. Intended meanings in official discourses shifted from an emphasis on "humanity" and "citizens" in the 2008 mourning to self-congratulatory narratives about the party's "strong and correct leadership" and the Chinese people's "great spirit of combating the earthquake (*kangzhenjiuzai*)" (*Guangming Daily* 2009). The earthquake response was depicted as a "victory," in that the Chinese people, rallying around the party-state, had "defeated" (*zhansheng*) a natural disaster.

The ritual marking the first anniversary also became a multisite, elaborate state ceremony. In 2008, out of urgency, the Chinese state followed the simple ritual elements suggested by public opinion. In 2009, by contrast, the whole cultural-management system could operate at full steam without being disturbed by public opinion. State media, central and local governments, and some big corporations worked together to stage a spectacle, which some Hong Kong commentators criticized as "anniversary celebrations" instead of anniversary commemorations (*Hong Kong Economic Journal* 2009). In the epicenter town, Yingxiu, the central government held a commemoration attended by Hu Jintao, other high-ranking officials, and foreign diplomats. The rite followed a prescribed procedure, in which the leaders were at the center and ordinary people played the role of a passive audience (*Guangming Daily* 2009).

In addition to the main official ceremony in Yingxiu, other commemoration rites were held in the most devastated places, such as the Beichuan county seat, Hanwang in Mianzhu, and Donghekou in Qingchuan. Commemoration rites were so ubiquitous on the anniversary day that major roads in the quake zone were jammed with traffic. On that day, I traveled with a group of journalists and NGO staff, planning to go to Beichuan to attend commemorative ceremonies before going to our final destination, Qingchuan. But after being stuck somewhere in An County, we had to drive off the highway and abandon our original plan. After returning to Chengdu, I met several journalists who had managed to enter Yingxiu to attend the anniversary ceremony. According to them, the tiny town was occupied by different groups that launched various kinds of rituals, such as CCTV's "Heart to Heart" show and a charity walk by entertainment stars, organized by Jet Li's One Foundation. Consequently, the town was packed with hundreds of thousands of people. It was so crowded and chaotic that journalists very nearly came to blows as they attempted to get a better position for videotaping.

To stage these shows and commemorations, the media and official commemoration organizers mobilized local school students and residents to play the role of an "active audience" who rehearsed to display certain feelings and to say scripted words when the state media "interviewed" them. On the day of the first anniversary, when I finally got to a village in Qingchuan, which had been destroyed by the earthquake, the official ceremony had already finished. Teachers in the nearby school told us the children had been awakened in the early morning to rehearse for the ceremony, which was held in the afternoon. While we were talking about this, their TV was showing a report on the ceremony. A student from the school was being interviewed by a TV journalist and said she was feeling stronger and happier now and also grateful to the government and people all over the country. One of the teachers I was conversing with said the journalist wrote the script and asked the student to memorize it.

On the other hand, not everyone affected by the earthquake was allowed to attend the spectacular commemorations. The parents of student victims in the most "sensitive places," where the parents had protested before, were detained at home or escorted out of town for "sightseeing" in order to prevent them from disturbing the orchestrated celebrations.

In both content and form, the official commemorative sites and rituals were "big." The anniversary commemorative rituals were large-scale, officially organized grand ceremonies, cordoned off by the police in multiple places. The memorials usually turned several devastated towns into huge commemorative and commercial complexes, which merged the sites of devastation into tourist attractions. At the center of all these "big" things were the anonymous, collective "people," described as "heroic," "optimistic," and "grateful."

ACTIVISM ON NAMES AND NUMBERS

In November and December 2009, Tan Zuoren and Ai Weiwei somewhat independently mobilized volunteers to launch a highly expressive activism through which the volunteers collected the student victims' names to resist the oblivion the state imposed on the public.

Tan Zuoren entered the quake zone after the earthquake as a volunteer and sometimes as a local guide for the overseas media. The more devastation he witnessed in various schools, the more firmly he believed there was a problem with the quality of construction. Standing by the collapsed building at Beichuan High School, he even swore in front of the media's cameras that he would demand justice for the children. In June, the central government decided to tighten control over the quake zone (see Chapter 3) and arrested a few activists who had spread information about the collapsed schools, including Huang Qi, a veteran dissident, and Liu Shaokun, a high school teacher. On July 2, the Chengdu Guobao (the Domestic Security Protection Team in the Public Security Bureau) interrogated Tan Zuoren and warned him not to have further interactions with the parents who had lost their children in their schools.[2]

At that moment, because of the imminent suppression, Tan was still hesitating over whether he should keep his promise to investigate the issue. During our interview, Tan confessed that he even secretly wished someone would take the lead in acting on the issue. After he made more trips to the quake zone, he felt he could not just walk away. After being silent for two months, he decided to devote himself to an investigation of the school collapse issue. He said that even if he were to die at any moment, he had no complaints or regrets. In retrospect, this was not empty rhetoric. Tan knew that when he decided to embark on this investigation, he was in effect sending himself directly to the Public Security Bureau.

All the volunteers—indeed, all Chinese—knew the potential risks of activism, but why would Tan Zuoren decide to devote himself to the name-collecting activism while other volunteers—for example, those described in previous chapters—did not? As I have already discussed, many volunteers had a similar or even stronger emotional attachment to the affected people. Tan also experienced moments of fear and hesitation. After Huang Qi and Liu Shaokun were arrested and he was interrogated, he could have retreated with a legitimate excuse, that of self-protection. But he did not. We can certainly attribute his decision to his courage. However, this undoubtedly true explanation still needs some sociological qualifications.

Social movement scholars have explored the various reasons why people engage in activism entailing different risks and costs; for example, network and organizational affiliation, identification, emotion, values, and prior engagement (Snow and Soule 2010). In Tan Zuoren's case, I believe, three major reasons besides personal courage explain his activism.

First, Tan was one of the core members of a "tiny public" of dissidents and intellectuals in Sichuan, which included politically active intellectuals as well as some internationally famous dissidents, such as Liao Yiwu, Wang Yi, and Ran Yunfei. They communicated through social media, such as blogs and microblogs, but also had frequent offline meetings. At the center of the network was the Chengdu Reading Club, a salon founded by Zhou Yuqiao and Wang Yi in 2003. The salon met regularly to talk about politics and current affairs. Members of the tiny public of intellectuals and dissidents also met informally. During my fieldwork in Chengdu, I attended several of those meetings, held in restaurants and teahouses. Some of the participants were from other cities; in fact, the meetings were usually initiated by those people's visits to Chengdu. Most participants knew each other by both their screen names and real names. Amid the pleasant aroma of food, liquor, and tea, the atmosphere of the conversations was usually jolly, filled with words cheering each other on as well as vulgar language condemning the government and gossip about those in the network.

Many members of this tiny public were politically active and daring. For example, Luxin and Shinan, two core members of this tiny public, went to Tianfu Square on June 4, 2009, wearing T-shirts that displayed the numbers from 0 to 9, but with the numbers 4 and 6 conspicuously missing, alluding to the June 4 (6/4) Tiananmen incident in 1989. Another member, Chen Yunfei, successfully tricked a young staff member at a local newspaper, who obviously did not know of the Tiananmen incident, to publish an advertisement saluting the "Tiananmen mothers." Most of them signed *Charter 08* and other petitions.[3] Almost all of them had been invited to "drink tea" (a euphemism for being interrogated) by the Guobao. A major topic of their meetings and conversations was their "tea-drinking" experiences. Some were arrested and detained by the police, and even sentenced to several years in prison. Open defiance was a convention and even an act of heroism for this tiny public; being detained or interrogated was a badge of honor.

On one occasion, I even witnessed a heated quarrel between an old-timer and a newcomer. The newcomer just got in touch with the group but was eager to demonstrate his credentials by bragging about the attention he got from the Hong Kong media ("*X Newspaper* from Hong Kong has run a whole page of reports on my activism on the school collapse issue") and his experience of being chased and interrogated by the government ("Zhou Yongkang and the Sichuan police sent several agents to kill my family by trying to fake car accidents"). The old-timer, who had been arrested and detained by the police a few times and enjoyed a high status in the tiny public, was apparently unimpressed and even annoyed. He bluntly told the newcomer to stop showing off because "everybody here had this kind of experience and only dumbasses (*shabi*) like you think it's a big deal." Offended by the old-timer's comments and emboldened by alcohol, the newcomer fired back with even stronger profanity. The exchange stopped short of a fist fight, thanks to other people's intervention.

In some sense, the tiny public developed a "group style" that turned conventional attitudes upside down: instead of shying away from politics, they prized open expression and acts of defiance. In this sense, Eliasoph's argument about the group style or speech norms of civic groups makes a great deal sense, because the tiny public in this case deviated from both the dominant official political culture and the widespread apathy. The difference between this tiny public and Eliasoph's American civic groups is that the former did not avoid politics; instead, it was devoted to politics. To some extent, the tiny public resembled the small enclaves of dissidents and intellectuals under East European socialism (Goldfarb 2006).

Second, birds of a feather flocked together. Members of this tiny public shared a set of clearly articulated ideas centering on individual liberty, democracy, and equality. They identified themselves--and were identified by others--as "liberal wingers" (*ziyoupai*) and had strong connections with a few liberal domestic media outlets--such as *Southern Metropolis Daily*—as well as overseas media, which usually sought their opinions on Chinese politics and needed their assistance in getting access to information. Some prominent members of the group, such as Ran Yunfei, often wrote articles for Hong Kong newspapers and magazines. Therefore, their ideas were consistent with those upheld by the liberal media, whose concern for ordinary people's lives and dignity had played a major role in public advocacy of the national mourning (see Chapter 2). But while the liberal media often had to tone down its defiance in order to survive, the tiny public did not refrain from challenging the state in a direct and radical way.

Tan Zuoren's writing clearly represented these values. For example, in August 2008 he posted to his blog a long article titled "Mount Longmen: Please Testify for the Beichuan Children." In a sorrowful tone, Tan's article attributed the collapse of Beichuan High School to mistakes in planning and shoddy construction. Outraged and disdainful of the government's crackdown on the parents and activists, he declared:

> I want to ask: When some people want to equate the investigation of "tofu-dreg" schools with the political issue of "confronting the Communist Party," do they mean that the party already collectively has decided

to side with corrupt people and criminals? Do they mean that the Chinese justice system does not protect social justice but serves the powerful? Do they mean that China will develop into a society with only power but no responsibility, only crime but no rule of law, only party but no people, only bayonets but no speech? (Tan Zuoren 2008)

On March 3, 2009, Tan posted an article on Ran Yunfei's blog calling for building an online archive of the 5.12 student victims. Soon after the article was posted, the government blocked Ran's blog. But the article itself had already been widely circulated through emails and online sharing. The post reached out to numerous anonymous netizens:

> Every Chinese with a conscience should feel guilty for their death and shoulder the responsibility. When the children suffer from misfortune and unfair treatment, can we do more specific things in addition to saying "sorry" from the bottom of our hearts?
>
> Only when we respect the deceased can we respect the living. Upon the anniversary of the 5.12 earthquake, we propose the following through the online media: Chinese netizens! Mobilize all your resources to participate in the compilation of the 5.12 Students Archive to demonstrate your respect for the student and teacher victims. (Tan 2009)

As social movement scholar Douglas McAdam argues, an intense identification with an established set of values pushes people to join in high-risk activism (McAdam 1986). More recent studies of movements and activism also demonstrate that moral sentiment and cultural values can empower otherwise weak activists (Goodwin, Jasper, and Polletta 2001; Jasper 2011). In Tan Zuoren's case, it was not compassion alone but compassion based on well-articulated political values that drove him to initiate and lead the activism. Most volunteers, by way of comparison, did not have the intense identification with the moral and political values necessary to turn their compassion into political activism.

Third, Tan was not an "ordinary volunteer," but a veteran activist, and was even more active than most members of the tiny public. According to my interview with Tan, his political engagement can be traced back to his youthful years as a Red Guard in Chengdu. Later, Tan participated in the 1989 Tiananmen movement and wrote a widely circulated article, "Witnessing the Last Beauty: A Witness's Square Diary," recounting the government's brutal crackdown on the movement. Since the Tiananmen incident, he participated in environmental activism. For example, on

May 4, 2008, right before the earthquake, Tan was a major participant in a protest in Chengdu against the Pengzhou Petrochemical project, the biggest petrochemical project in Sichuan, which was slated to be built on an earthquake fault line only 30 kilometers from Chengdu. It was believed that the plant would significantly affect Chengdu's air and water quality and, if an earthquake hits the area and leads to an explosion of the plant, chemicals released from the plant could jeopardize the city's safety.

Through his prior involvement in all kinds of activism, Tan gained the political skills needed to deal with local authorities, and a habit and the determination to initiate activism. Most volunteers certainly had no such experience and were less prepared for any activity that might deviate from their normal life trajectory. Moreover, he had already developed an informed anticipation of the consequences of his activism. Before he was arrested, he and his wife, Wang Qinghua, had already discussed, in front of their daughter, what to do if he was arrested. So, when the police came on March 28, 2009, Tan and his daughter appeared incredibly calm and prepared.

In sum, Tan Zuoren differed from ordinary volunteers in many ways. He was embedded in a tiny public of dissidents and liberal intellectuals, strongly identified with the values prevalent in that tiny public, and had experience in activism. In this sense, his earthquake activism was an extension of his previous political involvement, while ordinary volunteers lacked these conditions that could facilitate their transcendence of the split between volunteering and activism.

In December, he gathered a few volunteers to start the investigation. They used multiple methods—conducting interviews, collecting textual evidence, recording information from local bulletins, and so on—and cross-checked multiple types of data. Tan and his associate Xie Yihui made seven trips to the quake zone, and as one would imagine, were harassed by local police. They subsequently decided to use the Internet to collect data from students and their parents. On March 28, 2009, the police raided Tan's home and detained him. A month later, the Chengdu Public Security Bureau formally arrested him for "incitement to overthrow the state regime." More specifically, Tan was accused of "being dissatisfied with the party central's handling and definition of the 'June 4 incident' and carrying out all kinds of commemorative activities of the 'June 4' incident." The major activities listed in the indictment included

Tan's online article about his experience in Tiananmen, his correspondence with Wang Dan, one of the student leaders of the Tiananmen movement, and his call for blood donations on the anniversary of June 4. The indictment devoted only one sentence to describe Tan's earthquake-related activities: "After the '5.12' earthquake, the defendant Tan Zuoren had many interviews with overseas media and expressed many opinions that damaged the image of the party and the government."[4]

The indictment did not specify what "opinions" "damaged" the party-state's image. It failed to mention Tan's investigation of the child victims; instead, it highlighted his Tiananmen-related activities, which by any standard were minor and insignificant. Moreover, the indictment did not mention Tan's activism against Pengzhou Petrochemical, which, according to Tan himself, was a major reason for his arrest and was embedded in the complex power-money nexus related to Zhou Yongkang.[5]

Tan's trial on August 12, 2009, was quite a drama in which important figures in the tiny public converged on Chengdu. Pu Zhiqiang and Xia Lin, two prominent rights lawyers, served as Tan's lawyers. And many liberal intellectuals, dissidents, activists, and overseas journalists flocked to Chengdu to either support Tan or report on this sensational trial. The high-profile Ai Weiwei, who had already started his own student investigation, was certainly the most prominent person to try to attend the trial. The Chengdu police decided to curb this flow of people. Before the trial, they raided Ai Weiwei's hotel, and, according to Ai, one of the policemen even hit him in the face after Ai requested that they show their IDs. After denying they hit anyone, the policemen ordered all guests on that floor to line up in the hallway and then detained six of them, including Ai and his friends, until 2 p.m., when Tan's trial ended (*Apple Daily* 2009). A Hong Kong journalist from NOW TV also recounted that the police searched her hotel room because "someone reported there might be drugs in the room." The policemen started searching the room at 6 a.m., dawdling over every item the journalist possessed, and at 1 p.m. suddenly finished and retreated. Xie Yihui, Tan's collaborator in the student investigation, and Ran Yunfei were also detained by the police until the trial ended. Some parents of the child victims were put under house arrest. Despite the police's attempts at blocking them, a few hundred concerned people—parents, liberal intellectuals, and dissidents—still managed to gather in front of the Chengdu Intermediary Courthouse to demonstrate their support for Tan by applauding and shouting. They were surrounded by hundreds of uniformed and plainclothes police (Wan 2009).

Not surprisingly, the court did not play by the rules. The prosecutors and judges constantly interrupted the defense lawyers. They rejected the defense lawyers' request for more witnesses and dismissed some of the evidence as irrelevant and unreasonable. Finally, the court handed down a sentence of five years in prison, starting from the date Tan was arrested. In March 2014, Tan was released from prison but was still kept under close surveillance.

AI WEIWEI'S ACTIVISM

When Tan Zuoren went down to the quake zone to collect the students' names, Ai Weiwei began engaging in similar activism. Ai's activism was far more influential than Tan's, probably due to his fame, to his identity as one of the designers of the "Bird's Nest," the main stadium for the Beijing Olympics, and to his articulation of the meanings of the activism in his narratives and art objects. Right after the earthquake, he began to write blog posts commenting on the school collapse issue. In December 2008, Ai decided to do more than blogging. He and his associates began to collect information about the number and names of the student victims from press reports and online sources. In addition, they phoned the Sichuan Department of Education, Civil Affairs, Public Security, Provincial Government Office, local governments, and schools to request information about the death toll and the names of the student victims. Unsurprisingly, the governmental bureaus rejected their request, and did so in a way that ranged from rudeness and suspicion to indifference.

After coming up with a preliminary estimate of the death toll based on media and online sources, Ai recruited volunteers to go into the field and collect the students' names and ascertain the actual death toll. Unlike Tan Zuoren with his lone wolf strategy, Ai Weiwei used his prestige and influence to recruit volunteers from a large pool of college students, artists, and journalists. Moreover, he used his international prestige to promote his activism. According to Ai's blog, from March to May 2009, he gave forty-six interviews to domestic and international media outlets, including major presses and newspapers such as AFP and the *New York Times*.

The final result of this investigation was released in an online report in July 2009. The total number of student victims was 5,194. Among them, 4,803 deaths have been verified; the remaining 391 lacked critical information for verification. This number was lower than the official number of 5,335, and Tan's number of 5,679. From a technical perspective, Ai's investigation unnecessarily overlapped with Tan's in various ways, including methods, locations covered, and the time period. Their numbers also did not dramatically differ from the official count. Nevertheless, the investigation's moral-political implications were far more important than its technical accuracy.

The most striking feature of Ai's activism was that it was based on clearly articulated ideas about the political significance of names and individual rights. In his first blog post about the school collapse issue on May 18, 2008, six days after the earthquake, he took on the then prevalent "gratitude" narrative in the official media, which demanded that people thank the party, the state, officials, and soldiers for their devotion to the rescue and relief work. He believed all these thanks were unnecessary because, first of all, the state did not do a good job in protecting the students, and second, this work was what they were supposed to do in any case. On June 1, Children's Day, Ai wrote a more emotional blog post mourning the students and raising the issue of names and numbers:

> If there is a day when the innocent children begin to distrust the world and to be disappointed at human beings, it should be today. Twenty days ago, in a natural tremor, thousands of school buildings collapsed and buried more than six thousand students under bricks and concrete.
>
> Twenty days have passed, but there is no list of the names of the missing children, no accurate count of the death toll. People do not know who the dead children are, how their families are doing, and who built those schools by skimping on rebar . . . and using substandard concrete for foundations and columns.

In later posts, he continued to address the death toll issue. For example, he wrote in his blog on July 28, 2008: "In China, who can answer the question of how many students died of the tofu-dreg construction? Those bastards in Sichuan, is this also a state secret that must be concealed? Is it so hard to clarify things?"

In May 2009, a month before the first anniversary of the earthquake, Tianya, one of the biggest online forums in China, arranged a public online chat for Ai Weiwei to communicate with netizens about the meaning and activities of his citizen investigation. During the chat, when a netizen asked him about the meaning and purposes, he said:

> The government bureaus must release unambiguous information about the [dead students'] names, ages, causes of death, the place where they died, and the place of their *hukou*. A name is basic information about individuals and citizens. This basic information, regardless of whether the person is alive or dead, should be available in the government's records at any time. We do this because of the lack of transparency in the government's system. Moreover, we do this to demonstrate our fundamental respect for the deceased. A name is the most basic *value* and *right* of a person. A name is the smallest and most basic unit that we can verify about a person. If the deceased is reduced to a number, we do not show the most basic respect for their life. In our society, all these basic things are absent and unlikely to be available anytime soon. Thus, as citizens, we must shoulder our responsibility and ask the questions that we should ask. It is a necessary condition for society to progress. Therefore, we spontaneously started a "citizens' investigation." (Tianya 2009)

In this passage and other, similar statements, such as the one quoted in the beginning of this chapter, Ai Weiwei linked the name-collecting activism to ideas about citizens' basic human rights, the right to know and to be known. He believed that the collective term "people," substituted for individual names, was a device used by the state to impose collective forgetting. Therefore, the first and most important step to resist the forgetting, Ai argued, was to recover the victims' individual names.

A Western reader might not be surprised by this idea. In modern Western political culture, individual names "constitute signs of mourning, expressing individual and communal grief indifferent, if not actively hostile, to the ideology of patriotism and military glory." The inscription of names on monuments and memorials, such as the Vietnam Veterans Memorial, "enacts a kind of resistance to totalizing discourses that would subsume individuals into some single larger meaning" (Sherman 1998, 443–44). In various commemorative rituals, the names of the deceased are read aloud in solemn silence; sometimes, if casualties are heavy, the name reading can take hours. Inscribing or reading every name fosters a modern culture of equality, commemorating the deceased not according to the hierarchical order of their social ranks but according to a horizontal order, an idea fundamental to civil society (Putnam, Leonardi, and

Nanetti 1993). Remembering ordinary people's names not only constitutes resistance to the authoritarian state's grand narratives about the anonymous, collective "people," but also challenges the state's forced forgetting of unnamed individuals whose deaths could be attributed to the state's mistakes and misdeeds. Searching for their names is not just a commemoration but also a moral action that citizens should undertake to confront the authoritarian state and uphold the basic human rights of individual citizens.

Nevertheless, this idea was alien to Chinese political culture, in which the totalizing collective term "people" usually overshadowed individuals. The names of ordinary people who died in disasters, wars, and accidents were rarely revealed by the state to the public; only the names of those considered part of the state—heroes, leaders, and generals—were imprinted in the national memory. How then did this very Western idea, based on the recognition of individual rights, travel to China through people like Ai Weiwei?

Born into an intellectual family, Ai Weiwei did not follow the life path and ideals of his father, Ai Qing, a renowned patriotic poet, but instead went to the United States in the early 1980s, when China began to allow its citizens to travel to and study in the West. Ai lived in New York's East Village for about a decade, and, like many other New York artists, hopped from one odd job to another--from drawing portraits on the street to playing blackjack in Atlantic City casinos. He befriended beat poet Allen Ginsberg and was clearly influenced by Andy Warhol and Marcel Duchamp. He was among Chinese intellectuals and artists who went to the United States—many of them to New York City—in the 1980s to experience a dramatically different culture and seeking meaning outside their state-arranged life course: born in the 1950s, a generation that "grew up under the red flag" and went down to the countryside during the Cultural Revolution. Some of Ai's fellow Chinese who wandered in New York City and other US cities in the 1980s later became the most prestigious artists, intellectuals, writers, and musicians in and out of China: for example, Chen Yifei, Tan Dun, Chen Danqing, Wang Xiaobo, and Zha Jianying. Their American experience constituted a resocialization. They have not only achieved stunning success in their own professions but also collectively developed a cosmopolitan mentality based on liberal-democratic ideas about individuals' values and rights as opposed to the collective culture in which they were raised. This was evident in Ai

Weiwei's answer to a question in the aforementioned Tianya interview about the differences between his father, Ai Qing, and himself: "He [Ai Qing] is a person who has loved his country and people throughout his life. I am a person who cares about individuals' rights and possibilities of survival. We face different times."

Unlike Tan Zuoren, Ai Weiwei had minimal prior political engagement. He participated in a few protests in the United States but had not been politically active. The earthquake student investigation was his first serious engagement. Nevertheless, his lack of experience was compensated for by his prestige as an artist and his impressive ability to elaborate on the meaning of his activism. Thus, after his activism was widely known, he gained support and respect from ordinary netizens as well as from veteran dissidents. His cosmopolitanism, liberal ideas, and even anarchist lifestyle and manner attracted many young, educated Chinese who were born after the 1970s, enjoyed material abundance, were heavily influenced by Western culture, and felt dissatisfied with the social and political status quo. Their habitus matched Ai's political views and personal style. After launching his earthquake activism, Ai Weiwei became an icon of the tiny public. He was sometimes referred to as the God of Love (*aishen*), a play on his surname, Ai, a homonym for "love" in Chinese.

The liberal media's journalists and columnists, also members of the tiny public, articulated the importance of the names of the deceased as well. On April 15, 2009, the *Southern Metropolis Daily* published an editorial titled "Make the Names of the Earthquake Deceased Known to the Public." The editorial addressed the name issue by citing the National Human Rights Action Plan of China (2009–2010), which was released by the State Council on April 13, about two weeks after Tan Zuoren was arrested. The plan was little more than a self-congratulation of the Chinese state's respect for and protection of human rights, but the *SMD* editorial took the state at its word and linked the human rights issue to the names and numbers of earthquake victims. The piece started by acknowledging the government's effort to incorporate compiling information about the earthquake deceased into the human rights agenda, but went on to urge the state to actually implement the agenda in practice. It demanded the government respect and incorporate, instead of alienating, social organizations' efforts to collect lists of names, alluding to Ai Weiwei's activism. It also elaborated on the meaning of names using more poetic language than Ai Weiwei's, but the key ideas were the same:

> Every name represents a life, as a meteor represents the starry night sky. A name represents a life that once flourished but soon ended abruptly. If we let the names of the deceased fade, we are in fact ignoring ordinary people's lives. Human rights then have no basis.
>
> As for the Wenchuan earthquake, the victims were humans and, therefore, deserved a sincere commemoration as humans. Only when we trace their life trajectory through their names can we truly honor their lives. The worst scenario is that we lower our heads to mourn in front of a monument without names or that the citizens only mourn the casualties as a mass rather than as individuals. That would be an unbearable shame and would inscribe the word "dishonor" in history. (*Southern Metropolis Daily* 2009)

MEANINGS OF ACTIONS

How did the ordinary volunteers who joined the activism interpret the meaning of collecting the students' names when they actually interacted with government officials?

Ai Weiwei's volunteers made many phone calls to local governmental offices at the county, city, and provincial levels to request information about the students. Their ideas about citizens' rights clashed with governmental functionaries' indifference and rationalization. Officials usually asked: "Which *danwei* are you from?"; "What's the use of the name list [since the students are already dead]?"; "Why do you care about this?" The volunteers answered that they were individual citizens who instead of representing a *danwei* were using the names only for commemorative purposes, and cared about the victims because they were compatriots. These idealistic answers did not make sense to government officials, who did not believe that individual citizens without any *danwei*-based identity had the right to be engaged in public activities. If someone came to investigate a political matter only as a concerned citizen, they believed he or she was lying and must be acting as an agent for political forces from outside of China.[6]

A typical interaction can be found in the following phone conversation transcription. A female volunteer called the Stability Maintaining Team in Beichuan County, a task force in charge of monitoring and suppressing any happenings that posed a threat to "social stability." Activism on the school collapse issue was certainly within their scope. What followed was a head-on conflict.

After the volunteer told the official on the other end of the line that she was just a concerned citizen and not a representative of any *danwei*, the official refused to give her the names of the students because it was a rule not to give any private individuals that data. The volunteer then stressed that "we citizens have the right to know," but the official began to be suspicious of her motives, asking why she cared so much about the names. The volunteer answered that it was "our Chinese duty" to know. The conversation then became a heated debate:

O (official): I'm Chinese too! What if you are a spy sent by the Americans?

[The volunteer was infuriated and denied she was an American spy.]

O: Since our government already released it, it is okay now. You still keep asking. So I'm suspicious. I want to protect the country.

V (Volunteer): We are all protecting the country. But the country must protect the people!

O: Yes, but that's the government's job. It's none of your business.

V: We are citizens! We want you to shoulder your responsibility.

O: Is what you said all true? I now suspect that you are a female spy sent by the Americans!

The volunteer insisted on citizens' right to the information and their responsibility to care about their dead compatriots, a discourse based on liberal-democratic ideas about rights and moral responsibility. In contrast, the official emphasized bureaucratic rules and even the national interest and dismissed her work as not only nonsensical—since "that's government's job" and "none of your business"—but also subversive.

When the volunteers went down to the quake zone to conduct fieldwork, they were detained and interrogated by the local authorities and police, just as they had expected. The most interesting part of the interactions, however, was not the expected suppression but how both the volunteers and the local governments clashed over the meaning of the investigation, raising the same issues as those in the phone conversation: Who are you? What's your purpose? Why do you care about the names and numbers?

In one of these encounters, a policeman asked a young female volunteer, "What's the use of the investigation?" The volunteer replied: "I feel this [the students' names] is the only thing that can make people remember them [the children]. I simply want to know their names. I saw online what a mother said: she only wanted the whole world to know her beautiful daughter once happily lived in this world for seven years." The volunteer started to cry, and the policeman ended the interrogation. Later, a man from the government came to the police station and tried to do "thought work" (*sixiang gongzuo*, an attempt to persuade the volunteer to "correctly" interpret the issue). The official lectured the volunteer about the benefits the government's policies had already brought to the affected people, such as housing subsidies, loosening the birth control policy for the families who lost their children, and education subsidies. The official also warned the volunteer not to allow herself to be used by "outlaws and foreign adversarial forces." The pattern of this interaction resembled that of the phone conversation: the volunteer insisted on citizens' right to know, whereas officials and local law enforcement attempted to convince the volunteer that her actions undermined the state's laws and regulations and the nation's interests. Certainly, conversations like these were absent from many of the interactions, which mainly consisted of bullying, detaining, and expelling.

A few other volunteers did not directly participate in the field investigation, but actively addressed the issue of the collapse of schools and other issues in their own way. Zihou, whose experience I briefly described in the Introduction, was one of them. He turned his website from a scientific education site into a political forum, which provided public intellectuals with a space to discuss political issues, including the pressing school collapse issue. He said he was mostly apolitical before the earthquake; in addition to his private business, he was interested in discussion about scientific education only. His volunteering experience enabled him to see the dark side of social reality. Unlike other volunteers, who put themselves at the center of a heroic and compassionate narrative, he recounted his deep depression after witnessing the unimaginable tragedy unleashed by the earthquake.

As described in the Introduction, Zihou walked on the rubble at Juyuan Middle School and heard students calling for help from below. He could do nothing to help them. He also saw a parent who found his child's shoe and murmured, "This is her shoe" the whole night, with empty eyes and a trembling voice. Zihou said he almost broke down when he saw this. Later he felt so depressed that he went to see a psychiatrist, but it did not help. He then decided to cure himself by donating more money and participating in more volunteering work. He realized that schools had collapsed not because of natural forces but because of political forces, which a person like him was unable to ignore:

> The other day someone asked me: "Why were you like this [political]?" I said that 5.12 [the earthquake] changed me. In the first days after 5.12, I believed that the government would deal with the corruption problem, but now it's impossible for me to believe them. I dare say things will get worse, absolutely. Now it's like the June 4 [Tiananmen] movement. At a later stage, there was a crackdown, no room for negotiations or discussion. That model of suppression succeeded once and will continue to repeat itself. Now I feel society is doomed. I'm very disappointed and very frustrated. Too frustrated, too frustrated. How come society has no justice at all? Not even hypocrisy? They're blatantly shameless. It's terrible.[7]

Not surprisingly, as a Chengdu resident, Zihou quickly joined the tiny public of dissidents and intellectuals in Chengdu after he decided to turn his website into an online venue for political discussion.

COMMEMORATIVE OBJECTS

Ai Weiwei blended art and politics in his activism and life. His art works were not just a medium of commemoration but also a form of protest and resistance. At a deeper level, his activism had an expressive and performative aspect and became part of his art. Some works of art were direct extensions of his name-collecting activism. Before the second anniversary of the earthquake in 2010, Ai organized an online commemorative activity titled *niannian buwang* (reading to remember). Each participant selected a few names from his list of student victims, read them aloud, and audio-recorded it. Ai compiled the recordings into an art object titled *Nian*. About five thousand students' names were assigned to online users who volunteered to read. The final audio file was circulated through file-sharing services and on foreign social media websites like Twitter, which mainland users could access via proxies. In a letter to the participants, Ai elaborated on the meaning of this online commemorative activity: "This is an audio artistic object dedicated to the student victims of the Sichuan earthquake. This object is to commemorate the lives

FIGURE 9. Ai Weiwei's installation *Remembering* (2009) on the façade of the Haus der Kunst, Munich. © Ai Weiwei. Source: Jens Weber, Munich.

of the innocent victims and express our outrage over the concealment of the tofu-dreg [schoolhouses]. Respect life, and resist forgetting."[8] A similar commemorative object is *4851*, a video clip with names of 4,851 confirmed student victims slowly rolling up, accompanied by soothing music. Both *Nian* and *4851* were available online.

In addition to these unconventional online commemorative objects, Ai Weiwei also incorporated the theme of the earthquake into his traditional genres, such as installation art. Two art installations were particularly significant: *Remembering* (2009) and *Straight* (2013).

The inspiration for *Remembering* came from a sentence in a letter that a parent of a child victim, Yang Xiaowan, had written to Ai's investigation team: "She once lived happily for seven years in this society." This simple but heart-wrenching sentence was incarnated in a giant art installation consisting of nine thousand backpacks hung on the façade of the Haus der Kunst in Munich. The backpacks were painted in different colors and spelled out the sentence in Chinese, in a slightly revised version: "She lived happily for seven years in this world." The reader should have no difficulty figuring out the implications of the installation: the backpacks signify the children who died in schools that collapsed; the sentence was from a heart-broken mother; the installation turned the little girl and the simple sentence into a commemoration at a gigantic scale, highlighting human dignity and the importance of ordinary people's lives. This constituted a challenge and resistance to the "official memory," which reduced individuals to inaccurate numbers and concealed the state's misdeeds. Moreover, the installation is part of Ai's exhibit *So Sorry*, a title that reminded informed visitors of the lack of recognition and apology from the Chinese government regarding the earthquake issue.

The installation *Straight* was also executed at a colossal scale: it consisted of 150 tons of rebar recycled from the ruins of Sichuan. The artist had all the bent and broken rebars straightened and neatly arranged into big piles, which filled a whole room in Zuecca Project Space, a gallery in Venice, Italy. The title was meaningful in both the physical and symbolic senses. To make the rebars straight was to recover from the devastation; and the recycled rebars may be of practical use for future construction. The word "straight" also signified a political meaning: to get the facts "straight," particularly on the issue of the shoddy construction of the schools. Thus, the installation served as a memorial for the those killed in the earthquake and also as a political statement. Its political implications were even more apparent in the installation accompanying *Straight*, *S.A.C.R.E.D.*, which included six iron boxes reenacting Ai's incarceration.

In 2015 Ai Weiwei created new works with rebar as the motif again, but in a miniature size, quite a contrast to the supersized *Straight*. In an exhibit titled *Rebar in Gold* in a gallery in London, he showed a series of 24-carat gold jewelry pieces patterned to look like bent rebar, which visitors to the exhibit could purchase for £22,900–£45,500 (roughly $30,000–$60,000) and were encouraged to wear as a form of commemoration of the child victims. Ai explained the miniaturization: jewelry was so personal and intimately attached to human body that wearers could remember the child victims in a more personal way. Using gold also dramatized the stark contrast between the children's fragile lives, which had been largely forgotten, and the precious metal, which usually signifies eternity (Tsui 2015).

An interesting dimension of Ai Weiwei's activism was that he and his associates videotaped almost everything related to the activism and edited the clips into underground documentaries. *Disturbing the Peace* (its Chinese title, *Laomatihua*, was adapted from the name of a local Chengdu dish, literally meaning "Mom's slow-stewed trotters"), for example, recorded the whirlwind around the trial, including the police's beating of Ai and his other interactions with the government. *So Sorry*, a sequel to *Disturbing the Peace*, recorded his confrontation with the police and government after Tan's trial. The video clips in the documentaries were usually raw, and the documentaries had only limited artistic value. Both documentaries, however, were widely circulated online and used as a way of defying the government. Thus, the documentaries went from being mere recordings and representations of social reality to becoming part of social reality.

To some extent, Ai Weiwei consciously chose to blend his artistic practices with his activism. In an interview, he described his purpose as an "attempt to incorporate arts into today's life, into a country's miserable reality, and into individuals' ideals and expressions. Although I have paid a heavy cost for this attempt, the expressions are effective. The successful attempt makes it possible to incorporate individual artistic practices into social reforms and progress" (*Welt* 2015). A few artists and intellectuals shared the same ideas and also produced many commemorative objects. For example, Ai Xiaoming (no relation to Ai Weiwei), a professor of gender studies at Sun Yat-sen University, made a few documentaries about the earthquake school collapse issue and the name-collecting activism. As one of the most prominent activists in China, Ai Xiaoming had been engaged in activism and advocacy for various causes pertaining to the rights of disadvantaged populations, including peasants, women, prisoners, and AIDS/HIV patients, in addition to the earthquake victims. Before the earthquake, she had already made underground documentaries about some landmark incidents. *Taishi Village* (2005), for example, recorded the protest of peasants in Taishi Village in Guangdong against corrupt local cadres. *The Central Plains* (2007) and *Care and Love* (2007) addressed the spread of AIDS through government-backed blood selling.

Ai Xiaoming's first documentary about the Sichuan earthquake, *Our Children* (2009), presented the dispute over the collapse of schools and the parents' clashes with the government. With no voice-over narration and little editing, the documentary's use of many raw videos from

witnesses and parents' cell phones constituted a narrative directly opposite the official narrative, in both intended meaning and presentation.
The story started with some heart-wrenching video clips about the tragic
and chaotic scenes in several of the most devastated schools: Xinjian Elementary, Juyuan Middle, Beichuan High, and so on. Parents' narratives
and graphic images of crushed bodies made the documentary hard to
watch. The documentary also used interviews and the protesting parents'
videos to recount the parents' disputes, negotiations, and clashes with
the local government, as well as their suppression by the government.

The documentary was not—or more precisely, was not intended to
be—neutral. All the interviews were with the parents, supporting intellectuals, and human rights activists, but no interviews were conducted
with government officials, mostly because such interviews were impossible. In some sense, the documentary was melodramatic: perpetrators
and victims were clearly defined, and responsibility for the deaths was
determined through outside intellectuals' comments. The government's
voice and complicated local politics are not well documented. The same
representation pattern repeated itself in Ai Xiaoming's other documentaries about the Sichuan earthquake. *Citizen Investigation* recorded Tan
Zuoren's investigation of the school collapse issue. *Why Are the Flowers So Red?* told the story of Ai Weiwei's volunteers' investigation, while
River of Forgetting recorded Beichuan local residents' and students'
commemoration of the student victims on the first anniversary of the
earthquake.

All these documentaries drew a clear boundary between good and
bad, perpetrators and victims, heroes and villains. Their Manichean
presentation may lack depth since, as I have discussed in this book, the
collapse of schools was more a matter of the state's institutional failure
and collective wrongdoings than some people's moral shortcomings. The
documentaries raised the issue, and described the government's suppression and the activists' confrontations, but did not explore the complexity of the issue. In contrast, professional independent filmmakers'
documentaries were more emotionally controlled and presented more
diverse perspectives. For example, Pan Jianlin's *Who Killed Our Children?* used a relatively detached language to record disputes over various
issues surrounding Muyu Middle School right after the earthquake. On
every issue, there was a *Rashomon*-esque story: local residents' memories
and accounts dramatically differed from those of the school principal,

teachers, and local officials. Despite its seemingly provocative title, the documentary presented views and narratives from both sides of the dispute.

On the other hand, Ai Xiaoming's and Ai Weiwei's documentaries gave voiceless parents an opportunity to turn their private suffering into a public issue. The purpose of filming the documentaries was not to gain recognition in the professional field but to use them as a form of civic engagement, for citizens to participate in public affairs and for intellectuals to record citizens' civic engagement. Like Ai Weiwei, Ai Xiaoming elaborated on the meaning of the activism in an unambiguous way:

> Sometimes it was a difficult choice. We didn't want our life to be so restless or our work to be so overloaded. But when you were doing your work, a work ethic was involved: you should not lie. . . . In addition, in the citizens' investigation, you can see all of us were very hardworking and persistent. The biggest danger to our society is the collapse of values. From Tan Zuoren to Ai Weiwei to the volunteers, all were in fact repairing values. This group of people did not work for their own interests but to uphold values. The government did not understand our motives. We want to protect the core values of society, including human rights, justice, and equality. These values need people to promote, manifest, and protect them, through action. (Zhang 2010)

Not surprisingly, Ai Xiaoming was also under the state's regular surveillance, banned from leaving mainland China, and often under house arrest.

Another, quieter commemorative object was Chengdu-based architect Liu Jiakun's *Hu Huishan Memorial*, a small house in memory of a student victim, Hu Huishan, who died at Juyuan Middle School. From the outside, the house looked like a storage shed, but its inside walls were painted pink and decorated with the girl's backpack and toys. On the door was a small plate that read "Hu Huishan Memorial"; the inscription was written by Hu Huishan's mother. The house was located in a museum compound in Dayi, near Chengdu, which was developed by a local tycoon, Fan Jianchuan, Liu's friend. The local authorities forbade Liu's Hu Huishan Memorial to be opened to the public, so Liu had to hide it among trees beside one of the museum buildings. The door was locked, and only visitors introduced by Liu could get the key from the museum owner. The memorial was intended to be low profile to avoid sensationalism and the local government's attention. Casual tourists could easily miss it. Even a wandering tourist who happened to discover the hut might ask, "Who is Hu Huishan?" This inconspicuous hut was the only memorial to honor student victims in the entire quake zone.

Liu interpreted the meaning of the memorial in the following way:

> She [Huishan] did not have enough time to leave an imprint on society. She is not a famous person but an ordinary girl, a "pearl in her parents' palms." The commemoration in this memorial does not present a grand narrative of sacrifice or a loud celebration of heroism. It is just a memory of a girl at a flowering age. . . . This memorial is dedicated not only to this ordinary girl but also all the ordinary lives. Care for ordinary lives is the basis for a nation's revival. (Liu 2009, 41)

Without an explicit statement about justice and human rights, this memorial was less defiant than Ai Weiwei's installations and quieter than Ai Xiaoming's documentaries. Nevertheless, it was an example of Chinese architects actively engaging in public affairs. There had been a trend among architects to consider more than just aesthetics or commercial possibilities. Instead, many of them felt they should seek the social meaning of their work, including their concerns about all kinds of issues pertaining to ordinary people's lives, their communities, and the public spaces that surrounded them. Liu started this project almost by accident, but his inspiration was certainly enabled by this trend. After the earthquake, according to my interview with Liu, he went to the quake zone and met Hu Huishan's parents in Juyuan. Huishan's mother, Liu Li, presented him with Huishan's deciduous teeth and umbilical cord, which she had collected and put in a bag as a remembrance of her daughter. Liu decided to build a small memorial for Hu Huishan but still worried about the parents' potential response: Was this idea too "aesthetic" or "useless" for a couple who were struggling to rebuild their home and desperately needed more "practical" assistance? To his surprise, when he mustered up the courage to tell the parents of his idea, Liu Li immediately knelt down to thank him. Hu Huishan's father, a reserved middle-aged man, also agreed. At this emotional moment, the architect's otherwise empty slogan of "civic architecture" converged with the survivors' deepest sorrow and their desire to commemorate their loved one. Another of Liu's projects, *Revival Bricks* (*Zaisheng zhuan*), was imbued with these meanings of civic engagement. The *Revival Bricks* project aimed to provide the people affected by the earthquake with low-cost bricks, made from recycled materials from the ubiquitous earthquake rubble.[9]

At a deeper level, the memorial was not free of politics. It touched on the political meaning of death and ordinariness. Hu Huishan died in Juyuan Middle School, which collapsed immediately after the quake while all the other buildings around it remained standing. Visitors to the memorial who had known about the school would raise questions about the causes of the suffering, but the memorial itself did not make a loud statement. Thus, with its simple design and inconspicuous location, it constituted a silent challenge to the state's forced forgetting of ordinary people by highlighting the importance of an ordinary life and implicitly pointing to questions about the causes of the suffering.

MEMORY OUTSIDE AND INSIDE: INFLUENCE OF THE TINY PUBLIC

Within a few years the Sichuan earthquake became a focal point for members of the tiny public for expressing their ideas about politics and society. There was significant diversity among them: angry dissidents like Ai Weiwei, veteran activists like Tan Zuoren, quieter professionals like Liu Jiakun, and ordinary netizens and volunteers who read their writings, retweeted their tweets, and donated their money. However, they shared the same set of ideas: care about individuals' lives and resistance to the state-imposed forgetting.

Not surprisingly, the activists within the tiny public provoked suppression. Tan Zuoren, as we have noted, was imprisoned, and other activists were harassed, detained, and arrested. Ai Xiaoming was banned from leaving mainland China for a screening of her documentaries in Hong Kong. In 2011, Ai Weiwei was arrested because of his company's alleged tax evasion. Many believed the real reason for his arrest was his political activism. After 81 days of detention, Ai was released "on bail," and his company, under his wife, Lu Qing's, name, was ordered to pay a fine of 15.22 million yuan. In 2011, Ai's passport was confiscated. To vent his anger, Ai had put a flower in a basket on a bicycle outside his house every day after the confiscation.

From a practical perspective, Tan Zuoren's and Ai Weiwei's activism certainly failed, as the state easily cracked down on the tiny public. Yet the intent of their activism was expressive rather than substantive. It was not to achieve significant institutional change, but to commemorate the deceased, enhance public awareness of the issue, and challenge the state's moral authority. From this perspective, their activism in fact generated remarkable influence. It attracted tremendous media attention from outside of China and generated online participation in various commemorative activities. Tan's trial provoked a wave of moral outrage among liberal and oppositional sectors of civil society and made this otherwise little-known activist an icon as significant as Liu Xiaobo, a Nobel Peace Prize winner––at least in the eyes of liberal intellectuals, the liberal media, and dissidents.

Ai Weiwei benefited most from the earthquake activism. In *Art Review*'s "Power 100" ranking, a system that rates the influence of artists around the world, Ai Weiwei was ranked 71 in 2006 and 68 in 2007, fairly high positions. But his ranking jumped to 47 in 2008 and 43 in 2009, due to his high-profile activism. In 2011, when he was arrested, his ranking skyrocketed to number 1. *Art Review* described him "as . . . one of the world's leading (and wittiest) artists."

> Ai has become prominent for his social activism and repeated desire to hold the Chinese authorities accountable to the people, through his artworks, his interviews, or his blog posts (now collected in book form). In doing so he has been prominent in reconnecting art––the coverage of which is so dominated by questions of economic value in much of the mainstream media––with issues of social and cultural value, and their links to more conventional aesthetics. (*Art Review* 2016)

Since then, his ranking has decreased slightly, to 9 in 2012 and 13 in 2013, but he remains an international celebrity artist/dissident. Ai Weiwei's arrest immediately provoked a wave of criticism of the Chinese government from liberal and oppositional intellectuals and netizens in China and the media, the art community, politicians, and human rights organizations outside of China. *Time* nominated him as one of the runners-up for the Person of the Year 2011, together with Princess Kate, Paul Ryan, and William McRaven. Alison Klayman made a documentary, *Ai Weiwei: Never Sorry*, exploring his life and art. There are at least thirty English language books on his work and life, according to my search at the Emory University library. Almost every major media outlet in the world has reported on his artworks and activism and regularly sought his comments on Chinese art and politics.

Through his works and the media coverage, the memory of the Sichuan earthquake went beyond national boundaries and affected perceptions of the earthquake all across the globe. Almost every introduction to Ai Weiwei's works—related or not related to the earthquake—has included a brief or long narrative about his search for the students' names and numbers. For example, *Time* identified him mainly as a "dissident" instead of an artist when the magazine nominated him as a runner-up for the Person of the Year 2011: "The son of a revolutionary poet, Ai, 54, has grown more outspoken in recent years, expressing his anger at abuses of power and organizing online campaigns, including a volunteer investigation into the deaths of children in schools that collapsed during the 2008 Sichuan earthquake" (Beech and Ramzy 2011). Even in the blurbs of books about his artwork, his political activism plays a prominent role in the narrative about his identity and achievements. Again, the Sichuan earthquake is considered the most important part of his activism. For example, the blurb of *Ai Weiwei: Spatial Matters* reads:

> Outspoken, provocative, and prolific, the artist Ai Weiwei is an international phenomenon. In recent years, he has produced an astonishingly varied body of work while continuing his role as activist, provocateur, and conscience of a nation. Ai Weiwei is under "city arrest" in Beijing after an 81-day imprisonment; he is accused of tax evasion, but many suspect he is being punished for his political activism, including his exposure of shoddy school building practices that led to the deaths of thousands of children in the 2008 Sichuan earthquake. In 2009, he was badly beaten by the police during his earthquake investigations. (Ai and Pins 2014).

His stardom was also salient in the networked public. His provocative defiance, black humor, and even vulgarity attracted young, educated urban professionals and college students. After he was released and ordered to pay an enormous fine for his alleged tax evasion, Ai Weiwei decided to "borrow money" from netizens. His fans immediately responded, wiring about 9 million yuan to Ai's company account within ten days. Ai's fame came not only from his activism but also from his frequent interactions with his fans on social media. In an interview with *Time*, he said he spent a minimum of eight hours a day on Twitter and sometimes as much as twenty-four hours (Beech and Ramzy 2011).

Within this public of liberal and oppositional sectors of civil society and a significant number of netizens, as well as the wider public outside

China, the Sichuan earthquake was remembered mainly as a failure of the government to shoulder its responsibility in investigating the causes of students' deaths. In the wake of the earthquake, the overseas media cautiously praised the government's fast response and its leaders—particularly Wen Jiabao—for their compassion (Xu 2012). Only a few years later, however, when the major English language newspapers and news agencies mentioned the Sichuan earthquake they mostly associated it with the school collapse issue and repression of activists.

A personal anecdote also corroborates that, beyond China, memories were negative. Since the inception of my project, I have talked about it with various people in the United States and other countries. Except for Chinese nationals and a few scholars with expertise on Chinese civil society and related issues, most of the people I talked with promptly asked, "Is that the one with lots of collapsed schools?" In contrast, the Chinese response was more mixed. Questions often included "How is the reconstruction going on there?" or "Are you studying the volunteers?" or "How much of the donated money did those bastard officials put into their pockets?"

The reader of this book might reject the tiny public's oppositional memory as one-sided. It was. The dissidents and liberal intellectuals never intended to present a neutral image of the past, which is usually the job of a historian or a social scientist. They constructed the collective memory out of their moral outrage, resisting the polished, self-congratulatory official memory. The moral values they expressed through their actions were clearly articulated: solidarity with the affected people should be based on the values of equality and freedom. The dignity of the ordinary should be respected, and the causes of their suffering must be addressed. Their articulation of these moral values was the result of their life experience: leading activists either had experience living abroad, like Ai Weiwei, or had been engaged in social activism even before the earthquake, like Tan Zuoren. Their fellow travelers and followers had similar experiences and characteristics—they were well-educated urban professionals who espoused liberal ideology. Despite its tininess, the public was well connected to the outside world and effectively turned the outside memory of the Sichuan earthquake into a narrative about an unaccountable Chinese state.

The tiny public's commemorative activism also influenced the domestic memory of the earthquake. The liberal media and online

commentators, who were mostly supporters of--or at least sympathiz-
ers with--the tiny public of dissidents and intellectuals, reshaped the
domestic memory of the Sichuan earthquake. Since June 2008, the media
have been forbidden to report on the school collapse issue, but some of
them have used roundabout ways to remind readers of the issue. Whenever a disaster resulted in the collapse of a school, the major liberal media
carried reports and commentaries reminding people that school building safety was still an issue and that the government failed to take action
on it. The papers also used other countries' successful disaster mitigation to invoke the memory of the Sichuan earthquake. For example, after
Japan's 3/11 disaster in 2011, *Southern Metropolis Daily* and the *Beijing
News* published in-depth reports about Japan's school buildings, which
not only had withstood the earthquake, but also functioned as emergency shelters for local people. *SMD*'s report ended with a sentence with
an interesting allusion: "In Japan, if the government's inaction results in
the collapse of school buildings and heavy student casualties, the cabi-
net would step down" (Yang and Ma 2011). Other reports focused on
the technical aspects of school building safety without politicizing the
issue. For example, on the third anniversary of the Sichuan earthquake,
SMD carried an interview with civil engineering experts on the reasons
for the large number of school collapses, including flaws in design, the
low construction standards, and the contractors' failure to follow those
standards, deficient though they were (Yang 2011). The report certainly
gave credit to the government's new standard of earthquake safety, but
it stressed that more work had to be done to improve the implementa-
tion of these measures. Sometimes the school collapse issue converged
with other problems related to the Sichuan earthquake, such as the Red
Cross's mismanagement of the earthquake donations and the local governments' appropriation of the funds they received.

Nevertheless, the tiny public's strong connections to the outside world
and their influence on outsiders' memories of the Sichuan earthquake
made it particularly vulnerable to the state's suppression. Dissidents and
liberal intellectuals usually served as a major channel for outside media
to obtain alternative information to that in the official media. They were
willing to be interviewed by Hong Kong and foreign media; sometimes,
as in Tan Zuoren's case, they even assisted journalists in their investigations. The values they embraced were also highly consistent with those
of the overseas media. This strong connection gave the state an excuse

to accuse dissidents and intellectuals of "conspiring with anti-China forces" to subvert the regime.

Not only the state but also some ordinary Chinese people viewed the dissidents and intellectuals with suspicion. Those with a strong sense of national identity, although they may not have liked what the government did, viewed people like Ai Weiwei as "unpatriotic" and "used by outside forces." I have told the story of Jiajun (see Chapter 3) and his reluctance to discuss the school collapse issue with me, for fear I might relay the information to foreign political forces. During the years I have been working on this and other projects, I have repeatedly encountered people who openly criticized the dissidents and intellectuals as "anti-China." Sometimes they even accused my work of being "too negative" and "deliberately tweaked to please Western audiences"--although my "Western audiences" occasionally disliked my work because I failed to provide a Manichean picture of state versus society. In addition to encountering those accusations, my project more usually has led to awkwardness in interpersonal interactions. After hearing about my project, my friends, relatives, and acquaintances looked at each other, with strange smiles on their faces as if they were embarrassed; and usually one of them would break that polite but uncomfortable silence by saying, "So what you're doing is politically sensitive," before other people switched the topic of conversation. On rare occasions, close friends and relatives have warned me to "be careful," as if I was in imminent danger.

Those who were content with China's material abundance usually considered the tiny public's devotion as fanatic and stupid. Once I accompanied a few intellectuals and dissidents in Chengdu's tiny public to a dinner with a group of people with different occupations and backgrounds who had randomly gathered together through a network of friends. The clash of ideas began almost immediately after courteous introductions and a round of handshaking. One of them, a dealer for luxury brands like Lexus and BMW, challenged the dissidents by saying what they did was not only crazy but also useless. He said (not an exact quote but the words jotted down in my field notes):

> I bet you won't find any country without any social problems, even the United States. China has been progressing so much in the last thirty years, and many people are very satisfied with their living conditions. We have houses, cars, and tons of stuff in the supermarket. My friends,

you should read history! You probably won't find such a golden age [*shengshi*] in history. But you guys focus only on negative stuff. What's your point?

The dealer would find the inaccuracy in his comments if he had done a quick fact check: not everyone, not even most people have "houses, cars, and tons of stuff." As expected, his comments infuriated the intellectuals and dissidents and turned the dinner into a heated debate, which was also fueled by alcohol. The dissidents insisted that the car dealer twisted reality and urged him to think about the scenario that "if no one stands up to injustice, then one day you'll be the next victim." The car dealer and other people attempted to refocus the attention to the "bigger picture" (*daju*) and the progress that the country had made. The debate ended amicably after several rounds of beer and hard liquor. After the dinner, one of the dissidents told me that such a debate broke out almost every time they had conversations with people outside the tiny public. Though he had become used to it, he still felt frustrated by the apathy that prevailed in society.

In 2014, when I revisited Sichuan, I accompanied a few people within Chengdu's tiny public of liberal intellectuals to a college student summer program, in which students traveled around the country and discussed cultural and political issues with local intellectuals. The dissidents and intellectuals found a much friendlier and more supportive occasion to hold a discussion. Two of them were invited to speak to around fifty students about political issues. It was not an academic talk. The speakers drank beer, cursed, and sometimes even shouted. Yet, the students seemed amazed and impressed, expressing their admiration through constant applause and laughter.

After the talk, the intellectuals and students went to a low-end restaurant to have another round of drinks. The students cheered for the speakers, who already were widely known within the tiny public. This group consisted of a number of self-selected students, who were eager and idealistic enough to spend money and time on listening to not only practically "useless" but also politically dangerous talks and speeches. Compared to the middle-aged businessmen with whom the dissident intellectuals had an emotional debate, this group of young students who had not gotten a dose of reality were an ideal audience. After several rounds of drinks, one of the dissidents, apparently drunk, burst into raucous curses and laughter, and later, at midnight, was escorted home.

Conclusion

On April 4, 2010, about two years after the Sichuan earthquake, an earthquake hit Yushu, an impoverished prefecture in Qinghai Province. Measuring 7.1 on the Richter scale, the earthquake destroyed more than 80 percent of the houses in Jiegu, the capital of Yushu, and killed 2,698 people, as of May 31, 2010 (China News Service 2010).

A consensus crisis quickly formed in the wake of the earthquake. The quake's intensity and breadth were hardly comparable to Sichuan's, but it still utterly devastated a large area and killed thousands of residents. Yushu's complex geological features and high altitude hampered rescue and relief work. Both the state and civic associations took the opportunity to work together to pursue their common as well as different goals in a more conscious way than in Sichuan. For example, the Gesanghua Western China Education Aid Society, an NGO that had been working in Qinghai for five years, sent their first response team only 41 minutes after the earthquake, arriving in the quake zone that night. A local NGO, the Minhe Disability Assistance Center, after initial communications difficulties, managed to obtain and publicize information from local residents. The NGO coalition network 5.12 Relief formed after the Sichuan earthquake (see Chapter 1), sent a team to Yushu immediately (Guo 2011).[1] Shortly after the earthquake, One Foundation, which actively engaged in both the Sichuan and Yushu earthquakes, finally obtained legal status as a public foundation and, thus had the legal right to collect and manage donations. This opened the possibility for other private foundations to obtain government-approved status. Seven days after the Yushu earthquake, without being urged by the public sphere, the Chinese state mandated a one-day national mourning for the victims.

Nevertheless, the ethnic features of Yushu complicated the consensus crisis. Most residents of Yushu were ethnic Tibetans, who were also Buddhists. Buddhist monks became the major force in local civic engagement. They swiftly organized local rescue and relief work and provided emotional and spiritual care for survivors. Sometimes the government was engaged in a moral competition with the monks for the hearts and minds of the Tibetans. While the monks clearly had the upper hand in providing spiritual support, particularly through prayers and death rituals, the Chinese government's best bet was to provide as much material support as possible.

This complication put the Chinese government in an awkward situation. On the one hand, to respond to the disaster effectively, it had to mobilize resources from all non-state actors, including outside associations and monks. Moreover, the government attempted to demonstrate its generosity and paternalism by allowing the monks to engage with the community. On the other hand, it could not afford to allow the monks too much freedom for fear that they would steal the limelight in this political drama and construct an alternative force with probably a higher degree of legitimacy. Moreover, the monks were more likely to—and in fact, did—expose issues in the government's response to the foreign media.

A significant number of schools in Yushu collapsed, killing students. Images of the toppled schools and child victims rekindled the collective memory of similar scenes in Sichuan and provoked controversy. Top leaders, such as President Hu Jintao and Premier Wen Jiabao, took pains to demonstrate that they cared for the affected people, but their display of compassion was challenged and sometimes discredited by the public. Their hugging and kissing child survivors in Yushu reminded people of the child victims in Sichuan, especially since "Grandpa Wen" had not addressed the causes of their deaths in the two years since the Sichuan earthquake.

All these factors led to a more restrictive context for civic engagement in Yushu than in Sichuan. The state placed tighter constraints on the media for fear that reports on politically sensitive issues would tarnish its image. Even the liberal media muted their angry voices, reporting the school collapses in a matter-of-fact way, without any in-depth investigation. The consensus among the state, the monks, and outside volunteers only lasted for a brief period. Soon the monks began to complain to foreign media about the government's concealing of the death toll, the expulsion of the monks from relief work, and ineffective distribution of supplies. Conflicts also broke out between outside civic associations and the government. The government ordered the public foundations involved to submit the donations they collected to the Qinghai provincial government to "facilitate the management of donations." This practice was not substantively new since, as shown in Chapter 3, most of the donations for the Sichuan earthquake relief work eventually went to local governments. Such a blatant order, however, still infuriated even public foundations, which had been endeavoring to fit themselves into China's emerging civil society. Some claimed that this suggested "the death of charity" in China.

In sum, the civic engagement after the Yushu earthquake both resembled and differed from that in Sichuan. The Yushu earthquake provided otherwise restricted civil society—including outside civic associations and the Tibetan monks' religious organizations—with political opportunities and symbolic-moral resources to participate in large-scale public activities. This engagement, however, was constrained by a more unwelcoming context due to two political issues. First, the collapse of schools in Yushu rekindled the memory of the fall of school buildings after the Sichuan earthquake. Second, from the very beginning, the Tibetan monks constituted a competing force that operated independently from the state. Their cooperation with the government was brief and less substantive than that in Sichuan. Thus, their civic engagement intensified previous ethnic tensions and invited heavy restrictions by the state.

THE POLITICS OF MORAL SENTIMENTS

This book has told a story of Chinese citizens' self-organized, grassroots engagement in the aftermath of the Sichuan earthquake. The pages that follow recapitulate that story and highlight what we have learned from it.

Immediately after the Sichuan earthquake, Chinese citizens, mostly without being organized by the state, rushed to the quake zone to volunteer or collected donations on the street. It was an exuberant moment when ordinary Chinese felt they could do something to help their fellow citizens and make society a better place. Tragedy led to compassion, and compassion led to a can-do spirit. The resulting large-scale civic engagement was not only an outpouring of compassion, but also a large-scale collective action that expressed moral sentiments through actions, symbols, and words. All this was embedded in China's particular political context and shaped by the political opportunities and constraints the earthquake generated through its interaction with structural state–civil society relations.

For Chinese who had believed society to be devoid of any altruism and care, this wave of volunteering was delightfully surprising. However, as my analysis has shown, beneath this torrent of volunteering was a political logic that made such civic engagement possible and turned it into a reality in an authoritarian context. The earthquake led to a consensus crisis, a crisis in which the state needed services from society for practical and political purposes and the state and civil society reached a general agreement on goals and priorities. This consensus crisis compelled both the state and civic associations to solve pressing practical issues related to emergency response. Thus, civic associations were able to demonstrate the capacity they had built up in the preceding decades.

The earthquake triggered strong emotions related to suffering and death and put compassion at the center of the drama. Liberal intellectuals and the media vocally demanded that the state show compassion for its citizens through an unprecedented mourning ritual. For various structural and situational reasons, the state accepted the proposal and, for the first time in Chinese history, lowered the national flag for ordinary citizens. At the moment when flags flew at half-staff and a three-minute silence was observed, the large-scale civic engagement—including volunteering and public advocacy—reached its peak. It was a moment of sorrow and solidarity, but it was also a result of the combined effect of both the long-term development of the Chinese public sphere—both its structural conditions and its normative ideas about the dignity of individual lives—and state-society interaction in the immediate context of 2008.

In the ensuing months and years, however, the consensus crisis dissolved. A state-business alliance dominated recovery plans and squeezed out civic associations with little money or *guanxi*. As the school collapse issue became a national scandal, the state expelled and restricted associations that provided social services and suppressed activists such as Ai Weiwei, Tan Zuoren, and the volunteers they mobilized to address the causes of the collapse of schools. In the long run, the post-earthquake civic engagement did not lead to significant changes in structural relations between the state and civil society. On the contrary, civil society became even more fragmented.

People civically engaged in the post-earthquake relief and recovery work interpreted the meaning of their actions in diverse and multivocal ways. Most of them did not draw on the normative ideas of liberal democratic civil society. Nor did many of them follow the state's official altruism. Instead, more of them used nationalism, religion, individualism, and other cultural terms to talk about why they participated and how they felt about their volunteering experience. At the early stages of the disaster response, these diverse interpretations shared the common feature that they all expressed compassion for the suffering and solidarity with fellow volunteers. Such a multivocal commonality was manifested in their understanding of volunteering in the relief and their participation in the mourning ritual.

On the other hand, while all of the participants transcended particular group boundaries, many failed to turn compassion for suffering into a serious political discussion and actions that addressed the causes of the suffering. This apathy was mainly a result of the repressive political context, which shaped people's words and thoughts not only through prohibitions but also through a pervasive feeling of fear, a sense of helplessness, and an inability to speak about harsh reality. Only a tiny public of dissidents and liberal intellectuals consciously embraced classical civil society ideals such as individual dignity, liberty, and equality, and engaged in activism and commemorations to counter the state's forced forgetting and remembering.

The complexity, ambiguity, and paradoxes in the participants' actions and meanings suggest that the authoritarian political context shaped acts of compassion in deep and subtle ways. The volunteers had accomplished something remarkable by transcending their particular group boundaries, private interests, and day-to-day calculations. This huge wave of engagement was enabled by the political context at the time of the earthquake. The moral sentiments expressed in their words and actions were multivocal and pluralistic. But political conditions also prevented them from transcending more boundaries—moving from compassion to serious deliberation and political actions. Many of them, consciously or unconsciously, faced a series of moral dilemmas: Should one avoid talking about the causes of the suffering or speak out about them? Stay in the comfort zone of merely volunteering or take action to reveal the causes to the public? These dilemmas were especially intense in Sichuan, where suffering and death made it difficult for volunteers to be evasive.

CIVIC ENGAGEMENT: ACTION, CONTEXT, AND MEANING

The Sichuan earthquake did not generate important social changes. Nor was it a turning point in history. It was less a transformative event than a "template of possibility" (Sewell 1996). It belongs to those events that "are sociologically and politically important because they permit us to see relations and interconnections that speak to broader macro- and micro-level social processes" (Berezin 2012, 620).

More specifically, the story of the Sichuan earthquake provides us with a window on civic engagement in China in general. In scrutinizing civic engagement, our focus shifts from structural relations to actions, from organizations to people. Thus, civic engagement and its contexts and meanings come into sharp relief. Needless to say, this case analysis does not cover all the forms and dimensions of civic engagement in China today. In fact, no case analysis can do that. Instead, it highlights a topic significant for an in-depth understanding of Chinese civil society: the intertwined relations between the authoritarian context, Chinese citizens' grassroots engagement, and their interpretations of the meaning of their actions. The paragraphs that follow trace what we can learn from the case of the Sichuan earthquake about this aspect of civic engagement in China in general.

The Sichuan earthquake spotlighted otherwise less salient but pervasive civic engagement in China and, more importantly, showed how the authoritarian political context in China shapes—both enables and constrains—citizens' grassroots civic engagement. This power to shape varies across different types of engagement. Volunteering to provide social services is generally less restricted than activism, and thus becomes the safest way for citizens to participate in public activities. This can explain why volunteering has developed rapidly in both social-service-based and community-based organizations over the past decades. Some public advocacies may be tolerated and even encouraged, especially when the state needs symbolic support from society to buttress its legitimacy, as in the Sichuan mourning ritual advocacy. Even some types of political civic engagement, such as village elections, which are not covered in this book, are tolerated and even encouraged since they project an image of an open and reformist state (Shi 1999). Nevertheless, the state has posted a dead-end sign for those who aspire to get answers to politically troublesome questions. This variation in types of civic engagement is consistent with a major postulate in the complex coexistence approach that different sectors in Chinese civil society develop unevenly in responding to the state's "graduated control," that is, differential strategies of enabling and restraining (Kang and Han 2008).

The new thing I offer here, however, is another dimension of political context: that the constraining and enabling also vary across different *situations*, which interact with structural variations to generate more contingencies and ambiguities. I have demonstrated how the earthquake as a "consensus crisis" facilitated service-providing civic engagement even from dissident associations (for example, B-log) and how such a consensus crisis faded and gave rise to more divergent and contentious engagement. Beyond situations involving disasters, we find many cases in which the same association may be treated quite differently in different situations when the structural context does not change much. For example, Kou Yanding, director of Aiyi Cultural Development Center, an NGO providing social services for the disabled, which had been working in the quake zone for about five years (see Chapter 3), was suddenly arrested by the government in October 2014 (*Hong Kong Economic Journal* 2014). The specific reason for Kou's arrest was unknown, but it was speculated to be related to a workshop she organized to facilitate dialogue among civil society activists from Hong Kong, Taiwan, and mainland China. Workshops like this were common among Chinese NGOs, but the timing of the workshop organized by Kou could not have been worse: September 2014, when the Occupy Central movement, or the Umbrella Revolution, was at its peak in Hong Kong and Taiwan's Sunflower Movement had ended just several months earlier. Kou was not usually considered by other people or herself to be a dissident; instead, she was dedicated to developing democracy through "moderate and constructive" civic engagement (Zhao 2015). During my fieldwork, I accompanied Aiyi's disabled artists to a few activities, participated in their staff meetings, and visited their stations in the quake area. Despite initial difficulties, Aiyi's work stations had been running well, with support from local schools and governments. However, through my informants, I learned the stations were closed down right after Kou's arrest.

This development reminds us that even if there are cooperative interactions between service-delivering associations and the authoritarian state, as many scholars, as well as the present study, have demonstrated (Teets 2014), such cooperation largely relies on *situations* and is fragile. Aiyi, an organization with service-delivering functions, and Kou, a mild-mannered person and not a dissident, were able to actively participate in the recovery work by carefully managing their relations with local governments. When the political situation changed from normal to contentious, even organizations and individuals without explicitly oppositional goals were suppressed. Similarly, Oxfam Hong Kong, an NGO usually considered to have cooperative relations with the Chinese government, was accused by the Ministry of Education of "infiltrating the mainland with evil intentions" by recruiting college students (Radio Free Asia 2010). Nevertheless, in the wake of the Yushu earthquake, Oxfam Hong Kong was allowed to enter the quake zone and undertake disaster relief work. To some extent, this variation was a result of the Chinese state's situation-based strategy, or "adaptive governance" (Heilmann and Perry 2011): the state chooses the tactic of tightening (*shou*) or loosening (*fang*) control according to the perceived risks and opportunities in particular situations (Baum 1994). The situational variation adds one more dimension to the contingency and ambiguity in state–civil society relations in China.

Another little discussed dimension of contingency and ambiguity is the diversity in the participants' interpretations of the goals and meanings of their engagement. As my analysis has shown, even exuberant expressions of solidarity and compassion were multivocal, not to mention the divergence of meanings at the later stages of the earthquake response. On the one hand, such diversity is not surprising in an increasingly pluralistic society with a growing range of cultural ideas. On the other hand, a closer look at this diversity reveals that it is filled with political tensions and ambiguities, which are a result of the complex interactions between political context and action.

For example, only a small section of civil society, the tiny public of dissidents and intellectuals, upholds the notion of liberty and equality, and they are the people with the most affinity with Western journalists and intellectuals, who regularly seek their opinions and sometimes inflate their importance in the Chinese civil society. In the image common in the foreign media, they are the people standing in front of an array of tanks, as in the famous "tank man" picture.

Most civically engaged people, however, do not fit this tank man image. Such people, as we have seen, draw on various items in their cultural repertoire—including nationalism, individualism, religion, and even Communist altruism—to understand their actions. This finding corroborates the research on other civil societies, in both Western and non-Western contexts, in which the actual participants in civic engagement on the ground and discourses in civil spheres may not always follow the classical, democratic ideas of civil society (Lo and Fan 2010; Eliasoph and Lichterman 2003). It also strongly supports the idea of "moral ecology": values, vocabularies, and symbols used in civic participation are shaped by the particular political and cultural context (Madsen 1993). The East European countries in the 1980s and the United States in the 1990s represented two variants of moral ecology. In East Europe, political actors consciously attached ideas of democracy to some types of civic engagement, such as joining an independent union, creating small safe havens for political discussions, and starting a social movement (Goldfarb 2006). In those cases, civil society was not only the sphere in which they worked but also the ideal they were fighting for, a slogan shouted by crowds at rallies. By the same token, the civic engagement debate in the United States in the 1990s was also part of the larger debate over the role of the federal government in social life, in which advocates of civic republicanism rediscovered the Tocquevillian voluntary association at the local level (e.g., bowling groups) as a way to express their rejection of big government (Skocpol 1997).

Applying that concept to a different context without careful examination of its ideological implications may run the risk of merging a normative idea with an empirical analysis. If Chinese civil society in the 1980s somewhat resembled civil society in East Europe, the two later dramatically diverged. After the Tiananmen crackdown, civil society was painfully revived in "social organizations" (*shehui zuzhi*), which carried out some social service functions that the state was unwilling or unable to perform (Watson 2008), and to a limited extent in the market-oriented media and the Internet (see Chapter 2). The revival did not turn into a unifying oppositional force not only because of the fragmented structure of civil society but also because of a lack of consensus on the meanings and goals of the activities of social organizations. Some consciously pursue a civil society, whereas most identify their goal as contributing to social welfare (*shehui gongyi*).

Correspondingly, the state also practices graduated control over associations, not only with regard to their structural autonomy or dependency, but also their claims of goals and meanings. For example, small grassroots groups are autonomous: the Super Girl Fan Club, the mountaineers, and the Car Owners Club all operated outside of the state's reach. But they rarely troubled the state because the meanings and purposes they attached to their actions—helping others, doing good things, and contributing to public welfare—did not threaten the state's legitimacy. As long as such associations concentrate on their work and refrain from raising political issues, the state is likely to grant them some room. If, for example, an artists' group decides to make paintings about a politically sensitive issue, say, the Tiananmen incident, or if, as in Kou Yanding's case, a director of a service-delivering NGO is connected to politically sensitive issues, they step over the so-called red line and invite repression. In other words, the key political issue surrounding Chinese civic associations is not about autonomy but the causes they work for and their interpretations of their activities.

Sometimes the state determines associations' political sensitivity according to the terms they use to talk about their engagement. The same activity of delivering a social service can be framed as a means of improving "social welfare" or developing a "civil society" (*gongming shehui*). The two terms, however, receive quite different responses from the government. In May 2013 a document titled "An Announcement about the Current Situation in the Ideological Sphere" was widely circulated online and stirred up a storm. It was said to be an internal document that urged party members and college professors to resist the "erosion caused by Western ideas." The core part of this document consisted of seven "don'ts." College professors and propaganda departments alike should not talk about seven things: universal values, civil society, citizens' rights, the party's mistakes in the past, "power-elite capitalism," and an independent justice system. Civil society (*gongmin shehui*) was listed among the seven taboo topics because it was intended to "disin-tegrate the social foundation of the party's rule" (BBC Chinese 2013). In addition, the years since the Sichuan earthquake have witnessed numerous cases of arresting, harassing, and detaining self-proclaimed civil society actors, such as activists like Liu Xiaobo and other signers of *Charter 08*, human rights lawyers like Xu Zhiyong and Pu Zhiqiang, feminists, and so on. On the other hand, no evidence suggests the state imposes strict control over various public expressions along the lines of "public welfare" (*gongyi*); instead, the state has even incorporated the new discourse of *gongyi* into its political vocabulary.

Therefore, despite all the ambiguity and contingency, the authori-tarian state draws an unambiguous red line between nice, warm, and helpful *gongyi* activities and angry and "radical" public expressions of criticism. This structural condition enables public expressions with so-called positive energy (*zheng nengliang*)—talking about the positive side of society and refraining from discussing social problems—a term that was not as popular in 2008 as later but certainly had its equivalents then (for example, in Greentea's terms, "the positive side," *jiji de yimian*). It restricts public expressions that openly challenge the state and, more-over, cuts off defiant activists from the rest of civil society through the censorship and control system.

As a result, the diversity of participants' interpretations of their engagement comes into being at the expense of oppositional voices, which are silenced amid the loud and enthusiastic chorus of compassion. This paradox is manifested in the dilemmas in individuals' narratives, especially when individual participants are confronted with the "ele-phant in the room"--an obvious but disturbing incidence of tragedy and injustice (Zerubavel 2006). In anticipation of potential repression and with no possibility of changing the context, people may avoid talking about blatant injustice, let alone take action to address it. In some cases, ordinary volunteers like Siyi may have been unaware of the existence of bolder volunteers who struggled to change the context.

In this sense, a repressive context does not simply produce fear and so deter civic engagement from addressing political issues. It also generates a general inability to speak (Gaventa 1980). The story of the Sichuan earth-quake tells us that we must refrain from assuming that once "authoritarian obstacles"—the fear factor and the institutional restrictions—are removed, citizens will enthusiastically and immediately take part in politics and embrace democracy. That is untrue even in established democracies, where civic groups attempt to create an appearance of political apathy out of fear that they will be perceived as too much associated with dirty politics (Elia- soph 1998; Bennett et al. 2013). In an authoritarian political context, the state rules out alternative ways of thinking about and talking about politi- cal reality. Most volunteers who went to Sichuan did not ask questions that touched on anything beyond their care-giving even though suffering and injustice were ever present. They normalized their apathy, stayed within their comfort zone, and were unaware of the efforts of more daring people. As a result, a spiral of silence emerged after the Sichuan earthquake, even among public-spirited volunteers: the more repressive the context, the less you talked about the issue; the less you talked about the issue, the higher the cost of talking about it or acting on it. Eventually, you did not even have the desire to talk about it.

The biggest irony in the story of the Sichuan earthquake is that apathy went hand in hand with compassion. However, compassion was chan- neled into warm volunteering instead of open deliberation and public action to address the causes of the suffering. The same warm-hearted, public-spirited volunteers may have been indifferent to politically sensi- tive suffering, which they witnessed but tried to ignore. Do good deeds; show your compassion; feel good about yourself; and don't worry about things you can't change. As sociologist Nina Eliasoph puts it, "if we want to prevent the woes that caused the need for volunteers to begin with, we often have to look beyond personal care-giving to find out why it was missing in the first place" (Eliasoph 2013, 162). But Eliasoph warns that this is easier said than done. The Sichuan earthquake shows that in a political context like China even speaking about woes was not easy.

When Alexis de Tocqueville praised civic engagement for its "renew- ing feelings and ideas" and "enlarging hearts," he was alarmed by what he believed to be the centralization of state power in France and later worried by the paradoxical link between extreme individualism and oli- garchy. He thus had high hope for the associational life, in which ordi- nary citizens could develop "habits of the heart," work for the common good, and counter the impact of both the strong state and individualism. This idealistic and largely tentative argument was picked up and simpli- fied by various kinds of neo-Tocquevillianism—ranging from the East European to American versions—to justify an empirical-normative idea about the functions of civic engagement for democracy.

To carry the historical burden of democratization is, however, too demanding a task for civil society. The story of the Sichuan earthquake casts doubts on this great expectation, not only from a structural perspective, as the complex coexistence approach has aptly shown, but also from a cultural perspective—by listening to the "feelings and ideas" of the people who participated in civic engagement. In other words, the meanings and purposes of civic engagement under authoritarianism may not constitute a culture of democracy. Democracy may not be their goal; compassion may coexist with apathy. This happened not only in Sichuan but also elsewhere in China, since the political context is not conducive to serious political discussions. We have seen a boom of volunteering in China in various fields in recent decades, but we have also witnessed the tightening of control over civic associations' expressions of ideas of civil society and their links to foreign organizations. The state has constantly tightened its control over civic associations, from building party branches in NGOs to placing strict restrictions on foreign funds for civic associations, which is part of the content of a new law on social organizations (*Overseas NGO Management Law*, 2016). Civic engagement in China, as a form of practice and a discourse, entails many paradoxes, contradictions, and dilemmas. All this ambiguity and complexity leads us to refrain from predicting the future of civic engagement. Perhaps people without an explicit intention of pursuing democracy may still develop the art of association—skills of communicating with strangers, organizing public events, deliberating issues, electing leaders, and so on—which can be employed in more politically significant activities in the future. This "unintended consequence" argument makes sense in theory, but we must be cautious about the view that associational life as a social alchemy automatically turns associations without the common good as their purpose into democratic ones.

Any reader who has read this far should not have difficulty getting my normative message. The "real" Alexis de Tocqueville—not the Tocqueville of the neo-Tocquevillianism—never assumes a naïve linear causal relationship between civic engagement in bowling groups and the democratization of society. Instead, Tocqueville emphasizes political associations, which facilitate and guard civic associations to produce an art of associations:

I do not claim that there can be no civil associations in a country where political association is prohibited, for men can never live in society without becoming involved in some joint enterprise. In such a country, however, I do contend that civil associations will always be few in number, weak in conception, and lacking in leadership and will either refuse to entertain ambitious projects or fail in executing them. (Tocqueville [1840] 2004, 607)

Civil society will not develop into a decisive force if there is no fully developed sphere for political associations, or what Linz and Stepan term "political society"—the "arena in which the polity specifically arranges itself to contest the legitimate right to exercise control over public power and the state apparatus" (Linz and Stepan 1996, 8). Core constitutions in a political society include parties, elections, electoral rules, political leadership, interparty alliances, and legislative bodies. They protect civil society and ordinary citizens from the state's intervention and manipulation and enable citizens' long-term and stable public engagement as well as public expressions of their ideas and feelings. For all these institutions to emerge requires a transformation of political society instead of civil society.

The real problem is not about civil society per se but about the polity.

Notes

Introduction

1. The 2008 Sichuan earthquake is sometimes referred to, particularly in the Chinese government's documents and narratives, as the Wenchuan earthquake (*Wenchuan dizhen*) or the Great Wenchuan earthquake (*Wenchuan da dizhen*), named after the county at its epicenter. This name, however, often causes unnecessary confusion and misunderstanding among people unfamiliar with the earthquake. For example, some believe only Wenchuan was affected. In fact, the earthquake devastated many places outside Wenchuan, such as Beichuan, Dujiangyan, and Qingchuan. I refer to this disaster as the "Sichuan earthquake" to do justice to all the seriously affected places.

2. Pseudonyms are used for interviewees and the organizations they belonged to, unless they are widely reported public figures, such as Tan Zuoren. All interviews were conducted by me.

3. Interview with Zihou, June 14, 2009, Chengdu.

4. As I will show later in this book, an accurate number of casualties at Beichuan High is still unavailable because of political restrictions on investigations. We can estimate the percentage by examining some reports with information about the school's casualties, which were published before the reporting ban (Cong, Liu, and Wang 2008).

5. Interview with Zhou Yin, August 1, 2009, Chengdu.

6. Interview with Wu Hang, June 15, 2009, Chengdu.

7. *Shu* is the ancient name for an area that today is part of Sichuan Province.

8. Interview with Liang, July 7, 2009, Chengdu.

9. Unlike in other countries, in China the Red Cross is administered by the government, particularly the Ministry of Civil Affairs.

10. In this book, I use civil society as an *analytical* concept to examine a phenomenon with three dimensions (Edwards 2014). Civil society is firstly a form of organization, consisting mainly of civic associations, including nongovernmental organizations (NGOs) with formal organizational structures and regulations, small civic groups, and networks that consist of NGOs and groups. Civil society is a "public sphere," a discursive space for individuals and organizations to debate public issues and advocate social changes. Civil society is also

an ideal that is believed to represent positive norms and values, and an analytical concept intended to reveal how civil society actors understand the meanings of their actions and their own norms and values.

11. Disasters, as used in this book, refer to large-scale, "natural" or, more accurately, "nature-triggered" disasters, which generate a considerable national impact and are treated by the state's disaster management system with the highest level of response. Strictly speaking, "natural" is a misnomer, since all disasters are social. An earthquake is not a disaster, but a natural hazard. It is society that causes its own disasters: people build houses in places where they should not, or they do not build strong houses, for political, social, technological, and economic reasons (Kreps 2001; Perry 2006; Quarantelli 1998).

12. As a reviewer of the manuscript for this book correctly suggested, the term "consensus crisis" sounds like "crisis of consensus." However, the term is actually used in the opposite sense: a consensus that arises in the face of a crisis. This imperfect term has been widely used in the sociology of disaster, and I do not believe there is a need to change it.

Chapter 1

Portions of this chapter appeared in "Consensus Crisis and Civil Society: The Sichuan Earthquake Response and State-Society Relations," *China Journal* 71 (January): 91–108. 1324–9347/2014/7101–0005. Copyright 2014 by the Australian National University. All rights reserved. Reproduced with permission.

1. Interview with Luqiong, April 16, 2009, Shanghai.

2. Interview with Luxin, June 19, 2009, Chengdu.

3. China's first comprehensive national disaster management agency was the National Commission for the International Decade on Natural Disaster Reduction, established in 1989 in response to a UN resolution to establish such commissions worldwide. The commission was later renamed the China Commission for International Disaster Reduction in 2000, and in 2006 renamed again as the China National Commission for Disaster Reduction, the current national disaster management agency, which is responsible for coordinating disaster management with national bureaus and ministries.

4. Among the many civic associations I contacted and interviewed, the only one with disaster-related functions was an international organization, ShelterBox, which, with help from English-speaking Chinese volunteers, delivered prepackaged boxes of relief materials to the earthquake zone. Among the domestic associations I know of, only a few mountaineering associations had training that could be used to support disaster relief, such as outdoor survival skills.

5. "Zhong Zuwen" is a pen name suspected to stand for *Zhongyang zuzhibu wenjian* (the Organization Department's document). Editorials by Zhong

Zuwen are usually considered to be documents that convey messages from the Central Organization Department of the party to lower-level cadres.

6. Throughout the book, all US dollar equivalencies are based on the exchange rate in 2008, unless otherwise noted.

7. Interview with Xiaoli, March 31, 2009, Shanghai.

8. Interview with Shinan, August 3, 2009, Chengdu.

9. Douban (www.douban.com) is a Web 2.0 website for people to discuss books and movies, and organize online groups based on mutual interests.

10. Interview with Wenting, June 18, 2009, Chengdu.

11. Interview with Shinan, August 3, 2009, Chengdu.

12. Interview with Bojun, June 16, 2009, Chengdu.

13. Interview with Jiajun, August 4, 2009, Chengdu.

14. Interview with Yang Shuang, June 19, 2009, Chengdu.

15. Interview with Xiaoli, March 31, 2009, Shanghai.

16. Interview with Zhou Yin, August 2, 2009, Chengdu.

17. Interview with Hang Wei, March 17, Shanghai.

18. Interview with Xiaomi, June 16, Chengdu.

19. Interview with Soil, April 30, Shanghai.

20. Interview with Wenting, June 18, 2009, Chengdu.

21. Interview with Feizhu, April 28, 2009, Shanghai.

22. Interview with Shinan, August 3, 2009, Chengdu.

23. Interview with Guangchuan, August 2, 2009, Chengdu.

24. Interview with Luqiong, April 16, 2011, Shanghai.

Chapter 2

An earlier version of parts of this chapter appeared in "For Whom the Bell Tolls: State-Society Relations and the Sichuan Earthquake Mourning in China," *Theory and Society* 42 (5): 509–42, ©Springer Science+Business Media Dordrecht 2013, reproduced with permission.

1. Interview with Luxin, June 19, 2009, Chengdu.

2. Moreover, governments of all levels mobilized and controlled war-commemorative gatherings and rituals. On December 13 of every year, for example, the Nanjing municipal government has ordered all air raid sirens in the city to blare to commemorate victims of the Nanjing Massacre in 1937. Schools and governmental offices also have halted their activities to observe three minutes of silence.

3. In 1999 the Chinese government held a national mourning observance and lowered the flag for two Chinese journalists and the wife of one of them, who died in the NATO bombing of China's embassy in Belgrade. In some sense, it differed from previous war mourning because the victims were journalists. But in another sense, the mourning was a miniature war commemoration, in which

the journalists were officially called "martyrs" and honored in a way no differ-ent from fallen soldiers.

4. Sun Zhigang was a college graduate who started work at a company in Guangzhou. Because he did not have his ID with him when the police required him to verify that his legal residence was in the city, he was detained in a shelter center, where he had a confrontation with guards and was beaten to death. The authorities covered up the incident until a journalist from the *Southern Metrop-olis Daily* discovered the case in an online forum, later investigated the issue, and published an in-depth report (Feng 2005). The report instantly triggered a storm of criticism about the government's forcible detention and deportation of the homeless, beggars, and people without legal residence in the city. Pub-lic opinion enabled some intellectuals, particularly law scholars, to use normal channels of civic engagement to demand a policy change: they submitted their proposal to the National People's Congress to abolish the laws and regulations pertaining to homeless sheltering. Under the tremendous pressure of public opinion, the People's Congress and State Council finally accepted their pro-posal, abolishing detention centers and reforming relevant laws.

5. Interview with Ge Jianxiong, April 15, 2009, in Shanghai.

6. I searched both native and English language sources, including major newspapers, legislative records, and government documents, but could not find any particular reason for the Peruvian government's decision. A Peruvian expert suggests that the decision might have been the result of two aspects of Peruvian politics. First, since Peru is prone to major earthquakes, mourning for foreign victims has become a symbolic practice of international solidar-ity with countries that experience major natural disasters. National mourn-ing days have been held not only for the Chinese but also for victims of other disasters, such as the Haiti and Chile earthquakes in 2010. Second, Chinese are the biggest immigrant community in Peru, and the two countries have had strong cultural and economic connections. Therefore, it is understandable that the government used this event to show its concern with and respect for the Chinese (personal communication with Dr. Ricardo Gonzalez at Florida Inter-national University).

7. My request for an interview with the State Council did not get any response. My interviewee, Professor Ge Jianxiong, a prestigious intellectual with many contacts within the state system, told me that CCTV, China's official central television, attempted to interview members of the State Council about the decision when it was making a documentary about the earthquake. But its request too was rejected. I searched other sources and did not find any clues. This silence was quite typical, because information about the state's decision-making process was not usually revealed to the public, even when a decision was not politically sensitive. Core official media outlets, such as the *People's Daily* and the Xinhua News Agency, did not have any reports or comments about the mourning proposal until the decision was officially announced. Only one day after Peru reportedly decided to hold a national mourning day for the

Chinese victims, the Chinese government quickly decided on holding its own mourning observance, starting on May 19. The announcement was made in the late afternoon on May 18. Many local governments were obviously unprepared and had to summon emergency meetings to arrange the ritual practices, such as informing schools and government office to lower the flag. This silence and hastiness suggested that the Chinese state was unlikely to have had a conscious plan.

8. Interview with Shinan, August 3, 2009, Chengdu.

9. I collected 167 video clips about the commemorations by searching the keyword *aidaori* (mourning day) from a popular online video-sharing website (www.youku.com). These include 70 clips of central square gatherings (indicated by C-# in the analysis), 19 clips of gatherings organized by corporations and government offices (indicated by G-#), and 78 clips of the three-minute observance of silence (indicated by S-#). I analyzed the video clips by coding important ritual elements qualitatively, such as actors, actions, scenes, and symbols. Some of these codes are used in a content analysis about the observances. A potential criticism of this method is that the videos do not represent a representative sample. This criticism is valid, but the advantages exceed the flaws, with two being particularly important. First, the videos provide a unique set of data for examining people's detailed interactions during the ritual. Second, the videos were taken in a variety of cities (19) and places (from within cars to big squares) and demonstrate variations in the way people observed the commemorations. Many of these variations are not shown by other types of data--for example, press reports, which mainly focused on public gatherings in mostly ceremonial places. This richness makes the unrepresentative videos a valid data source for examining the details of interactions that are not obtainable through textual data.

10. March 23, 2009, field notes.

11. On the second and third mourning days, no sirens wailed, and an announcement transmitted through the public-address system politely asked people to leave the square in an orderly manner. The voice said, "Compatriots, let us turn our sorrow to power and use our real actions to support the people in the affected zone. Please leave the square in good order. Thank you for your cooperation" (Clip C-6 and C-7 of Youku videos). The crowd left the square but marched onto the streets around it, and the police did not restrain them except to keep the line in order.

12. *Xiongqi*, a local Sichuan catchword originally intended for cheering at soccer games, means "Go! Go!," "Stay strong," or "We will tough this out!"

13. Interview with HL in Chengdu and S1 and S2 in Shanghai; clips C13, 16, 17, 18, which depict activities in Tiananmen Square in Beijing.

14. Phone interview with BT, June 29, 2010.

Chapter 3

1. China Data Online (www.chinadataonline.org).
2. Interview with Feizhu, April 28, 2009, Shanghai.
3. Interview with LD, August 5, 2009, Chengdu.
4. Interview with Gaoyan, June 13, 2009.
5. Interview with Guangchuan, August 2, 2009, Chengdu
6. Interview with Greentea, August 4, 2009, Chengdu.
7. Phone interview with Siyi, May 11, 2010.
8. Interview with Jiajun, August 4, 2009, Chengdu.

Chapter 4

Parts of this chapter appeared in "Commemorating a Difficult Disaster: Naturalizing and Denaturalizing the 2008 Sichuan Earthquake in China," *Memory Studies*, 2017 (online first). DOI: 10.1177/1750698017693669. I retain the copyright of the article but thank SAGE for granting me the right to reuse the material.

1. Throughout this chapter, blogs, journals, and reports about Ai Weiwei's investigation are cited from his personal website, http://aiweiwei.com/projects/5-12-citizens-investigation/name-list-investigation/index.html, unless otherwise noted. Many files are in pdf format. The translations are mine.
2. Interview with Tan Zuoren, August 12, 2014.
3. Charter 08 was a manifesto signed by pro-democracy intellectuals and dissidents advocating a series of political reforms, including establishing an independent legal system, eliminating the one-party system, and other reforms.
4. Probably due to its political sensitivity, Tan's criminal verdict (No. 273 Criminal Verdict, 2009, Chengdu Intermediate People's Court) is unavailable in any official databases of legal documents in China. The only available text can be found online (for example, https://zh.wikisource.org/zh-hans/四川省成都市中级人民法院（2009）成刑初字第273号刑事判决书) and foreign media reports (BBC's Chinese-language report: http://www.bbc.com/zhongwen/trad/china/2010/06/100609_china_tan_zuoren_appeal.shtml).
5. Tan said the people behind both cases—the collapse of schools and Pengzhou Petrochemical—were the same: two "Jiangs" and one "Zhou": Jiang Jiemin, then chairman of the China Petroleum, Jiang Jufeng, then governor of Sichuan Province, and Zhou Yongkang. He even believed that Pengzhou was more important than the school collapse issue because Pengzhou Petrochemical was the focal point of an extensive network of money and power. Anyone opposing the project could expect to be "eliminated." This explanation has not been verified.

6. Narratives of the volunteers' interactions with the local authorities can be found in a pdf file on Ai Weiwei's blog (http://aiweiwei.com/projects/5-12-citizens-investigation/name-list-investigation/index.html) .

7. Interview with Zihou, June 14, 2009, Chengdu.

8. Ai Weiwei's tweet: https://twitter.com/aiww/status/200969592238112770.

9. Interview with Liu Jiakun, August 7, 2009, Chengdu.

Conclusion

1. For a short time the local government in Yushu discouraged civic associations from entering the quake zone in order not to jam the already-congested roads to the area. Some Hong Kong newspapers interpreted this as a restriction on associations' access to the politically sensitive Tibetan area. But no strong evidence supports this political interpretation, because the associations that had already been in Yushu before the traffic control measure, and those that went into the area after the traffic control was lifted, were not expelled. Those associations included Oxfam Hong Kong, which continued to undertake some long-term projects in the area.

References

Adams, Vincanne. 2013. *Markets of Sorrow, Labors of Faith: New Orleans in the Wake of Katrina*. Durham, NC: Duke University Press.

Ai Weiwei and Anthony Pins. 2014. *Ai Weiwei: Spatial Matters: Art, Architecture, and Activism*. Cambridge, MA: MIT Press.

Alexander, Jeffrey C. 2003. *The Meanings of Social Life: A Cultural Sociology*. New York: Oxford University Press.

Almond, Gabriel A., and Sidney Verba. 1989. *The Civic Culture: Political Attitudes and Democracy in Five Nations*. New ed. Newbury Park, CA: Sage.

Ang, Audra. 2008. "Parents of China Quake Victims Express Anger." Associated Press, June 12.

Angel, Ronald, Holly Bell, Julie Beausoleil, and Laura Lein. 2012. *Community Lost: The State, Civil Society, and Displaced Survivors of Hurricane Katrina*. New York: Cambridge University Press.

Anna, Cara. 2008. "Chinese Police Drag Grieving Parents from Protest." Associated Press, June 3.

Apple Daily (Pingguo ribao). 2009. "Gongan wufa wutian ouda weixie zhengren" (The unlawful Public Security assaults and bullies witnesses). *Pingguo ribao*, Hong Kong, August 13, A31.

Art Review. 2016. "Ai Weiwei." https://artreview.com/power_100/ai_weiwei/ (accessed September 21, 2016).

Asian Development Bank. 2008. *People's Republic of China: Providing Emergency Response to Sichuan Earthquake*. Technical Assistance Consultant's Report, December. Mandaluyong, Philippines: Asian Development Bank.

Baiocchi, Gianpaolo. 2006. "The Civilizing Force of Social Movements: Corporate and Liberal Codes in Brazil's Public Sphere." *Sociological Theory* 24 (4): 285–311.

———. 2013. *The Civic Imagination: Making a Difference in American Political Life*. Boulder, CO: Paradigm.

Barriaux, Marianne. 2008. "Beijing's Political Heart Leads Nation in Mourning Quake Victims." Agence France-Presse, May 19, 2008.

Barton, Allen H. 1969. *Communities in Disaster: A Sociological Analysis of Collective Stress Situations*. Garden City, NY: Doubleday.

Baum, Richard. 1994. *Burying Mao: Chinese Politics in the Age of Deng Xiaoping*. Princeton, NJ: Princeton University Press.

BBC Chinese. 2013. "Xi Jinping's New Policies: Sixteen Points after the Seven Don'ts." http://www.bbc.com/zhongwen/simp/china/2013/05/130528_china_thought_control_youth (accessed September 21, 2016).

Beech, Hannah, and Austin Ramzy. 2011. "Ai Weiwei: The Dissident." *Time*, December 14. http://content.time.com/time/specials/packages/article/0,28804,2101745_2102133_2102331,00.html (accessed September 21, 2016).

Beijing News (Xin jing bao). 2008a. "Li yizuo kezhe yunanzhe mingzi de jinianbei" (Establish a monument with the victims' names). *Xin jing bao*, May 21, A02, Editorial.

———. 2008b. "Dizhen jiyi bianyuan: Yingxiu shisheng fuke" (On the margin of earthquake memory: Yingxiu's teachers and students resume class). *Xin jing bao*, August 29, A20.

Bennett, Elizabeth A., Alissa Cordner, Peter Taylor Klein, Stephanie Savell, and Gianpaolo Baiocchi. 2013. "Disavowing Politics: Civic Engagement in an Era of Political Skepticism." *American Journal of Sociology* 119 (2): 518–48.

Berezin, Mabel. 2012. "Events as Templates of Possibility: An Analytic Typology of Political Facts." In *The Oxford Handbook of Cultural Sociology*, edited by Jeffrey C. Alexander, Ronald N. Jacobs, and Philip Smith, 613–35. Oxford: Oxford University Press.

Beyerlein, Kraig, and David Sikkink. 2008. "Sorrow and Solidarity: Why Americans Volunteered for 9/11 Relief Efforts." *Social Problems* 55 (2): 190–215.

Billig, Michael. 1995. *Banal Nationalism*. Thousand Oaks, CA: Sage.

Boltanski, Luc. 1999. *Distant Suffering: Morality, Media, and Politics*. New York: Cambridge University Press.

Brook, Timothy, and B. Michael Frolic, eds. 1997. *Civil Society in China*. Armonk, NY: M.E. Sharpe.

Brownell, Susan. 2012. "Human Rights and the Beijing Olympics: Imagined Global Community and the Transnational Public Sphere." *British Journal of Sociology* 63 (2): 306–27.

Brunkhorst, Hauke. 2005. *Solidarity: From Civic Friendship to a Global Legal Community*. Translated by Jeffrey Flynn. Cambridge, MA: MIT Press.

Brunsma, David L., David Overfelt, and J. Steven Picou, eds. 2007. *The Sociology of Katrina: Perspectives on a Modern Catastrophe*. Lanham, MD: Rowman & Littlefield.

Cable News Network. 2008. "As Children's Bodies Are Found, Firecrackers Pop." http://edition.cnn.com/2008/WORLD/asiapcf/05/13/china.scene/index.html (accessed April 9, 2011).

Cai Qinyu. 2005. *Minjian zuzhi yu zaihuang jiuzhi: Minguo huayang yizhenghui yanjiu* (Social organizations and disaster relief: A study of

Chinese-foreign relief associations in the Republic of China). Beijing: Shangwu yinshuguan.

Cai, Yongshun. 2008. "Power Structure and Regime Resilience: Contentious Politics in China." *British Journal of Political Science* 38: 411–32.

———. 2010. *Collective Resistance in China: Why Popular Protests Succeed or Fail.* Stanford, CA: Stanford University Press.

Calhoun, Craig J. 1994. *Neither Gods Nor Emperors: Students and the Struggle for Democracy in China.* Berkeley: University of California Press.

———. 2002. "Imagining Solidarity: Cosmopolitanism, Constitutional Patriotism, and the Public Sphere." *Public Culture* 14 (1): 147–71.

Cao Jinqing. 2003. *Huanghebian de Zhongguo: yige xuezhe dui xiangcun shehui de guancha yu sikao* (The China by the Yellow River: A scholar's observation and thoughts about rural society). Shanghai: Shanghai wenyi chubanshe.

Chen, Gang. 2012. "China's Management of Natural Disasters: Organizations and Norms." In *China's Crisis Management,* edited by Jae Ho Chung, 130–48. New York: Routledge.

Chen Guidi and Tao Chun. 2004. *Zhongguo nongmin diaocha* (An investigation of Chinese peasants). Beijing: Renmin Zhongwen wenxue chubanshe.

Chen Min. 2008. "Zhenxiang bi rongyu geng zhongyao" (Truth is more important than honor). *Nanfang zhoumo,* May 29, A07.

Chengdu Business Daily (Chengdu shangbao). 2008. "Zhongguo dizhenju: dizhen shang bunen zhunque yubao" (China Earthquake Bureau: Earthquakes cannot be accurately predicted). *Chengdu shangbao,* May 14, *jinri yaowen.*

China Development Brief. 2009. "Aiyi Cultural Development Center." *China Development Brief* (47): 78–80.

China News Service *(Zhongguo xinwenwang).* 2008. "Wei Hong: Sichuan zhengfu zhongshi jiazhang tichu de xiaoshe zhiliang wenti" (Wei Hong: Sichuan government pays attention to the school construction quality issue raised by parents). http://cd.qq.com/a/20081121/000274.htm (accessed September 19, 2016).

———. 2010. "Qinghai shengzhengfu queren Yushu dizhen zuizhong siwang renshu wei 2698 ren" (Qinghai provincial government confirms 2,698 dead in the Yushu earthquake). http://www.chinanews.com/gn/news/2010/05-31/2314359.shtml (accessed February 28, 2017).

China Youth Daily (Zhongguo qingnian bao). 2008a. "Siming tuanganbu de zhenhou 28 xiaoshi" (Four Youth League cadres' 28 hours after the earthquake). *Zhongguo qingnian bao,* May 14.

———. 2008b. "Tuanzhongyang youguan fuzheren: xiwang zhiyuanzhe buyao mangmu qianwang dizhen zaiqu" (Officials of the Youth League Central: Volunteers should not go to the quake zone blindly). *Zhongguo qingnian bao,* May 16.

Chinese Ministry of Civil Affairs. 2008. *Jiuzai guanli banfa* (Regulations on the management of disaster relief donations).

Cohen, Jean L., and Andrew Arato. 1992. *Civil Society and Political Theory.* Cambridge, MA: MIT Press.

Cohen, Stanley. 2001. *States of Denial: Knowing about Atrocities and Suffering.* Cambridge: Polity.

Collins, Randall. 1975. *Conflict Sociology: Toward an Explanatory Science.* New York: Academic Press.

———. 2004. "Rituals of Solidarity and Security in the Wake of Terrorist Attack." *Sociological Theory* 22 (1): 53–87.

Cong Feng, Liu Shuyun, and Wang Jintao. 2008. "Chuanyue siwang de shouhu: huanyuan dizhen qianhou Beichuan zhongxue jiaoshi qunti" (Protection in the face of death: Teachers at Beichuan High School before and after the quake). Xinhuanet. http://news.xinhuanet.com/newscenter/2008–05/22/content_8226814.htm (accessed September 16, 2016).

Coser, Lewis A. 1956. *The Functions of Social Conflict.* Glencoe, IL: Free Press.

Davis, Deborah, and Helen F. Siu, eds. 2006. *SARS: Reception and Interpretation in Three Chinese Cities.* New York: Routledge.

Deng Guosheng. 2009. *Xiangyin Wenchuan: Zhongguo jiuzai jizhi fenxi* (Responding to Wenchuan: An analysis of relief mechanisms in China). Beijing: Beijing daxue chubanshe.

Diamant, Neil Jeffrey, Stanley B. Lubman, and Kevin J. O'Brien, eds. 2005. *Engaging the Law in China: State, Society, and Possibilities for Justice.* Stanford, CA: Stanford University Press.

Diehl, David, and Daniel McFarland. 2010. "Toward a Historical Sociology of Social Situations." *American Journal of Sociology* 115 (6): 1713–52.

Durkheim, Emile. [1912] 1995. *The Elementary Forms of Religious Life.* Translated by Karen E. Fields. New York: Free Press.

Dynes, Russell, and E. L. Quarantelli. 1971. "The Absence of Community Conflict in the Early Phases of Natural Disaster." In *Conflict Resolution: Contributions of the Behavioral Sciences,* edited by Clagett G. Smith, 200–204. Notre Dame, IN: University of Notre Dame Press.

Dynes, Russell Rowe, and Kathleen J. Tierney, eds. 1994. *Disasters, Collective Behavior, and Social Organization.* Newark, DE: University of Delaware Press.

Edwards, Michael. 2014. *Civil Society.* 2nd ed. Cambridge: Polity.

Ehrenberg, John. 1999. *Civil Society: The Critical History of an Idea.* New York: New York University Press.

Ekiert, Grzegorz, and Jan Kubik. 1999. *Rebellious Civil Society: Popular Protest and Democratic Consolidation in Poland, 1989–1993.* Ann Arbor: University of Michigan Press.

Elegant, Simon. 2008. "China: Roused by Disaster." *Time,* May 22.

Eliasoph, Nina. 1998. *Avoiding Politics: How Americans Produce Apathy in Everyday Life.* New York: Cambridge University Press.

———. 2013. *The Politics of Volunteering.* Cambridge: Polity.

Eliasoph, Nina, and Paul Lichterman. 2003. "Culture in Interaction." *American Journal of Sociology* 108 (4): 735–94.

Erikson, Kai. 1976. *Everything in Its Path: Destruction of Community in the Buffalo Creek Flood.* New York: Simon and Schuster.

Eyerman, Ron. 2015. *Is This America? Katrina as Cultural Trauma.* Austin: University of Texas Press.

Eyre, Anne. 2007. "Remembering: Community Commemoration after Disaster." In *Handbook of Disaster Research,* edited by Havidán Rodríguez, E. L. Quarantelli, and Russell Rowe Dynes, 441–55. New York: Springer.

Feng Chen. 2005. "Yiqie fasheng zai yiliao zhiwai: Sun Zhigang shijian caifangji" (Everything was unexpected: The story behind the Sun Zhigang incident). *Jinchuanmei* 3: 28–29.

Feng Xiaojuan. 2010. *Beichuan wuyu* (Silent Beichuan). Chengdu: Sichuan wenyi chubanshe.

Fewsmith, Joseph. 2008. *China since Tiananmen: From Deng Xiaoping to Hu Jintao.* New York: Cambridge University Press.

Fine, Gary Alan. 2012. *Tiny Publics: A Theory of Group Action and Culture.* New York: Russell Sage Foundation.

Fine, Gary Alan, and Brooke Harrington. 2004. "Tiny Publics: Small Groups and Civil Society." *Sociological Theory* 22 (3): 341–56.

Fleischer, Friederike. 2011. "Technology of Self, Technology of Power: Volunteering as Encounter in Guangzhou, China." *Ethnos* 76 (3): 300–325.

Fortun, Kim. 2001. *Advocacy after Bhopal: Environmentalism, Disaster, New Global Orders.* Chicago: University of Chicago Press.

Freudenburg, William R., Robert Gamling, Shirley Laska, and Kai T. Erikson. 2009. *Catastrophe in the Making: The Engineering of Katrina and the Disasters of Tomorrow.* Washington, DC: Island Press/Shearwater Books.

Gao Jianguo. 2010. *Yingdui juzai de juguo tizhi* (The whole-country system of disaster response). Beijing: Qixiang chubanshe.

Gaventa, John. 1980. *Power and Powerlessness: Quiescence and Rebellion in an Appalachian Valley.* Urbana: University of Illinois Press.

Geertz, Clifford. 1973. *The Interpretation of Cultures: Selected Essays.* New York: Basic Books.

Geng Shu [Shu Keng] and Hu Yusong. 2011. "Tufa shijian zhong de guojiashehui guanxi: Shanghai jiceng shequ 'kangfei' kaocha" (State-society relations in a crisis: An investigation of the "combat against SARS" by local communities in Shanghai). *Shehui* (*Chinese Journal of Sociology*) 31 (6): 41–73.

Gerring, John. 2001. *Social Science Methodology: A Criterial Framework.* Cambridge: Cambridge University Press.

Goffman, Erving. 1969. *Where the Action Is: Three Essays.* London: Allen Lane.

———. 1974. *Frame Analysis: An Essay on the Organization of Experience.* Cambridge, MA: Harvard University Press.

Goldfarb, Jeffrey C. 2006. *The Politics of Small Things: The Power of the Powerless in Dark Times*. Chicago: University of Chicago Press.

Goldman, Merle. 2005. *From Comrade to Citizen: The Struggle for Political Rights in China*. Cambridge, MA: Harvard University Press.

———. 2007. *Political Rights in Post-Mao China*. Ann Arbor, MI: Association for Asian Studies.

Gonos, George. 1977. "'Situation' Versus 'Frame': The 'Interactionist' and the 'Structuralist' Analyses of Everyday Life." *American Sociological Review* 42 (6): 854–67. doi: 10.2307/2094572.

Goodwin, Jeff, James M. Jasper, and Francesca Polletta, eds. 2001. *Passionate Politics: Emotions and Social Movements*. Chicago: University of Chicago Press.

Gries, Peter Hays. 2004. *China's New Nationalism: Pride, Politics, and Diplomacy*. Berkeley: University of California Press.

Griswold, Wendy, Gemma Mangione, and Terence E. McDonnell. 2013. "Objects, Words, and Bodies in Space: Bringing Materiality into Cultural Analysis." *Qualitative Sociology* 36 (4): 343–64.

Gu Zhuomin, Shi Hongbin, Li Cheng, and Cao Yiting. 2008. "Wangluo de yanshe zuotian shi heibai" (The Internet turned black and white yesterday). *Shanghai qingnianbao*, May 20, 2008.

Guangming Daily (*Guangming ribao*). 2009. "Qingshan jijing qingting shenqie simian, Mingjiang benteng jiyang fenjing Liliang: jinian Wenchuan teda dizhen yizhounian huodong longzhong juxing" (Blue mountains listening to the silent remembrance, the Ming River became a raging torrent of advancement : The first anniversary commemoration of the Sichuan Wenchuan earthquake). *Guangming ribao*, May 13, 1, News. (In Chinese).

———. 2012. "Yuanjian xin Beichuan zhongxue gongcheng tongguo yushuan" (New Beichuan High School project passed budget audit). *Guangming ribao*, January 20, 06.

Guo Ting. 2011. "From Wenchuan to Yushu." *China Development Brief* (46): 27–30.

Habermas, Jürgen. 1989. *The Structural Transformation of the Public Sphere: An Inquiry into a Category of Bourgeois Society*. Cambridge, MA: MIT Press.

He, Yinan. 2009. *The Search for Reconciliation: Sino-Japanese and German-Polish Relations since World War II*. New York: Cambridge University Press.

He Zhenghua. 2008. "Guoqi zhangxian shengmin de zuyan" (The national flag demonstrates the dignity of life). *Renmin ribao*, May 19.

Heilmann, Sebastian, and Elizabeth J. Perry, eds. 2011. *Mao's Invisible Hand: The Political Foundations of Adaptive Governance in China*. Cambridge, MA: Harvard University Asia Center.

Hildebrandt, Timothy. 2013. *Social Organizations and the Authoritarian State in China*. Cambridge: Cambridge University Press.

Hong Kong Economic Journal. 2009. "What Is the Most Important Thing about Rebuilding after the Earthquake?" *Hong Kong Economic Journal,* May 13, P02.

———. 2014. "More Than 40 Intellectuals Were Arrested for Supporting Occupy Central." *Hong Kong Economic Journal,* October 13, A26.

Huang Chengju. 2007. "Editorial: From Control to Negotiation: Chinese Media in the 2000s." *International Communication Gazette* 69 (5): 402–12.

Hurst, William. 2009. *The Chinese Worker after Socialism.* Cambridge: Cambridge University Press.

Jager, Sheila Miyoshi, and Rana Mitter, eds. 2007. *Ruptured Histories: War, Memory, and the Post–Cold War in Asia.* Cambridge, MA: Harvard University Press.

Jasper, James M. 2011. "Emotions and Social Movements: Twenty Years of Theory and Research." *Annual Review of Sociology* 37: 285–303.

Jia Haifeng. 2008. "Jiang Weixin zhenqu guilai: jiang yanchai xiaoshe zhiliang" (Jiang Weixin back from the earthquake area: School buildings will be investigated closely). *21 shiji jingji baodao,* May 19, 11.

Jiang Wei. 2008. "Zheshang yuzai zaiqu yuanjian daxing shangcheng" (Zhejiang merchants plan to build large malls in the quake zone). *Huaxi dushi bao,* June 4, 2008.

Kang Xiaoguang and Han Heng. 2008. "Graduated Controls: The State-Society Relationship in Contemporary China." *Modern China* 34 (1): 36–55.

Keane, John. 1988. *Civil Society and the State: New European Perspectives.* London: Verso.

Klein, Naomi. 2007. *The Shock Doctrine: The Rise of Disaster Capitalism.* New York: Metropolitan Books/Henry Holt.

Kleinman, Arthur, and James L. Watson, eds. 2006. *SARS in China: Prelude to Pandemic?* Stanford, CA: Stanford University Press.

Klinenberg, Eric. 2002. *Heat Wave: A Social Autopsy of Disaster in Chicago.* Chicago: University of Chicago Press.

Kreps, Gary A. 2001. "Sociology of Disaster." In *International Encyclopedia of the Social and Behavioral Sciences,* edited by Neil J. Smelser and Paul B. Bates, 3718–21. Amsterdam: Elsevier.

Kriesi, Hanspeter. 2004. "Political Context and Opportunity." In *The Blackwell Companion to Social Movements,* edited by David A. Snow, Sarah A. Soule, and Hanspeter Kriesi, 67–90. Malden, MA: Blackwell.

Lai Haoning and Guo Shaofeng. 2008. "Xiaoshe zhiliang juedui neng chaqingcu; Dujiangyan guanyuan biaoshi xiaoshe jianzhu ziliao yijing baochun" (The issue of the quality of school building construction absolutely can be determined: Dujiangyan officials said construction archives have been stored). *Xin jing bao,* May 30.

Lee, Ching Kwan. 2007. *Against the Law: Labor Protests in China's Rustbelt and Sunbelt.* Berkeley: University of California Press.

Lei, Ya-Wen. 2011. "The Political Consequences of the Rise of the Internet:

Political Beliefs and Practices of Chinese Netizens." *Political Communication* 28 (3): 291–322.

Li Changping. 2002. *Wo xiang zongli shuoshihua* (I tell the premier the truth). Beijing: Guangming ribao chubanshe.

Li, Cheng. 2012. "The End of the CCP's Resilient Authoritarianism? A Tripartite Assessment of Shifting Power in China." *China Quarterly* 211: 595–623.

Li Datong. 2005. *Bingdian gushi* (The story of Freezing Point). Guilin: Guangxi shifan daxue chubanshe.

Li Guangmin. 2011. "Wenchuan zaihou: NGO shengchun nengli mianlin kaoya" (After the Wenchuan earthquake: the NGOs' ability to survive is being tested). *Fenghuang zhoukan*. http://news.ifeng.com/mainland/special/chuandizhensanzhounian/content-2/detail_2011_06/09/6902345_0.shtml (accessed September 19, 2016).

Li Hongbing. 2008. "Qingwei dizhen sinanzhe jiang banqi" (Please lower the flag for the earthquake victims). *Xinmin wanbao*, May 16, A-11.

Li Wenhai and Xia Mingfang, eds. 2007. *Tianyou xiongnian: Qingdai zaihuang yu Zhongguo shehui* (The predestined calamities: Disasters and Chinese society in the Qing dynasty). Beijing: Sanlian shudian.

Li Xueju, Yang Yanyin, and Yuan Shuhong, eds. 2005. *Zaihai yu yingji guanli* (Disaster and emergency management). Beijing: Zhongguo shehui chubanshe.

Li Yongfeng, Zhang Jieping, Zhu Yixin, and Zhang Xiaoya. 2008. "Dadizhen huanxing Zhongguo renxin; feixu zhong zhanqi gongmin liliang" (Great earthquake awakened Chinese; citizens' power emerged from ruins). *Yazhou zhoukan* (*Asia Weekly*), Hong Kong, June 1.

Li Zixin, ed. 2009. *Zainan ruhe baodao* (How to report a disaster). Guangzhou: Nanfang ribao chubanshe.

Lichterman, Paul. 2005. "Civic Culture at the Grass Roots." In *The Blackwell Companion to the Sociology of Culture*, edited by Mark D. Jacobs and Nancy Weiss Hanrahan, 383–97. Oxford: Blackwell.

———. 2006. "Social Capital or Group Style? Rescuing Tocqueville's Insights on Civic Engagement." *Theory and Society* 35 (5–6): 529–63.

Lichterman, Paul, and Nina Eliasoph. 2014. "Civic Action." *American Journal of Sociology* 120 (3): 798–863.

Linz, Juan J., and Alfred C. Stepan. 1996. *Problems of Democratic Transition and Consolidation: Southern Europe, South America, and Post-Communist Europe*. Baltimore: Johns Hopkins University Press.

Liu Jiakun. 2009. "Hu Huishan jinianguan" (Hu Huishan memorial house). *Xin jianzhu* 2009 (6): 131–33.

Liu Tie. 2010. *Duikou zhiyuan de yunxing jizhi jiqi fazhihua: jiyu Wenchuan zaihou huifu chongjian de shizheng fenxi* (Operation mechanisms of the duikou support system and its legalization: An empirical analysis of recovery and rebuilding work after the Wenchuan earthquake). Beijing: Falü chubanshe.

Lo, Ming-Cheng. 2010. "Cultures of Democracy: A Civil-Society Approach." In *Handbook of Cultural Sociology*, edited by John R. Hall, Laura Grindstaff, and Ming-Cheng Lo, 504–13. New York: Routledge.

Lo, Ming-Cheng M., and Yun Fan. 2010. "Hybrid Cultural Codes in Nonwestern Civil Society: Images of Women in Taiwan and Hong Kong." *Sociological Theory* 28 (2): 167–92.

Lu Feng. 2008. "Jintian, rang women gongxin moai" (Today, let's mourn with a single heart). *Pingguo ribao* (*Apple Daily*), Hong Kong, A08.

Lu, Yiyi. 2009. *Non-Governmental Organizations in China: The Rise of Dependent Autonomy*. New York: Routledge.

Ma, Qiusha. 2006. *Non-Governmental Organizations in Contemporary China: Paving the Way to Civil Society?* New York: Routledge.

Madsen, Richard. 1993. "The Public Sphere, Civil Society and Moral Community: A Research Agenda for Contemporary China Studies." *Modern China* 19 (2): 183–98. doi: 10.2307/189379.

———. 1998. *China's Catholics: Tragedy and Hope in an Emerging Civil Society*. Berkeley: University of California Press.

Martin, Dan. 2008. "China Seals Off Ruined Schools Amid Parent Anger." Agence France Presse, June 4.

McAdam, Doug. 1986. "Recruitment to High-Risk Activism: The Case of Freedom Summer." *American Journal of Sociology* 92 (1): 64–90.

Ministry of Housing and Urban-Rural Development. 2008. *Guanyu jiaqiang Wenchuan dizhen zaihou huifu chongjian chunzhen guihua bianzhi gongzou de tongzhi* (Announcement about strengthening planning work of villages and towns in the Wenchuan earthquake recovery period).

Mitter, Rana. 2000. "Behind the Scenes at the Museum: Nationalism, History and Memory in the Beijing War of Resistance Museum, 1987–1997." *China Quarterly* 161: 279–93.

Nan Xianghong. 2009. *Juzai shidai de meiti caozuo: Nanfang duishibao Wenchuan dizhen baodao quanjilu* (Media operations in the age of disaster: The Southern Metropolis Daily reports on the Wenchuan earthquake). Guangzhou: Nanfang ribao chubanshe.

Nathan, Andrew J. 2003. "Authoritarian Resilience." *Journal of Democracy* 4 (1): 6–17.

National Public Radio. 2008. "Shattered School Shows Power of Chinese Quake." http://www.npr.org/templates/story/story.php?storyId=90379917 (accessed September 19, 2016).

O'Brien, Kevin J., ed. 2008. *Popular Protest in China*. Cambridge, MA: Harvard University Press.

O'Brien, Kevin J., and Lianjiang Li. 2006. *Rightful Resistance in Rural China*. New York: Cambridge University Press.

Oliver-Smith, Anthony. 1999. "The Brotherhood of Pain: Theoretical and Applied Perspectives on Post-Disaster Solidarity." In *The Angry Earth:*

Disaster in Anthropological Perspective, edited by Anthony Oliver-Smith and Susannah M. Hoffman, 156–72. New York: Routledge.

Oliver-Smith, Anthony, and Susannah M. Hoffman, eds. 1999. *The Angry Earth: Disaster in Anthropological Perspective*. New York: Routledge.

Peng Shujie and Feng Bing. 2009. "5.13–5.23 Qianzhi de shiyige riri yeye: Wenchuan dadizhen qianfang baodao zhihuibu gongzuo shouji" (Eleven days and nights in the headquarters at the front: Xinhua front headquarters work log in the great Wenchuan earthquake). Xinhuanet. http://news. xinhuanet.com/newscenter/2008-06/15/content_8374730.htm (accessed September 19, 2016).

Perry, Ronald W. 2006. "What Is a Disaster?" In *Handbook of Disaster Research*, edited by Havidán Rodríguez, E. L. Quarantelli, and Russell Rowe Dynes, 1–15. New York: Springer.

Pfaff, Steven, and Guobin Yang. 2001. "Double-Edged Rituals and the Symbolic Resources of Collective Action: Political Commemorations and the Mobilization of Protest in 1989." *Theory and Society* 30 (4): 539–89.

Polletta, Francesca. 1998. "'It Was Like a Fever': Narrative and Identity in Social Protest." *Social Problems* 45 (2): 137–59.

Post, P., R. L. Grimes, A. Nugteren, P. Pettersson, and H. Zondag. 2003. *Disaster Ritual: Explorations of an Emerging Ritual Repertoire*. Leuven: Peeters.

Putnam, Robert D. 2000. *Bowling Alone: The Collapse and Revival of American Community*. New York: Simon & Schuster.

Putnam, Robert D., Robert Leonardi, and Raffaella Nanetti. 1993. *Making Democracy Work: Civic Traditions in Modern Italy*. Princeton, NJ: Princeton University Press.

Qi Leyi. 2008. "Doufuzha xiaoshe jianding jieguo jiang chulu" (Tofu-dreg school building assessment results will be out). *Zhongguo shibao*, Taiwan, June 17, A13.

Qian Gang. 2008a. "Xianzai shi jiemin yu daoxuan de guanjian santian" (Now it's the most critical three days to save people). *Nanfang dushibao*, May 14, A02.

——. 2008b. *Tangshan da dizhen* (The great Tangshan earthquake). Beijing: Dangdai Zhongguo chubanshe.

Qian Gang and David Bandurski. 2011. "China's Emerging Public Sphere: The Impact of Media Commercialization, Professionalism, and the Internet in an Era of Transition." In *Changing Media, Changing China*, edited by Susan L. Shirk, 38–76. Oxford: Oxford University Press.

Qian, Licheng, Bin Xu, and Dingding Chen. 2017. "Does History Education Promote Nationalism in China? A 'Limited Effect' Explanation." *Journal of Contemporary China*. 26 (104): 199–21.

Quarantelli, E. L. 1970. "Emergent Accommodation Groups: Beyond Current Collective Behavior Typologies." In *Human Nature and Collective Behavior: Papers in Honor of Herbert Blumer*, edited by Tamotsu Shibutani, 111–23. Englewood-Cliffs, NJ: Prentice-Hall.

———, ed. 1998. *What Is a Disaster? Perspectives on the Question*. New York: Routledge.

Radio Free Asia. 2010. "Beijing zuzhi daxuesheng canjia Xianggang Leshihui zhaoping huodong" (Beijing prohibits college students from attending Oxfam Hong Kong's recruitment activities). http://www.rfa.org/mandarin/yataibaodao/leshihui-02232010104608.html (accessed September 21, 2016).

People's Daily (*Renmin ribao*). 1976a. "Hebei sheng Tangshan, Fengnan yidai fasheng qianlie dizhen: zaiqu renmin zai Mao Zhuxi gemin luxian zhiying xia fayang rending shentian de gemin jingsheng kangzhen jiuzai" (Strong earthquake in Tangshan and Fengnan in Hebei: The affected people are guided by Chairman Mao's revolutionary line and uphold the revolutionary spirit of "man conquering nature" and battle the earthquake). *Renmin ribao*, July 29, 1.

———. 1976b. "Shoudu baiwan qunzhong huaizhe jiqi chentong he wuxian congjing de xinqing longzhong juxing weida de lingxiu he daoshi Mao Zedong zhuxi zuidao da hui" (With extreme sorrow and great admiration, a million people in the capital hold a memorial meeting for the great leader and mentor Chairman Mao Zedong). *Renmin ribao*, September 19, 1.

———. 2008. "Zhou Yongkang zai Sichuan zhidao kangzhen jiuzai gongzuo shi qiangdiao qieshi weihu shehui wending wei duoqu kangzhen jiuzai quanmian shengli tigong youli baozhang" (In directing disaster relief work in Sichuan, Zhou Yongkang emphasizes maintaining stability to ensure the success of combating the earthquake). *Renmin ribao*, June 10, 1.

Renminwang [People.cn]. 2008. "Tebie cehua: 5.12 Wenchuan dizhen zaiqing zonghe fenxi" (Special issue: Impact of the May 12 Wenchuan earthquake). http://scitech.people.com.cn/GB/7332696.html (accessed September 7, 2016).

Riley, Dylan, and Juan J. Fernández. 2014. "Beyond Strong and Weak: Rethinking Postdictatorship Civil Societies." *American Journal of Sociology* 120 (2): 432–503.

Saich, Tony. 2000. "Negotiating the State: The Development of Social Organizations in China." *China Quarterly* 161 (March): 124–41.

Samuels, Richard J. 2013. *3.11: Disaster and Change in Japan*. Ithaca, NY: Cornell University Press.

Schofer, Evan, and Marion Fourcade-Gourinchas. 2001. "The Structural Contexts of Civic Engagement: Voluntary Association Membership in Comparative Perspective." *American Sociological Review* 66 (6): 806–28.

Schudson, Michael. 2009. "The Varieties of Civic Engagement." In *The Civic Life of American Religion*, edited by Paul Lichterman and C. Brady Potts, 23–47. Stanford, CA: Stanford University Press.

Schwartz, Jonathan. 2009. "The Impact of Crises on Social Service Provision in China: The State and Society Respond to SARS." In *State and Society Responses to Social Welfare Needs in China: Serving the People*, edited by Jonathan Schwartz and Shawn Shieh, 135–55. New York: Routledge.

Scott, James C. 1990. *Domination and the Arts of Resistance: Hidden Transcripts*. New Haven, CT: Yale University Press.

Sewell, William H. 1992. "A Theory of Structure: Duality, Agency, and Transformation." *American Journal of Sociology* 98 (1): 1–29.

———. 1996. "Historical Events as Transformations of Structures: Inventing Revolution at the Bastille." *Theory and Society* 25 (6): 841–81.

Shan Chunchang, ed. 2011. *Yingji guanli: Zhongguo tese de yunxing moshi yu shijian* (Emergency management: Models and practices with Chinese characteristics). Beijing: Beijing shifan daxue chubanshe.

Shaw, Rajib, and Katsuhiro Goda. 2004. "From Disaster to Sustainable Civil Society: The Kobe Experience." *Disasters* 28 (1): 16–40.

Sherman, Daniel J. 1998. "Bodies and Names: The Emergence of Commemoration in Interwar France." *American Historical Review* 103 (2): 443–66.

Shi, Fayong, and Yongshun Cai. 2006. "Disaggregating the State: Networks and Collective Resistance in Shanghai." *China Quarterly* 186: 314–32.

Shi Lan. 2008. "Moai, women xuyao jinianbei jituo aisi" (We need monuments to express our sorrow). *Nanfang dushi bao*, May 20, A34.

Shi, Tianjian. 1999. "Village Committee Elections in China: Institutionalist Tactics for Democracy." *World Politics* 51 (3): 385–412.

Shieh, Shawn, and Guosheng Deng. 2011. "An Emerging Civil Society: The Impact of the 2008 Sichuan Earthquake on Grass-roots Associations in China." *China Journal* 65 (January): 181–94.

Shu Shenxiang. 2008. "She quanguo aidaori shi dui shengming de zunzhong" (Holding national mourning is to respect lives). *Yangcheng wanbao*, May 17.

Sichuan Daily (*Sichuan ribao*). 2008a. "1.67 wanyi, qingni lai gongying" (1.67 trillion: An invitation for you to have a win-win result). *Sichuan ribao*, September 11, International News.

———. 2008b. "Guanyu kangzhen jiuzai qijian guifan shehui mujuan xingwei de tonggao (Announcement about regulating social donations during the disaster period). *Sichuan ribao*, May 21, 1.

———. 2008c. "Waishang qiye: touzi Sichuan de xingxin buhui gaibian" (Foreign enterprises: Our confidence in Sichuan will not change). *Sichuan ribao*, May 31, B04.

———. 2008d. "Yali bujian, xiwang youchun" (Pressure remains; so does hope). *Sichuan ribao*, July 18, Headlines.

———. 2008e. "Zhua daxiangmu jiushi zhua touzi zhua fazhan" (To attract investment and boost development [we] need big projects). *Sichuan ribao*, October 8, Domestic News.

Sichuan Provincial Government. 2008. "Sichuan sheng reminzhengfu zhiding '5.12' Wenchuan zaihou nongfang chongjian gongzuo fangan" (The Sichuan provincial government draws a work plan for rebuilding rural houses after the 5.12 Wenchuan earthquake). http://www.sc.gov.cn/zt_sczt/mzzxd/smzjjxd/200806/t20080627_292736.shtml (accessed September 19, 2016).

Sijia. 2008. "Zoujing Shimenkan: canyu 08 xuezai jiuzhu jingyan fenxiang ji wenti fansi" (Sharing experience and reflection on relief work after the snowstorm). Shimenkan. http://www.shimenkan.org/sj/m/ (accessed September 19, 2016).

Sin Chew Daily. 2008. "Junfang fengsuo min'gan diqu shoujing dizhen baodao xianzhi" (Military seals off sensitive areas and tightens control on reporting on the earthquake). *Sin Chew Daily,* Malaysia, June 8, International News.

Skocpol, Theda. 1997. "The Tocqueville Problem: Civic Engagement in American Democracy." *Social Science History* 21 (4): 455–79.

———. 2003. *Diminished Democracy: From Membership to Management in American Civic Life.* Norman: University of Oklahoma Press.

Skocpol, Theda, and Morris P. Fiorina. 1999. *Civic Engagement in American Democracy.* Washington, DC: Brookings Institution Press; Russell Sage Foundation.

Skocpol, Theda, Marshall Ganz, and Ziad Munson. 2000. "A Nation of Organizers: The Institutional Origins of Civic Voluntarism in the United States." *American Political Science Review* 94 (3): 527–46.

Smith, Adam. [1759] 2009. *The Theory of Moral Sentiments.* 250th anniversary ed. New York: Penguin.

Snow, David A., and Sarah Anne Soule. 2010. *A Primer on Social Movements.* New York: W.W. Norton.

Sorace, Christian. 2014. "China's Vision for Developing Sichuan's Post-Earthquake Countryside: Turning Unruly Peasants into Grateful Urban Citizens." *China Quarterly* 218: 404–27.

Southern Metropolis Daily (Nanfang dushi bao). 2008a. "Wenchuan 'touqi' baiwan ren wangji" (Millions of netizens commemorate victims in the first week of the Wenchuan earthquake). *Nanfang dushi bao,* May 20, 41, A.

———. 2008b. "Aidaori: rang guojia kaojin renqing lin quanli zouxiang renxing" (The mourning days: Let the state get closer to human sentiments and power step forward to humanity). *Nanfang dushi bao,* May 20, AA02.

———. 2008c. "Juanjian shiyu xiao wuyi daota; Xianggang cishan jigou miaopu xingdong shou wangyou zuipeng chengzhan" (None of the sponsored schools collapsed: Hong Kong Sowers Action praised by netizens). *Nanfang dushi bao,* May 30, A48.

———. 2009. "Yi renquan de minyi gongkai zhenwangzhe da mindan" (In the name of human rights, make the names of the earthquake deceased known to the public). *Nanfang dushi bao,* April 15, A02, Editorial.

Spires, Anthony J. 2011. "Contingent Symbiosis and Civil Society in an Authoritarian State: Understanding the Survival of China's Grassroots NGOs." *American Journal of Sociology* 117 (1): 1–45.

State Council Information Office of the People's Republic of China. 2008a. "Guoxinban jiu Wenchuan dizhen ji zaishun pinggu qingkuang juxing fabuhui" (State Council Information Office press conference on the

Wenchuan earthquake and evaluations of the losses). http://www.scio.gov.
cn/tp/xwfb/Document/347527/347527.htm (accessed September 19, 2016).

———. 2008b. "Guoxinban shouquan fabu jiuyue ershiwu ri kangzhenjiuzai
qingkuang" (State Council Information Office authorized to report on the
development of earthquake relief). http://www.scio.gov.cn/zxbd/nd/2008/
Document/310218/310218.htm (accessed September 19, 2016).

Stockmann, Daniela. 2013. *Media Commercialization and Authoritarian Rule
in China*. New York: Cambridge University Press.

Sun Chengbin. 2008. "Dang he zhengfu yiding hui bangzu zaiqu renmin
duguo nanguan: Hu Jintao zongshuji zai Sichuan teda dizhen zaiqu Shifang kanwang weiwen shouzai qunzhong he jiuyuan renyuan" (The party
and the government will help the affected people to tough out this hardship—Hu Jintao visited affected people and responders in Shifang). *Renmin
ribao*, May 19, 1.

Swidler, Ann. 1986. "Culture in Action: Symbols and Strategies." *American
Sociological Review* 51 (2): 273–86.

———. 2001. *Talk of Love: How Culture Matters*. Chicago: University of Chicago Press.

Tan Hao. 2008. "Qingbuyao yong leishui lai huida wo" (Don't answer my question with tears). *21 shiji jingji bao (21st Century Business Herald)*, May 28,
02.

Tan Zuoren. 2008. "Longmenshan: qing wei Beichuan haizi zuozheng" (Mount
Longmen: please testify for the Beichuan children). http://www.huanghua-
gang.org/hhgForum/year2008/august2008/longMengShang_8-22-08.html
(accessed October 10, 2008).

———. 2009. "Guanyu jianli 5.12 xuesheng dangan de changyishu" (A proposal to establish an archive for students who died in the 5.12 earthquake).
http://www.edu11.net/space-291-do-blog-id-193565.html (accessed March 3,
2017).

Tang, Lijun, and Helen Sampson. 2012. "The Interaction between Mass Media
and the Internet in Non-Democratic States: The Case of China." *Media,
Culture & Society* 34 (4): 457–71.

Taylor, Charles. 1995. *Philosophical Arguments*. Cambridge, MA: Harvard
University Press.

Teets, Jessica C. 2013. "Let Many Civil Societies Bloom: The Rise of Consultative Authoritarianism in China." *China Quarterly* 213: 19–38.

———. 2014. *Civil Society under Authoritarianism: The China Model*. Cambridge: Cambridge University Press.

Teng Xiaomeng. 2008. "213 ren tuan: Zhongguo dizhen jiuyuan dui quan
jiemi" (A group of 213: China earthquake rescue team). *21 shiji jingji baodao*, May 15, 6.

Theiss-Morse, Elizabeth, and John R. Hibbing. 2005. "Citizenship and Civic
Engagement." *Annual Review of Political Science* 8: 227–250.

Thornton, Patricia M. 2009. "Crisis and Governance: SARS and the Resilience of the Chinese Body Politic." *China Journal* (61): 23–48.

———. 2013. "The Advance of the Party: Transformation or Takeover of Urban Grassroots Society?" *China Quarterly* 213: 1–18.

Tianya. 2009. "Zuoke Tianya 1" (Interview with Ai Weiwei). https://aiweiweiai. wordpress.com/page/75/ (accessed October 10, 2009).

Tierney, Kathleen J., and James D. Goltz. 1998. *Emergency Response: Lessons Learned from the Kobe Earthquake.* University of Delaware Disaster Research Center.

Tierney, Kathleen J., Michael K. Lindell, and Ronald W. Perry. 2001. *Facing the Unexpected : Disaster Preparedness and Response in the United States.* Washington, DC: Joseph Henry Press.

Tocqueville, Alexis de. 1969. *Democracy in America.* 2 vols. Garden City, NY: Doubleday.

———. [1840] 2004. *Democracy in America.* Translated by Arthur Goldhammer. New York: Library of America.

Tong, Jingrong. 2007. "Guerrilla Tactics of Investigative Journalists in China." *Journalism* 8 (5): 530–35.

Tsui, Enid. 2015. "Little Jewels: Ai Weiwei Remembers Quake's Child Victims in Intimate Scale." *South China Morning Post,* November 12. http://www. scmp.com/lifestyle/arts-entertainment/article/1877884/little-jewels-ai-weiwei-remembers-quakes-child-victims (accessed September 19, 2016).

Tu Chonghang. 2008. "17 ren dangang 20 yi shankuan zhizhong" (17 people handled 2 billion donations). *Xin jing bao,* June 10.

Tumarkin, Nina. 1983. *Lenin Lives! The Lenin Cult in Soviet Russia.* Cambridge, MA: Harvard University Press.

Turner, Ralph H. 1967. "Types of Solidarity in the Reconstituting of Groups." *Pacific Sociological Review* 10 (2): 60–68.

Unger, Jonathan. 2008. *Associations and the Chinese State: Contested Spaces.* Armonk, NY: M.E. Sharpe.

Unger, Jonathan, and Anita Chan. 1995. "China, Corporatism, and the East Asian Model." *Australian Journal of Chinese Affairs* 33 (January): 29–53.

United States Geological Survey. 2016a. "Earthquakes with 1,000 or More Deaths 1900–2014." http://earthquake.usgs.gov/earthquakes/world/world_ deaths.php (accessed September 7, 2016).

———. 2016b. "Poster of the Eastern Sichuan, China Earthquake of 12 May 2008—Magnitude 7.9." http://earthquake.usgs.gov/earthquakes/eqarchives/ poster/2008/20080512.php (accessed September 7, 2016).

Vinitzky-Seroussi, Vered, and Chana Teeger. 2010. "Unpacking the Unspoken: Silence in Collective Memory and Forgetting." *Social Forces* 88 (3): 1103–22.

Wakeman, Frederic Jr. 1985. "Revolutionary Rites: The Remains of Chiang Kai-shek and Mao Tse-tung." *Representations* 10 (Spring): 146–93.

Walder, Andrew G., and Gong Xiaoxia. 1993. "Workers in the Tiananmen

Protests: The Politics of the Beijing Workers' Autonomous Federation." *Australian Journal of Chinese Affairs* (29): 1–29.

Wan Qiu. 2009. "Tan Zuoren an de nanyan zhiying" (Unspoken secrets of Tan Zuoren's case). *Ming Pao*, Hong Kong. August 16, P02.

Wang Guanli. 2008. "Xuezai goule chude NGO nengli bianjie" (The snowstorm demonstrated the limitations of NGOs' capacity). *Zhongguo fazhan jianbao* 38 (Summer). http://www.chinadevelopmentbrief.org.cn/news-13189.html (accessed, March 3, 2017).

Wang Ming, ed. 2011. *Emerging Civil Society in China, 1978–2008*. Leiden: Brill.

Wang Yueyun. 2009. "Huigu yu fansi: cong Zundao moshi dao cheli Zundao" (Retrospection and reflection: From the Zundao model to leaving Zundao). *Zhongguo fazhan jianbao* 42: 28–30.

Watson, Andrew. 2008. "Civil Society in a Transitional State: The Rise of Associations in China." In *Associations and the Chinese State: Contested Spaces*, edited by Jonathan Unger, 14–47. Armonk, NY: M.E. Sharpe.

Watts, Jonathan. 2008. "Chinese Earthquake: Tragedy Brings New Mood of Unity: Government Wins Praise for Reaction as the Young Lead Surge in Patriotic Sentiment." *Guardian*, June 10, 15, International.

Weiss, Jessica Chen. 2014. *Powerful Patriots: Nationalist Protest in China's Foreign Relations*. Oxford: Oxford University Press.

Welt. 2015. "Ai Weiwei: "Ich bin nicht bereit, China zu verlassen." https://www.welt.de/kultur/article13947429/Ich-bin-nicht-bereit-China-zu-verlassen.html (accessed September 19, 2016).

West China Metropolis Daily (*Huaxi dushi bao*). 2008a. "Mianyang: dizhen yizhi jiangcheng zhongyao jingguan" (Mianyang: Earthquake ruins become tourist spots). *Huaxi dushi bao*, June 8, 2008.

———. 2008b. "Beichuan chongjian: xinlao xiancheng shuangda lüyou pai" (Recovery of Beichuan: The new and old county seats develop tourism). *Huaxi dushi bao*, July 28, 2008.

Whyte, Martin King. 2010. *Myth of the Social Volcano: Perceptions of Inequality and Distributive Injustice in Contemporary China*. Stanford, CA: Stanford University Press.

Whyte, William Foote. [1943] 1993. *Street Corner Society: The Social Structure of an Italian Slum*. 4th ed. Chicago: University of Chicago Press.

Wilson, John. 2000. "Volunteering." *Annual Review of Sociology* 26: 215–40.

Winter, Jay. 1995. *Sites of Memory, Sites of Mourning: The Great War in European Cultural History*. New York: Cambridge University Press.

Wuthnow, Robert. 1987. *Meaning and Moral Order: Explorations in Cultural Analysis*. Berkeley: University of California Press.

———. 1991. *Acts of Compassion: Caring for Others and Helping Ourselves*. Princeton, NJ: Princeton University Press.

———. 1998. *Loose Connections: Joining Together in America's Fragmented Communities*. Cambridge, MA: Harvard University Press.

Xenos, Michael, and Patricia Moy. 2007. "Direct and Differential Effects of the Internet on Political and Civic Engagement." *Journal of Communication* 57 (4): 704–18.

Xinhua News Agency. 2008. "Hu Jintao fu zaiqu weiwen shouzai qunzhong zhidao kangzhen jiuzai qiangdiao jiuren renshi dangwuzhiji zhongzhong zhi zhong" (Hu Jintao went to the quake zone to comfort affected people and direct the response: Emphasizing that rescuing is still the most urgent and important of important tasks). Xinhua News Agency, May 17.

Xu, Bin. 2009. "Durkheim in Sichuan: The Earthquake, National Solidarity, and the Politics of Small Things." *Social Psychology Quarterly* 72 (1): 5–8.

———. 2012. "Grandpa Wen: Scene and Political Performance." *Sociological Theory* 30 (2): 114–29.

———. 2013. "Mourning Becomes Democratic." *Contexts* 12 (1): 42–46.

———. 2016. "Moral Performance and Cultural Governance in China: The Compassionate Politics of Disasters." *China Quarterly* 226: 407–30.

———. 2017. "Commemorating a Difficult Disaster: Naturalizing and Denaturalizing the 2008 Sichuan Earthquake in China." *Memory Studies* online first (February). doi: 10.1177/1750698017693669.

Xu, Bin, and Xiaoyu Pu. 2010. "Dynamic Statism and Memory Politics: A Case Analysis of the Chinese War Reparations Movement." *China Quarterly* 201: 156–75.

Xu, Ying. 2013. "Volunteer Participation and the Development of Civil Society in China: A Case Study of Jinan." *Nonprofit Policy Forum* 5 (1): 139–68.

Xu Yongguang. 2008. "2008: Zhongguo gongmin shehui yuannian" (2008: The birth year of Chinese civil society). http://politics.people.com.cn/ GB/1026/7336201.html (accessed September 16, 2016).

Yang Binbin, Zhao Hejuan, Li Zhigang, Chang Hongxiao, Zhang Yinguang, and Chen Zhongxiaolu. 2008. "Xiaoshe yousi lu" (Reflections on school buildings). *Caijing* 12 (June 9).

Yang Chuanmin. 2011. "Jianzhu zhenhai qishi: ruhe zaochu geng jiangu de jianzhu" (Reflections on building damage in earthquakes: How to build stronger houses). *Nanfang dushi bao*, May 11, AIII04.

Yang, Dali L. 2004. *Remaking the Chinese Leviathan: Market Transition and the Politics of Governance in China.* Stanford, CA: Stanford University Press.

Yang, Guobin. 2003. "The Internet and Civil Society in China: A Preliminary Assessment." *Journal of Contemporary China* 12 (36): 453–75.

———. 2009. *The Power of the Internet in China: Citizen Activism Online.* New York: Columbia University Press.

Yang, Jisheng. 2012. *Tombstone: The Great Chinese Famine, 1958–1962.* 1st American ed. Edited by Edward Friedman, Guo Jian, and Stacy Mosher. Translated by Stacey Mosher and Guo Jian. New York: Farrar, Straus and Giroux.

Yang, Mayfair Mei-hui. 1994. *Gifts, Favors, and Banquets: The Art of Social Relationships in China*. Ithaca, NY: Cornell University Press.

Yang Xiaohong and Ma Jinyu. 2011. "Budao de xuexiao" (The schools that don't fall). *Nanfang dushi bao*, March 16, AIII04.

Yu Wei. 2008. "Jiaoyubu yancha doufuzha xiaoshe" (Department of Education will investigate tofu-dreg school buildings). *Nanfang dushi bao*, May 17.

Yu Yuhua. 2008. "Renhe kunnan du nanbudao yingxiong de Zhongguo renmin" (No difficulty can deter the heroic Chinese people). *Xinmin wanbao*, May 21, Editorial.

Zerubavel, Eviatar. 2006. *The Elephant in the Room: Silence and Denial in Everyday Life*. New York: Oxford University Press.

Zhang Jieping. 2010. "Ai Xiaoming de chuanzhen jilupian zhenhan" (Ai Xiaoming's documentaries about the Sichuan earthquake). *Asia Weekly*, January 24. http://www.yzzk.com/cfm/content_archive.cfm?id=1365136921695&docissue=2010-04 (accessed: March 7, 2017).

Zhang Meng. 2008. "Kaifashang miaoshang zaihou chongjian" (Real estate developers' eye on the recovery plan). *Takung Pao*, June 8, B07.

Zhang Ning, ed. 2012. *Kexue fazhanguan yu shiliu da yilai de lilun chuangxing* (The theory of scientific development and theoretical innovations since the 16th Congress). Beijing: Zhongyang wenxian chubanshe.

Zhang Xiaozhong. 2008a. "Dujiangyan Juyuan zheng 200 duo jiazhang jianchi wei sinan xuesheng 'taogongdao'" (200 parents in Juyuan, Dujiangyan seek justice for student victims). *Lianhe zaobao*, Singapore, July 1, 18.

———. 2008b. "Sichuan shengzhengfu pai liangge xuexiao kuata diaochazu" (Sichuan provincial government sends two investigation teams). *Lianhe zaobao*, Singapore. May 30, 22.

Zhao, Dingxin. 2001. *The Power of Tiananmen: State-Society Relations and the 1989 Beijing Student Movement*. Chicago: University of Chicago Press.

Zhao, Sile. 2015. "Kou Yanding: The Irremediable Moderate Constructionist." *China Digital Times*. November 21, 2015. http://tinyurl.com/zp6qj3a (accessed September 21, 2016).

Zhao, Yuezhi. 1998. *Media, Market, and Democracy in China: Between the Party Line and the Bottom Line*. Urbana: University of Illinois Press.

———. 2008. *Communication in China: Political Economy, Power, and Conflict*. Lanham, MD: Rowman & Littlefield.

Zhong Zuwen. 2008. "Dangyuan ganbu yao zhanzai kangzhenjiuzai diyixian" (Party cadres must be on the front line). *Renmin ribao*, May 14, 2.

Zhou Xiaopu. 2008. "08 bianzhengfa" (08 dialectics). In *Zhenhan: meiti huixiang* (Shock: Reflections on the Media), edited by Liang Xiaotao. Beijing: Zhongguo minzhu fazhi chubanshe.

Zhou Xun, ed. 2012. *The Great Famine in China, 1958–1962: A Documentary History*. New Haven, CT: Yale University Press.

Zhu Jiangang, Wang Chao, and Hu Ming. 2009. *Zeren, xindong, hezuo: NGO canyu Wenchuan dizhen gean yanjiu* (Responsibility, action, and cooperation: Case studies of NGO participation in the Wenchuan earthquake). Beijing: Beijing daxue chubanshe.

Zuo Lin. 2008. "Sichuan Wenchuan dizhen zaihou lüyouye huifu chongjian guihua zheng minyi Sichuan lüyou qiye ni mianshui liangnianban" (Sichuan post-earthquake tourism recovery plan: Seeking the public's opinions; tax free for tourist enterprises in Sichuan). *Xin jing bao*, July 5, A18.

Index